BABIES WITHOUT BORDERS

Adoption and Migration across the Americas

KAREN DUBINSKY is a professor in the Department of Global Development Studies and the Department of History at Queen's University.

Babies without Borders

Adoption and Migration across the Americas

KAREN DUBINSKY

NEW YORK UNIVERSITY PRESS
Washington Square, New York

First published in the U.S.A. by
NEW YORK UNIVERSITY PRESS
Washington Square
New York, NY 10003
www.nyupress.org

Library of Congress Cataloging-in-Publication Data
Dubinsky, Karen.
Babies without borders : adoption and migration
across the Americas / Karen Dubinsky.
p. cm.
Includes bibliographical references and index.
ISBN–13: 978–0–8147–2091–2 (cl : alk. paper)
ISBN–10: 0–8147–2091–9 (cl : alk. paper)
ISBN–13: 978–0–8147–2092–9 (pb : alk. paper)
ISBN–10: 0–8147–2092–7 (pb : alk. paper)
1. Intercountry adoption—America.
2. Interracial adoption—America.   I. Title.
HV875.58.A45D83   2010
362.734097—dc22   2009046696

Manufactured in the United States of America

c 10 9 8 7 6 5 4 3 2 1
p 10 9 8 7 6 5 4 3 2 1

Desde que existe el Mundo
Hay una cosa cierta
Unos hacen los muros
Y otras las puertas

Carlos Varela, 'Muros y Puertas'

Contents

Acknowledgments

I've worked on this book for almost a decade. Almost always, it's been a pleasure, because it has expanded my world and my heart. I'm happy to here recount my debts and honour my friends.

I'll start in Havana, for it was there that the idea for this book was launched, early in 2001, when my colleague and friend Susan Lord invited me to crash her research trip. Our conversations there helped to transform some unruly strands of ideas about the global politics of babies into something that could be planned, funded, researched, and now written. Sharing a sabbatical term in Havana in 2004 with Susan and Paul Kelley in order to research the Cuban chapter of this book is one of the smartest ideas she's had (and she's had many). Several years later, Havana has become a second home. When I, and my unusual family, return, we are always greeted with a hot meal, bananas (which taste like bananas), and a neighbourhood of familiar faces. For their hospitality, assistance, and countless conversations about politics, history, flan, and child-rearing, I thank Aldo Peña Morejon and Vanessa Chicola, Vivian Rocaberti, Franky Garcia González, and Vilma Vidal, and Sonia Enjamio, Inés Rodríguez, Lourdes Pérez, and Danys Montes de Oca. My *hermanas Cubanas*, Maria Caridad Cumaná and Mirta Carreras Diaz, are among the best gifts this project has given me. Caridad's scholarly generosity is legendary, and forever appreciated. At the University of Havana, I was welcomed by the Centro de Estudios de Migración Internacional and its director, Dr Miriam Rodríguez. And I am especially and monumentally indebted to Professor Ramón Torreira, who was generous with his time, his substantial personal archive, and, along with his wife, Reina, his hospitality as well. My *hermano*, Carlos Varela, provided the soundtrack as well as insights into history only the poets possess. Jorge Olivares has supported this project from the beginning, and by introducing me to Miami's Little Havana, he also helped to deepen and complicate my understanding of Cuban history.

In Guatemala, my thanks to Thelma Porros at the Centro de Investigaciones Regionales de Mesoamérica (CIRMA) in Antigua, one of the most beautiful archives in which I have worked. During my research time in Guatemala, Rene Calderon did triple duty, acting as translator, driver, and, using his vast network of contacts, arranger of interviews for me. It is possible he knows everyone in Guatemala City. After a few days of immersion in the past and present of Guatemalan crime and violence, I started calling Rene my bodyguard as well, and I was only half joking. Even more reassuring than the presence of a tall Guatemalan male, however, was Rene's ability to maintain both humour and dignity in the face of catastrophic history, and I thank him, and Rona Donefer, for their inspiration and their answers to countless questions.

In North America I am grateful to a number of individuals who facilitated my research at institutions and archives : Johanne Proulx and Claude Laurendeau at Batshaw Youth and Family Centre in Montreal; Heather Falconer at the Lakeshore Unitarian Church in Beaconsfield; Shelley Sorin at the Manitoba Department of Family Services in Winnipeg; David Klassen at the Social Welfare History Archives, University of Minnesota, in Minneapolis; Sister Dorothy Jehle at the Archives and Special Collections at Barry University, Miami Shores, Florida; and Lesbia Orta Varona at the University of Miami Cuban Heritage Collection.

I worked with a talented group of research assistants on this project: Karen Dyck, Katherine Harvey, Brittany Luby, Michele Donnelly, Danielle Beaton, Scott Rutherford, Jennifer Stacey, and Jennifer Westcott. I received translation help from Tara Bickis, Raquel Vásquez, Karen Cocq, and Rona Donefer. Mary Caesar compiled the bibliography. From this accomplished list (and I blanch as I write this, wondering why it possibly took me so long to complete this book when I had so much great help), I want to note especially the work of Scott Rutherford, demon researcher. One example, of many: the day Guatemala finally passed its long-awaited adoption reform bill, Scott sent me the AP wire story; as I read it, I realized he'd sent it to me exactly seventeen minutes after the wire service posted it (and this, incidentally, long after the grant ran out). Thanks to the Social Science and Humanities Research Council and the Queen's University Advisory Council on Research for grants that permitted me to pay these people. My research travels were made more comfortable by my various hosts: Aldo Peña Morejon and Vanessa Chicolo in Havana, Kwame Barko and Pamela Leach in Winnipeg, Ted Ho in Toronto, Laurie Stern and Dan Luke in Minneapolis, Marie Delattre in Antigua, and Katherine Harvey in Montreal.

My Spanish teachers, Angeles Sanchez Toussaint, Judit Luengo Martinelli, and Max Lizano in Kingston, and Caridad Peñalver in Havana, helped me to fall in love with a new language, but no one is responsible for my inability to grasp the subjunctive tense.

Friends, students, and colleagues have given me more than my share of conversations about my ideas and critical readings of my work. For reading all or parts of the manuscript, talking me through problems, and passing on a mountain of references and reading tips, I thank Mary Louise Adams, Mary Caesar, Kelly Dubinsky, Jennifer Hosek, Braden Hutchinson, Kristin Ireland, Cathie Krull, Annalee Lepp, Michael Lima, Susan Lord, George Lovell, Steven Maynard, Ian McKay, Sean Mills, Suzanne Morton, Adele Perry, Ishita Pande, Scott Rutherford, Ariel Salzmann, Laurie Stern, and Cynthia Wright. For fifteen years, Geoff Smith has been an expert and enthusiastic editor (not to mention a great friend); I am again enormously grateful. I have also benefited from the insights of an emerging international community of adoption scholars. Karen Balcom, Laura Briggs, Sara Dorow, Ellen Herman, Tobias Hubinette, Barbara Katz Rothman, and Veronica Strong-Boag also read all or part of the manuscript, and, by their work and their example, made this a better book. So, too, did the anonymous readers at University of Toronto Press and New York University Press. My long-time mentor and friend Roberta Hamilton helped to initiate me into adoption and its complexities, both personal and scholarly. Her wisdom and good sense are here on every page.

I was lucky to find two great publishers for this book: University of Toronto Press and New York University Press. Len Husband at UTP is a prince. Many academics in Canada already know this; it's nice to get to say it in print. Thanks also to UTP's expert editorial staff, Frances Mundy and Ken Lewis. Eric Zinner and Ciara McLaughlin at NYU Press have also been exemplary, and great to work with. Pat Goudvis kindly shared her image archive with me.

Susan Belyea has lived with this book with intelligence and generosity – as she has with many projects – but this one by its nature was an intimate, often intrusive, companion. Lucky for me, and for this book, she's as interested in, and opinionated about, these issues as I am.

This is a book about children and the meaning we make of (and for) them, and since I began my work on it, I've been inspired by many. From a long list, I have especially enjoyed the wisdom of Wilson Lahey Dubinsky, Kurt Kelley Lord, Paul Barko, Gavin Stacey, Oscar Evans, Laurence and Murley Herrle Fanning, Robbie and Danny Smith McCarthy, and Fadzai Katsenga in Canada; Diego Luke in the United States; Gerardo Cruz and Sergio Caal in Guatemala; and David and Daniel Chicolo Peña, Mauricio Garcia Vidal, and Lia and Lis Montes de Oca in Cuba.

Of course, this book is for Jordi, the sunshine of my life. More than once I've felt the irony: the book about symbolic children ('your book about me,' as he calls it) regularly took me away from the real thing. I hope he understands how much he inspires this book and his mothers. This is also for his other mothers: Hilda, Mariela, and Susan.

BABIES WITHOUT BORDERS
Adoption and Migration across the Americas

CHAPTER ONE

Children and the Stories We Tell about Them

Some people keep a lock of their baby's hair, or their first lost tooth. I keep a Guatemalan newspaper from 30 April 2000, the day after a Japanese tourist was stoned to death by villagers who mistook him for a baby-snatcher. I read the headline, 'Linchan a japones,' over someone's shoulder in a crowded bus in Guatemala City, where I had just arrived to meet the baby my partner and I adopted. It has become part of the archives of our son's life and my research. A week later, we arrived at the Toronto airport and proceeded to the immigration office. Unlike many, we breezed through, but not before a woman at an information desk fixed us with a look and said, 'That baby is very lucky.' We heard this constantly for the next few years.

This was my introduction to the contested politics of adoption: kidnap or rescue.

Since that time I've done plenty of research, and this book is full of what historians call 'evidence.' I'll offer up tales from the hundreds of adoption case files I've read, and the many archives I've visited. I'll explain that the core of my project is to move our understandings of interracial and international adoption beyond the false dichotomy of imperialist kidnap or humanitarian rescue. I'll highlight the powerful and deeply historic symbolism of children – bearers, but never makers, of social meaning. I'll ask why it is we look to children to illuminate, gauge, and solve social problems. But I began to learn about symbolic children because I *have* one.

As I've made my way through archives and interviews and airports, crossing several borders and meeting lots of babies, I have gathered many such tales. As an academic historian, it's okay for me to recount a few of these, as long as I keep them in the first few pages of my book.

'There is something disquieting about the confessional historian ...,'
Michael O'Brien writes in a recent round table on the subject. 'History is
supposed to begin not with the historian, but with the past.'[1] Of course,
some people have raised doubts about the voice of the omniscient, ob-
jective narrator, and perhaps it's not a coincidence that feminist historians have been in the forefront of this critique. It was female historians,
after all, who found themselves locked out of the libraries, archives, and
seminar rooms as the scientific model of historical scholarship emerged
in the nineteenth century and consigned women to jotting fiction or
'amateur' popular tracts.[2] Today, self-reflection isn't foreign to historians, but it's not exactly popular. On the whole, historians are still more
interested in the limitations, rather than the possibilities, of scholarly/
personal combinations. We admit our full range of humanness only in
the first few pages of our books, the acknowledgments pages.

Confessional mothers, especially adoptive mothers, also evoke skepticism. To some, invested research is, by definition, stigmatized research. The self, after all, is the ultimate closed archive; who's to say if
I'm telling the truth, working out my own guilt, tooting my own horn,
or committing that unforgivable sin, self-indulgence? Mothers are
a tortured lot, and there are many guilty adoptive mothers out there
these days, writing articles with titles like 'Did I Steal My Daughter?'[3]
Perhaps the revelation that I am an adoptive mother – winner in the
zero-sum game of adoption as it is currently structured – might provide
sufficient information to predict the history I'll tell. A young woman at
the Toronto Women's Bookstore recently answered my query about a
novel I was looking for, about adoptions in Guatemala, by telling me
that they would *never* stock this title. Her vehemence surprised me. We
don't carry books written by adoptive parents, she explained.

I write both as a historian *and* an adoptive parent, and I hope to con-
found the stereotypes of both. The zealous young feminist at the bookstore is, of course, correct in one respect. Adoptive parents have had
their share of air time on this topic, and often they speak in the language
of defensive entitlement (my baby, right or wrong) or wilful naivety
(how can it be wrong to love a child?). By comparison, other voices
are muted. North American birth parents have a handful of spokespeople; on the other hand, birth parents outside North America have
virtually none. The voices of adoptees are a remarkable new feature of
adoption's history.[4] I place myself in the small but inspiring company
of those who write critically about the institution in which they participate. I embarked on this book in part to help create more space for

reflection among those who, as theorist Leela Ghandi has put it speaking of an earlier generation, reject 'possessive nationalism' in favour of political critique.[5] 'I profit from American racism,' declares Barbara Katz Rothman, a white adoptive mother of a black child. 'More than almost anyone I know, I am a beneficiary.'[6] This makes her no less critical of the conditions that brought her a daughter. Neither did adoptive parenthood blind Canadian justice Edwin Kimelman, who led a pathbreaking government inquiry into the adoption of Aboriginal children in the 1980s, and gave the phrase 'cultural genocide' official legitimacy. His voluminous study No Quiet Place was an important source of research for this book, and I learned that he was the adoptive father of four children only when he died, in September of 2007. His obituaries could only puzzle at the apparent paradox: Canada's most famous adoption critic was himself an adoptive father? To me it made perfect sense.

I've found considerable openness towards, and sophistication about, placing the self in the story among anthropologists. By insisting on their presence in their own texts, anthropologists humanize their subjects *and* themselves. Through self-reflection, by recognizing the profound subjectivity of social observation, anthropologists have created a new and useful subject position for the researcher: what Ruth Behar calls 'the vulnerable observer.' Her subtitle is even better: 'Anthropology That Breaks Your Heart.'[7]

I haven't set out to write 'History That Breaks Your Heart,' but this book tells a sad story. My original contribution to an ever-expanding pile of smart books on adoption is to place its history in a wider analysis of the political symbolism of children. The social category 'child' is at once real and metaphorical – powerful as a cultural construct, but equally as forceful in flesh and blood. Children carry enormous cultural weight on their shoulders. A generation of women's historians have shown us how, to paraphrase Judith Walkowitz, 'what is socially peripheral is frequently symbolically central.'[8] The insight that women acted as 'bearers, but rarely makers of social meaning' can be applied even more strongly to children. I think if we recognized the symbolic power of children, we might find our way out of the impasse we're currently in about transnational and transracial adoption.

Children are nothing if not representational; they provide countless opportunities for judgments. I've drawn vast (sometimes involuntary) conclusions about parents I see pushing baby strollers while smoking, or screeching at their children in public. No doubt people have also made quick character sketches of me when I've been rendered incompetent by my child collapsing in a screaming frenzy of refusal at a shopping mall or (once unforgettably) on an airplane. Visibly unusual family formations also provide opportunities for easy conclusions. 'Anyone who saw me with my parents already knew way too much about me,' writes black transracial adoptee Catherine McKinley of her childhood in rural New England.[9] My brown son, growing up in small-town Ontario with two white mothers, may well echo this someday. These are all examples of symbolic children, those whom we look not *at* but *through*. Through children we collect data or form ideologies or make judgments about something small – embarrassed mothers in shopping malls – or large – race relations or the well-being of nations. My choice of stories for this book is necessarily idiosyncratic, as there are plenty of other symbolic children around the world. The symbolic child isn't a recent invention. However, the move towards a globalized notion of 'childhood' through the twentieth century has created many more opportunities for national self-definition through the bodies of children. The United Nations report *The State of the World's Children*, for example, published annually since 1980, is simultaneously an inquiry into the health and welfare of children, *and* of the nations in which they live.[10]

This book brings three sets of symbolic children under one roof: the 'National Baby,' the 'Hybrid Baby,' and the 'Missing Baby.'

The National Baby

The 'National Baby' was an orphan of the Cold War. Between January 1961 and October 1962, over fourteen thousand Cuban children under the age of sixteen, unaccompanied by their parents, departed Cuba for Miami. 'Operation Peter Pan,' so dubbed by the Miami press, was a clandestine scheme organized by the Catholic Church in Miami and Havana, working in conjunction with the CIA and anti-Castro forces in Cuba. Parents were motivated to send their children out of Cuba for several reasons, primarily because of rumours (organized by Fidel Castro's opponents) that the new revolutionary government was planning on nationalizing children and sending them to the Soviet Union for indoctrination or worse. (It is popularly understood in Cuba today that people were led to believe that their children would be sent to the Soviet Union and returned as tinned meat to Cuba.) The children were housed in camps and shelters in Miami, while their parents awaited Castro's imminent demise. As U.S.-Cuba relations deteriorated, and parents were unable to rejoin their children, many youngsters – about half, or seven thousand – found their way into long-term foster care or orphanages throughout the United States. In a story replete with ironies, one remains glaring: parental custody rights were indeed abrogated, but not by the Cubans. As one former Peter Pan child has put it, ' … we ended up in camps after all. We were saved from Prague but were sent instead to naval bases in Opa-Locka, orphanages in Toledo, camps in Jacksonville.'[11]

Almost fifty years later, when one child was found off the coast of Florida, a survivor of an ill-fated journey from Cuba, this history guaranteed that a run-of-the-mill family feud over his custody would take on huge political significance. Elián González became the most famous 'national baby' in recent history, and once more the fate of an actual child served as a compelling metaphor for a fractured nation. Could there be a better poster child for traumas over babies and borders? How many children have not one but two museums – one in Cuba, the other in Florida – dedicated to their story, before they turned ten years old?

I have researched this story on both sides of the Cuban/American divide, in Havana and Miami, in order to appreciate the place of Operation Peter Pan – and the National Baby, in general – in Cuban historical memory. Social upheavals – revolutions, moments of mass migration – unleash enormous anxieties. Rumours of disappearing children have made their appearance since at least the French Revolution, during which, it was said, children were abducted, forced to emigrate, or even stolen by the monarchy, who used their blood for miracle medical cures. Australia's literary history is filled with children 'lost' to the wilds of the outback; in colonial Canada and the United States, children were 'lost' and held captive by untamed Aboriginals.[12] Fears of the communist baby snatcher have emerged during several great ideological contests of the twentieth century: the Spanish Civil War, the Greek Civil War, the Korean War. The protagonists are children, but the social and political dramas they express are always created by and about adults. Operation Peter Pan highlights the particular cultural weight borne by children, how perceptions of the helplessness and innocence of children underscore continued political tensions inside the severed Cuban nation, and why the National Baby captures the imagination. When we look deeper than 'rescue' and see the enduring national traumas that are sometimes enacted over the bodies of migrating children, we can perhaps understand that straightforward 'humanitarianism' is not the only, or best, framework for analyzing these events.

In the next chapter, I'll offer this story as an argument for the centrality of children to the history of nations. When international or foreign policy conflicts are fought through and over the bodies of children, the enormous but often unacknowledged symbolic power of children ensures that such conflicts will have a very long life. So, for example, when anthropologist Marshall Sahlins recently declared, '... no Elián, no war in Iraq' (and obviously he was referring to the mobilization of Cuban Americans as a Florida voting bloc just before the election in 2000), we could take this as a slightly ironic example of the symbolic power of a seven-year-old boy.[13] But we could also acknowledge this as another example of the links between family and foreign policy, and how familial conflicts can, over time and under the right circumstances, metastasize and sustain grievances for years to come.

The Hybrid Baby

The 'Hybrid Baby' is my term for those children produced by the movement for interracial adoption which developed in North America after the Second World War. As adoption was professionalized, legalized, and regulated, agencies observed a strict colour and religious bar. For much of the twentieth century, 'non-adoptability,' a loose but popular concept in child welfare practice, placed black, Aboriginal, and mixed-race children outside the adoption system, in the same category as those with physical disabilities and diseases.[14]

One of the pioneers in breaking North American adoption's colour bar was Montreal's Open Door Society, founded in 1959 by three white couples who had adopted black children. The Open Door Society worked closely with a Montreal agency, the Children's Service Centre, to popularize interracial adoption and place black children in white families. They also maintained strong relations with Montreal's black community, in order to educate white parents about black history and culture. They attempted something new: a unifying, rather than colonizing, philosophy of adoption. Before long, Montreal was what activists called the 'mecca' for interracial adoption, and the Open Door Society hosted international conferences, promoted some of the first academic research on the topic, and advised adoptive parents all over the United States and Canada about how to do it 'right.' Canadian media spoke proudly of adopted black children as 'innocent bearers of racial reconciliation,' and of their families as the embodiment of civil rights ideals.[15] Martin Luther King Jr himself declared his support for

Montreal's adoption pioneers. When criticism of interracial adoption mounted in the United States, most famously in a 1972 declaration by the National Association of Black Social Workers, Canadian adoption activists were puzzled, but continued to feel secure that their own connections to Montreal's black community determined a different, better, future for their families. The black Hybrid Baby still makes the occasional appearance in Canada, including a recent feature in a national newspaper which positioned Canada as a land of 'racial tranquility,' more suitable for U.S. adopted black babies than the 'muggy heat and segregation of the Deep South.'[16] As always, the United States functions as Canada's racial foil, to reflect multicultural tolerance back, and the Hybrid Baby is the perfect conduit.

The adoption of Aboriginal children is also a product of this era, and in this story the symbolism of children plays out very differently. In Canada, this era is known as the 'sixties scoop.' This was a period of massive intervention by child welfare authorities into Aboriginal communities, and the subsequent adoption of Aboriginal children by white families. Yet unlike black children, the Aboriginal Hybrid Baby rarely acquired the status of cherished civil rights symbol. As the term suggests, the 'sixties scoop' defines cross-racial adoption as an instrument of colonization. White social workers outdid the missionary, the priest, and the Indian agent; they took Native children and attempted to erase their history and raise them as white.[17] Here the United States looms as the more progressive country – a rare thing in Canadian political discourse, especially on social welfare or race relations. In both countries, Aboriginal groups and their supporters were appalled by the high rates of children 'in care.' But the United States acted first to investigate and then halt cross-racial placements, passing the Indian Child Welfare Act in 1978. What accounts for these different understandings of adopting across racial lines?

The universal ideal of childhood, and the practices of modern adoption, have, for the past couple of centuries, 'scooped' white children as well. Modern adoption is premised on inequality. 'When the material circumstances of biological kin are good,' writes historian Veronica Strong-Boag, 'formal adoption is almost non-existent.'[18] European child welfare policies intruded in communities defined in class, rather than racial or ethnic, terms. In this sense, Europeans most definitely 'colonized' their own kind.[19] Paradoxically, while racialized groups were more likely to suffer massive intervention in their familial lives and eventually their citizenship status, ethnically defined communities of people were also more likely to resist colonizing child welfare systems. In this book, we'll see that the sheer visibility of adoption across racial borders helped to open adoption's closet. The idea that adoption should be hidden behind visibly similar family members kept it – and its ugly stepsisters, illegitimacy and infertility – out of public view for decades. I wanted to find out more about how this changed, about the children who crossed racial lines in the early years, the kinds of parents who lost them, and the parents who gained them. I'm a historian, so I went to the source, and to my surprise was granted access to confidential adoption case files by two adoption agencies: one in Montreal which worked with black children, and another in Winnipeg which worked with Aboriginal children. In chapter 2, I'll recount what happened when adoption crossed the colour bar, based on the stories I read in almost one thousand case files from the 1950s, 1960s, and 1970s. I'll also contrast the politics of interracial adoption, and the varying symbolic meanings of Hybrid Babies, among different communities in the United States and Canada.

The Missing Baby

International adoptions are now an inescapable feature of the cultural landscape in North America, and oddly configured families like mine leap from Kodak and Benetton ads. Anthropologists and others are busy exploring what they call these 'new geographies of kinship.'[20] Child welfare experts tell us, generally, that adoption is not 'bad for' children, but what is the effect on nations? What does adoption look like from the perspective of 'sending' countries? I'll answer this by examining how foreign adoptions have been discussed in contemporary Guatemala, the country with currently the world's highest per-capita adoption rate.

Nowhere are the ambiguities and anxieties about adoption more apparent than in Guatemala, a country that has experienced intense conflicts about missing babies for decades. Rumours began to circulate in Guatemala in the 1980s that children leaving the country for adoption were actually being sold into prostitution or sex slavery, or killed and their organs harvested. These rumours were fuelled by some specific features of the Guatemalan adoption system, which, until it was reformed in 2007, was decentralized and gave a handful of lawyers tremendous scope and profit. 'Guatemala is the perfect case study of how international adoption has become a demand-driven business,' declared a UNICEF Guatemala consultant in 2008.[21] These anxieties led to the lynching of Guatemalans (and the occasional foreign tourist) suspected of baby theft, as well as to two United Nations inquiries and dozens of media exposés into adoption scandals. At least one Guatemalan researcher, studying corruption in adoption practices, has herself gone missing.[22] Critics of adoption in Guatemala, such as the child welfare organization Casa Alianza, liken the country to a 'child supermarket' or 'a baby factory for rich countries.'[23]

Powerful words and actions like these express much more than concern about internal adoption regulations. In Guatemala, suspicion about foreign adoptions arose in the aftermath of an intense period of civil war, the prolonged consequence of the U.S. overthrow of Guatemala's elected president in 1954. Intense levels of poverty, and the public presence of thousands of street children in Guatemala, as in other Latin American nations, heighten the perception that children's lives are precarious. Guatemalans actually have experienced enormous loss, including countless children. When one lives in what anthropologist Nancy Scheper-Hughes calls a 'chronic state of panic,' perhaps it becomes reasonable to assume the worst.[24]

Awful things do happen to children. But there are dimensions of this anxiety that operate beyond strict questions of truth or falsehood, and veracity is not always the most revealing (or even possible) question. The Missing Baby is real, as those coming to terms with Guatemala's violent history are documenting. Little evidence exists to substantiate organ-stealing rumours – which have emerged throughout Latin America and parts of Africa – but global health statistics and the political economy of medical care make such fears eminently reasonable. The Missing Baby derives its power from Guatemala's tragic history. What I've termed a culture of 'missingness' did not end with the signing of peace accords in 1996. Inside the country, transnational adoption has become a profound statement about Guatemala's failure in handling the complexities of modern life. 'Have you seen what's going on in the airport?' asked a representative of a Guatemalan women's group I interviewed; it was her sad response to my question about the impact of adoption on Guatemalan society. Indeed I had. As the country was in the throes of a long debate on adoption reform, lawyers and agencies were working overtime to process children – twenty a day, by some estimates – headed to the United States, the only country which had yet to suspend Guatemalan adoptions. In chapter 4, I'll explain how foreign adoptions helped create the Missing Baby, and have been considered by many observers to imperil, rather than rescue, Guatemalan children.

Bringing the Stories Together

Symbolic children cross geographic borders, political spectrums, and historical eras. No one nation or political ideology has a monopoly on imagining itself through its children. But the paradoxical combination of enemy-making and global linkages that characterized the eras of the Second World War and the Cold War heightened domestic insecurities and hence the visibility of the symbolic child. During the Cold War, children's 'natural' needs for security and protection called for the construction of complex defence systems. Whether shielding them from atomic radiation or sexual psychopaths, the effect was the same: (silent) symbolic children, like women a century earlier, were idolized and elevated. Cold War children were a product of, and indeed advertising for, Cold War fault lines. Historian Odd Arne Westad highlights the 'teleological functions' of the American symbolic imagination at that time: '… what is America today will be the world tomorrow.' If we broadened the symbolic landscape from Westad's list (faith in technology, fear of state power, anti-communism, the free market) to include the domestic realm (homophobia, male breadwinners, dependent wives, quietly model children), the universalizing mission of First World nations in the modern era is even more apparent (and not just confined to the United States).[25]

The symbolic, contested babies of the Cold War appeared everywhere. When no less an authority on revolution than Che Guevera declared in 1960, 'Cuba will not be another Guatemala,' he had armed U.S. intervention, not baby-snatching, in mind. Guevera was in Guatemala in 1954 and witnessed the CIA-orchestrated overthrow of democratically elected reform-minded President Jacobo Arbenz. The course of Cuban revolutionary history was in no small measure modelled to prevent the repetition of Guatemala's tragic example. Some, such as historian Greg Grandin, argue that Guatemala was the staging ground for Latin America's participation in the Cold War, that 'winning' Guatemala proved even more important to U.S. foreign policy planners than 'losing' Cuba.[26] But like all politics, the Cold War operated on levels both formal and familial. One of the CIA's chief advisors in Guatemala, David Atlee Phillips, worked in Havana a few years later on the Peter Pan project, helping to spread the rumour that bearded communists were about to nationalize Cuban children. As we'll see, a few decades later, when baby-stealing and organ theft rumours swirled around Guatemala, fuelling lynchings and wreaking havoc in the tourist industry, the American state department blamed Soviet and Cuban propaganda for planting the rumours that inflamed Latin American suspicions about foreigners. Yet at almost the same time anxious Cuban parents were seeking safe haven for their children from what they feared was communist persecution, a group of parents in Canada sought asylum for their children in, of all places, Khrushchev's Russia. The Doukhobor Sons of Freedom, a religious group, waged a constant battle with Canadian authorities over compulsory school attendance. Tired of periodically losing parental custody to the Canadian state, the Doukhobors dispatched a delegation to the Soviet Union in 1958 to seek permanent residence and thus save their children from Canadian persecution.[27] Children also figured in the ideological divisions between communist North Korea and capitalist South Korea. At one particularly bitter moment in their contested history, North Korea seized on South Korea's high rates of adoption – initiated during the Korean War – as an 'appalling example of flunkeyism.' Characterizing adoption solely as economic trade, adopted Korean children in the United States and Europe were, from the perspective of the North, 'house slaves' to their former colonial exploiters.[28]

Children also symbolize social progress, or its absence. Civil rights era violence against black children, for example, undermined the global leadership and moral authority of the United States during the Cold War. From the *London Times* to *Pravda*, the story of 'lonely isolated Negro children' attacked by 'fascist thugs of the KKK' for simply walking into a school, contradicted the story the United States wanted to tell the world about democracy and freedom.[29] Canada sat out the massive child migration schemes that followed the Korean War and the Cuban Revolution. Rather, its involvement in Cold War child rescue was to provide a beacon of hope, abundance, and modern family life – especially child-rearing practices – for massive numbers of immigrants fleeing a Europe ruined by war and tyrannized by Communism.[30] Yet, domestically, the poverty-stricken Aboriginal child emerged as a powerful symbol of the limits of plenty and democracy at home. The Aboriginal child meeting death ('trapped, screaming, defenceless') in a burning tarpaper shack was invoked by an especially mournful editorialist as a fitting Canadian symbol of racial inequality, similar to the burning cross in the U.S. South.[31]

'Childhood,' of course, has a unique history and culture in different parts of the world. But, for at least the past several decades, 'childhood' has transcended politically bounded territories and in fact connects various parts of the world together. For this reason, a study of symbolic children becomes comprehensible only as a transnational project. My examples are drawn from different places, and therefore illustrate a central premise of transnational history: that historical processes are constructed 'in the movement between places, sites and regions.'[32] By considering several controversial moments in the movement of children, we'll see that childhood is, as Elizabeth Chin has explained, both 'globalized and an instrument of globalization.'[33] We couldn't have modern transnational adoption if we didn't have a single, global imagination for the 'child.' In this sense, today's adopted child joins other globally controversial, symbolic children, such as the labouring child and the child soldier.

'Missing' Guatemalan babies, 'Hybrid' Canadian babies, and 'National' Cuban babies are linked by their symbolic heft. Each has taken their place in the limelight at a particularly contested moment in national and international history, and came to bear, I argue, the anxieties and aspirations of the adults around them. Children can be, as political scientist Helen Brocklehurst suggests, 'a compelling illustration of wrongdoing.'[34] Sometimes they also illustrate right-doing: Cold War hearts were warmed by the sight of Peter Pan children 'free' on U.S. soil, just as Canadian liberal hearts were cheered by images of black children ensconced in white families. Yet, as Brocklehurst also points out, when children symbolize a story, they actually explain very little. Instead, the symbolic child typically acts to smooth out or even submerge complicated political issues under the veneer of sentiment.

These stories are linked by their historical moment, and by the force of the political controversies they generate. They are also linked by my own choices, observations, and preoccupations. I'm a Canadian historian with a Guatemalan son who spends time in Cuba. In North America, adoption illustrates how racial hierarchies and encounters were refashioned after the Second World War, a compelling topic for a Canadian historian. The Canadian dimensions of this story became even more interesting as I discovered the paradoxical history of the Hybrid baby: a source of both national pride (in the case of black children) and shame (in the case of Aboriginal children). Cuba welcomed me first as an earnest young student activist attending an international youth conference in 1978 and, continually thereafter, now as a researcher and teacher. For those interested in the politics of babies, the place is a gold mine. Symbolic children leap out from every corner of Havana, from the names of daycare centres ('The Dreams of Che,' or 'Future Combatants') to the face of Elián González, still visible on the occasional worn T-shirt. Yet it's also the place where I've witnessed and, especially with my son, *experienced* the profound truth of the words on these pages: there are very different cultures of childhood in different parts of the world. 'Los niños nacen para ser felices,' Cubans are fond of quoting from José Marti: children are born to be happy. (Often, in my experience, this is said ironically, when a child is misbehaving.) History and culture have produced a nation that integrates children into adult life and politics (for good and for ill) at the same time as bestowing upon them an intense, genuine affection. It's a powerful combination, unlike anything I have experienced in North America. And finally, Guatemala. Initially, I didn't choose a country; I chose an adoption agency, recommended by many for its ethics and its lack of homophobia. The agency worked in Guatemala. So while Guatemala was important to me for the simple reason of my son's origins, it quickly became more significant as I probed the contested politics of transnational adoption. As I'll explain in this book, I entered Guatemala's adoption system at a critical juncture. An adoption reform movement inside the country was building; a number of countries, including my own, were on the verge of withdrawing their participation in adoptions from Guatemala; and a long history of missing children was heightening controversies about corrupt adoption practices. Conditions for critical social and self-reflection could not be better.

A few of the common themes I'll explore:

How social fears operate through the bodies of children: What is it about contemporary configurations of the child, asks theorist Claudia Castañada, 'that make it available to such a wide range of constituencies and for such divergent uses?'[35] I believe the answer to this intriguing question lies in the history of the concept of childhood innocence. In the past several centuries, childhood has been understood as essentially vulnerable. The more adult society seemed 'bleak, urbanized and alienated,' British historian Hugh Cunningham writes, the more childhood appeared as a garden, 'enclosing within the safety of its walls a more natural way of life.'[36] Viviana Zelizer calls this the 'sacralized' child – excluded from the cash nexus, children became instead objects of sentiment.[37] This ideal of a safe, happy, protected childhood is a product of the social concerns and priorities of the capitalist countries of Europe and North America. Innocence is the reigning ideology of modern childhood. We expect, promote, and defend childhood innocence on all fronts: sexual, economic, legal, and political.[38]

'Childhood' as we know it today was invented in the West and then, through the hard work of social reformers, non-governmental organizations, and policy-makers, universalized, spread around the world. When children appeared on the international political stage in the early twentieth century, our notions of children's rights moved from legal reforms (replacing labour with schooling) to the broader sense that all children had a right to a childhood, a period of innocence.[39] The invention of a single standard of childhood was by no means a completely top-down process. The gap between the promise of innocent, protected childhood and the reality of most children's lives – First and Third World – provided an important space for marginalized groups to press their case for equitable treatment. The U.S. civil rights movement in the 1960s, for example, was just one of many social movements which attempted to melt stony hearts with the iconography of sentimentalized children. It's no coincidence that Brown vs. the Board of Education, the legal decision that eventually dismantled segregation, was a children's case, or that Martin Luther King's iconic 'I Have a Dream' speech spoke in sentimental terms of the future for 'my four little children.'[40] To those who see in the universalization of childhood solely exported and imposed models, which counter authentic local tradition, Afua Twum-Danso asks us to consider just whose traditional culture is being upheld. Universal instruments, such as the UN Convention on the Rights of the Child, are interpreted and implemented, Twum-Danso reminds us, by local communities, framed through often competing 'local, cultural and religious belief systems and understandings.'[41]

The psychic and political space occupied by the sacral child is enormous. Today, nations are increasingly judged by their ability to provide for their citizens a universal, normative, tightly defined 'childhood.' Children's 'rights,' however, belong only to those who can appear to value them. Despite the obvious fact that there are vast differences between children *within* wealthy countries, today children stand as representative icons of civilized Western subjectivity, in contrast to Third World 'others.'[42] That's one of the reasons people wished me well for adopting my 'lucky' Guatemalan baby; it is perceived that I had provided him with something we recognize in North America as a 'childhood,' something that registers here differently – and, we assume, better – than it does in a place like Guatemala. To the First World, writes historian Vijay Prashad, the 'darker nations' have long seemed like children themselves. 'The people of the colonies cannot save themselves,' he writes, 'so they must be saved.'[43]

The sheer ordinariness of these ideas about modern children becomes evident only in times of stress. Thus when anti-Castro forces planted rumours that the revolutionary government planned to revoke parental custody rights, nationalizing children along with sugar mills and factories, they invoked, but did not invent, the vulnerable child. Similarly, when Guatemalans, living through the carnage of civil war in the 1990s, saw charts, published in a mainstream national newspaper, which listed the prices purportedly paid by foreigners for various stolen organs, we can perhaps understand why a female tourist backpacking through a highland village seemed like more of a threat to children than a visiting U.S. president.

Children as emblems of the nation: Politicians kiss babies for a reason: children make for great symbols of the nation's political aspirations. Indeed, the two concepts – the child and the nation-state – share a similar origin story. The modern child, separated and protected from civic life, emerged at the same time as the modern nation-state, and, as Caroline Levander points out, helped historically to 'constitute and buttress the nation.'[44] Feminists have long pointed to the ways in which women (Mother Russia, Miss Canada) function symbolically to represent the nation's identity and honour.[45] When we focus on the place of children in the national imagination, we can see the psychic and emotional underpinnings of politics even more clearly. In the 1950s, for example, Americans were encouraged to rescue, through donations and adoption, Korean children. This personalized U.S./Asian relations in terms of familial love and elevating adoption as an effective means to fight the Cold War.[46] The campaign to find foster care for the stranded Cuban Peter Pan children a few years later drew on the same themes, as a huge network of Catholic volunteers in the United States were encouraged to 'fight communism one child at a time' by caring for a child refugee. Many such child refugees spent their childhood in the United States as miniature icons of anti-communism, appearing at American Legions and Catholic Church functions, for example, to narrate their stories as anti-Castro parables. 'High politics,' such as relations between nation-states, is often rendered culturally intelligible through metaphors of family. As Melani McAlister argues, this effectively depoliticizes conflicts between nations; identification with the private sphere is 'the guarantee of "innocence."'[47] When the foreign is made familial, abstract or frightening things like missile counts or terrorism become recognizable: the child who needs a hug.

International adoption extends the sentimentalized child around the globe, making, as Emily Noonan has put it, 'entire countries seem unsuitable for children.'[48] To receiving countries, the adopted child is reconstituted with Western interpretations of the culture from which he/she comes, and inscribed with specific forms of Western child-life. To sending countries, the departing 'orphan' can become a cultural resource, a 'child' with rights. Since the 1940s, the offspring of thousands of unmarried Irish women had quietly (and illegally) found adoptive homes in the United States until a high-profile adoption by U.S. film star Jane Russell in 1951 retold the story in starkly nationalist (and populist) terms: Ireland had become a 'hunting ground for foreign millionaires who believe they can acquire children to suit their whims.'[49] Karen Balcom recounts a similar story, showing how Canadian children were protected by a social welfare system to which the ubiquitous 'rich American' often stood as a menacing presence.[50] Like a cliché we never tire of repeating, Madonna's recent controversial adoption merely replayed this same story in Malawi fifty years later.

Some of the most developed research on transnational adoption comes from the experience of Korean adoptees. South Korea has participated in transnational adoption systems since the 1950s; it is the 'sending' country with the highest number of adopted children. By the 1980s, this created a public discourse of shame: adopted children were a painful symbol of national backwardness. In the 1980s, the government began to sponsor 'roots visits' of returning adoptees, who are invited to participate in public rituals of essentialized 'Koreanness.' In so doing, South Korea has sought a new meaning for adoption, embedded in an economic discourse in which the South Korean nation aspires to First World status. The economic success of overseas Korean adoptees parallels the newfound economic strength of the Korean nation. Now the nation can incorporate – even celebrate – its abandoned children, while at the same time ignoring, as Tobias Hubinette observes, the patriarchal sexual politics that produced them.[51]

As we'll see, national shame is currently the leading framework in the public discussion of adoption in Guatemala, but this is not the only possibility. In China, for example, another primary sending nation, shame coexists with a peculiar nationalist/racialist combination: Westerners, some imagine, like Chinese babies because they are beautiful and smart.[52] In Argentina there is still anther way of thinking about children and adoption. During the 'Dirty War' of the 1970s, children were stolen from political prisoners and, in a truly perverse twist, sometimes raised by police or military families. There is now an active movement, initiated by the families of 'disappeared' political prisoners, to reclaim the history and identity of those children. By linking the search for individual identity and demands for widespread social reckoning with the crimes of the war years, the symbolic child in contemporary Argentina is refigured as a source of national inclusion, the foundation for a new and active democracy.[53]

Kidnap and rescue as dominant frameworks in adoption history: Themes of kidnap and rescue dominate our thinking about children and adoption. Think of the sad-eyed Third World children who gaze forlornly in charity or child-sponsorship ads. Laura Briggs calls this the 'visual iconography of rescue': a visual culture of needy children which has provided a portal for middle-class whites in the West to imagine the problems of the poor – domestic and international – and to position themselves as their champion.[54] Child saving has always conferred a kind of nobility: there are vast and blinding pleasures attached to rescue. Adoption today is characterized by openness and an interest in maintaining familial and/or cultural ties of birth, but North American adoption culture has little room for 'celebrating' the political and economic forces that produce adoption – domestic or international – and shape contemporary integrated families. We have inherited an adoption system premised on rescue. In the early twentieth century, as adoption was formalized, regulated, and made the special orbit of professionals, reformers formulated an ideology in which, as historian Ellen Herman puts it, 'they were the exclusive defenders of vulnerable children against a universe of threats and abuses.'[55]

Following Sherene Razack's inquiries into another sort of contemporary rescue, the Western preoccupation with the 'imperilled' Muslim woman, I want to ask what discourses of rescue erase, and what they produce.[56] Children are amazing magicians; they can make the hard edges of poverty, war, and other disastrous effects of economic and foreign policies simply disappear. The self-presentation of most adoption agencies operating in North America – with names like 'Heart to Heart Adoption' or 'Children's Hope' – trades on the vulnerability and cuteness of waiting children, always pictured isolated, alone, devoid of parents, communities, and nations, and waiting for rescue. If I fancied, I could buy myself a T-shirt or a coffee cup or a mouse pad that proclaims, 'I found my son in Guatemala.' The fantasy of the global cabbage patch – filled with what U.S. celebrity 'orphan doctor' Jane Aronson once described as 'lovely, delicious children in the midst of chaos' – is seductive indeed.[57]

The kidnap narrative has its own complicated history. Of course, the 'trafficked' child today is the slave or indentured labourer of the past, and a historical perspective on child migration makes the contradictions of modern times even plainer.[58] Linda Gordon uncovered an important moment in the history of kidnap when a group of angry Anglo-Protestants in 1911 Arizona could not abide the possibility that Mexican Americans might make suitable parents for a trainload of Catholic orphans who had been sent to them, as was the custom then, from an orphanage in New York.[59] The Great Arizona Orphan Abduction was probably reproduced episodically, if less dramatically, through the twentieth century. The kidnap narrative emerged most famously, however, as a response to the 1960s era integrationist fervour for interracial adoption. It's been revived in the testimonies and political activism of domestic birth mothers, survivors of that cruel era when white girls, at least, could find redemption only if they relinquished their babies and forgot their history.[60] A recent, rare study of birth mothers in South India confirms that pregnant single women face shame and punishment around the globe.[61]

Transnational adoption produces its own kind of common-sense kidnap narrative. Children move from south to north, east to west, poor to rich, brown to white; over 50 per cent of them end up in one country alone, the United States. David Eng calls international adoption the most privileged form of immigration in the world today; with the stroke of a pen, a 'needy object' is transformed into a 'treasured subject,' worthy of economic protection, political rights, and social recognition.[62] At the same time, adoptive families embody – some more consciously than others – the unequal conditions that establish the basis for modern multiculturalism. The enthusiastic embrace of adopted children stands in stark, and perverse, contrast to the immigration policies aimed at others from their countries. We seem, as historian Paula Fass delicately puts it, 'increasingly willing to grant to children what we are far more reluctant to grant to their parents, a universal appeal.'[63] How could 'sending' nations *not* begin to imagine their babies as bananas: first you destroy our country, and then you rescue our children.

The point of this book is not to join, but rather to complicate, this tug-of-war. Kidnap and rescue speak to certain truths, but they are incomplete, partial, and abstract. Both rely on unreflective thinking about essentialized, sacral children, who remain mute (until, of course, they grow up and write their own stories). Babies are not just so many bananas, and the intense emotional attachments between adults and children in our world are too complicated to fit into simple binaries; certainly almost none of the hundreds of adoption case files I've examined could be described solely in the stark terms of kidnap and rescue. But ultimately the real problem with the Hybrid Baby, the National Baby, and the Missing Baby is that they, as with all symbolic children, simply bear too heavy a cultural burden. Real people, particularly birth parents, disappear when the story is told too abstractly. Symbolic children have come to represent an unequal world, with little consideration of the circumstances – created by adults – which produced them. Journalist E.J. Graff recently termed transnational adoption 'the lie we love.'[64] She is referring to the widespread but erroneous belief that all adopted children are orphans, and that a 'world orphan crisis' lies behind the phenomenon of transnational adoption. A prior lie, however, which facilitates this one, is the myth of universal, dependent childhood that stands apart from political and economic conflicts.

In this book, I make room for the many stories, such as – but by no means only – my own, in which neither kidnap nor rescue makes sense. I 'found' my son, not in a Guatemalan cabbage patch, but in a network of people who loved and cared for him. He has a birth mother who, accompanied by her brother, came to meet my partner and me and say goodbye to her son; a foster mother who sends him birthday cards; a foster brother with whom he recently spent a day imitating the monkeys at a zoo in Guatemala City. We don't meet on even ground. But we do meet, and neither kidnap nor rescue explains the conditions that brought us all together.

CHAPTER TWO

The National Baby: Creating Monumental Children in Cuba, from Operation Peter Pan to Elián González

In Havana, my morning run along the city's seawall, the Malecón, takes me past the oddly named U.S. Special Interests Section – essentially the embassy in a country which has not had a U.S. diplomatic presence since 1961. Having borne the dreams of the left and the nightmares of the right for five decades, Cuba fairly screams symbolism at every turn, and these days the area around the Special Interests Section is ground zero in a global battle for signification. I usually visit Havana in December, for me a respite not only from Canada's cold but also from Christmas, an event which, in its North American incarnation, I have grown to loathe. (I believe I join many parents of small children here.) But one especially memorable year I realized I could not outrun Christmas, even in godless, mall-less Cuba. Passing the embassy, I could see on display behind the heavily guarded fence a peculiar American holiday tableau: a decorated Christmas tree, a crèche, a neon-lit menorah, and several flags with Islamic crescents. Answering back, across the street the Cuban government had erected a huge billboard that depicted the now-familiar silhouette of the hooded Abu Ghraib prisoner, a swastika, a photo of Arab children at gunpoint, and a caricature of George Bush with a Hitler mustache. Quite a sight: in one spot, I took in the Cold War, the 'War on Terror,' and the Second World War (not to mention an overdose of various December holidays). Of course, such posturing between nations is nothing new, though Americans and Cubans occasionally demolish the line between 'statecraft' and schoolyard taunting. 'Naturally, if they are going to fuck with us, we will fuck them too,' well-known Cuban political commentator Randy Alonso Falcón told U.S. journalist Jon Lee Anderson in 2006, speaking of the war of symbols outside the embassy.[1] But just to the side of – perhaps even metaphorically underneath – this flag-waving and finger-pointing sits a vast apparatus of child symbolism. This, I believe, has sustained these national animosities as much as missile crises, bombings, and assassination plots have. Next door to the Special Interests Section is the 'Anti-Imperialist Tribunal,' a large open-air plaza built during the Elián González crisis, perfect for staging the many rallies and speeches which were organized in Cuba demanding Elián's return from his extended family in Miami to his father in Cuba. At one end of the plaza stands a statue of Cuban nationalist hero José Marti, holding a child protectively in one hand, pointing an angry, accusing finger towards the United States with the other. Post-González, this plaza still comes in handy and is used for a variety of political and cultural events. (There are always good reasons, in Cuba, to point accusing fingers at the United States.) Yet why, after years of political conflicts between Washington and Havana, did the custody battle over a single child occasion the construction of this permanent tribute? What makes this incident – of all others – monumental?

In this chapter, I'll explore the significance of Elián González's ill-fated journey across the Strait of Florida and the subsequent intra-familial and international debate about where he ought to grow up. The high point of the saga was the period between González's dramatic rescue from the inner tube he clung to after losing his mother and several others when their boat capsized in November 1999, and his equally dramatic return from Miami to Havana in April 2000, when his Cuban father's request for custody was finally enforced by the U.S. government, literally at gunpoint. But the story has important, on-going resonance, on both sides of the Cuban-American divide. While I think Marshall Sahlins's quip cited in the Introduction – '... no Elián, no war in Iraq' – overstates the case (and talk about a symbolic burden!), we shouldn't underestimate the chain reaction of political events González's story triggered, in both countries. But I'll focus most of my attention on Elián's precursors, rather than his legacy, for I believe the key to understanding the commotion caused by *one* migrant Cuban child lies in the backstory – the tale of the fourteen thousand who went before him.

Operation Peter Pan: The View from Cuba

By the end of 1960, relations between the United States and Cuba were unravelling. One of the Cuban Revolution's first initiatives was a land reform package, which redistributed existing landholdings and forbade foreign ownership in the future. Immediately after this was announced, in May 1959, the Eisenhower administration issued a public note of protest, and launched a private campaign to bring about, in the polite words of the National Security Council, 'a new government favorable to U.S. interests.'[2] From here, of course, the escalating skirmishes between the two countries are well documented and well known: the U.S decision to cut Cuban sugar imports, the Cuban nationalization of U.S. properties such as oil refineries and hotels, the U.S. economic embargo, the Cuban decision to accept Soviet military and economic relations, and the failed U.S.-supported Bay of Pigs invasion in April 1961.

The invasion was but one volley in a complex and multi-faceted campaign against the Cuban Revolution, a program of sabotage, bombings, assassinations, and other covert activities. Even after years of researching this topic, this chapter of Cold War history still occasionally seems absurd to me, as though I'm reading (or even writing) a lurid spy thriller, not a footnoted history book. Operation Peter Pan still creates tremendous disagreements, and the lines are drawn even in the terminology used. Counter-intuitively, perhaps, in Cuba it's known by its English name *Peter* Pan, a nickname, given by a Miami newspaperman, that stuck. In Miami, it's now more commonly known by its Spanish name, *Pedro*. The significance of these different names was made clear to me during my research time in Miami. I learned the story first in Cuba as 'Peter' (the name I continue to use), but in Miami I was often corrected for this and had the impression that my use of 'Peter' was, at best, impolite. The puzzle lies in the politics: *Peter* implies English-speaking, American government, CIA manipulation; *Pedro* connotes Spanish-speaking, Cuban parents making their own immigration decisions about what, and where, was best for their children. So is the context for this story the history of CIA-sponsored 'dirty tricks' against Cuba, or does it lie in the history of immigration? Can it be both?

If the story of either Peter or Pedro seems too much a product of left-wing paranoia or clichéd novels, consider this: In November 1960, Radio Swan, the CIA-funded station created to broadcast anti-Castro messages to Cuba, aired a remarkable story. 'Cuban mothers,' it began, 'don't let them take your children away! The Revolutionary Government will take them away from you when they turn five and keep them until they are eighteen.' A later broadcast warned parents that their children would become 'materialist fiends,' and Fidel Castro was poised to become 'the Mother Superior of Cuba.'[3] Parents were encouraged to go to their churches and receive further instructions from their clergy. A month later, the first Peter Pan children boarded flights from Havana to Miami.

The director of Radio Swan was David Phillips, an important player in what he called the CIA's 'propaganda shop.' Phillips learned his craft organizing and broadcasting fake reports from 'internal opposition' to the leadership of reform-minded President Jacobo Arbenz in Guatemala in 1955, to whom the government of the United States and the United Fruit Company – not always easily distinguished from each other – had taken a dislike. (The station, 'Voice of Liberation,' purported to emanate from freedom-loving Guatemalans hiding out in the highlands. In reality it was Phillips and a handful of Guatemalans based in Nicaragua.) As Phillips himself explained, his CIA training taught him that 'rumor campaigns were decisive in affecting political and military events,' and after six weeks of broadcasting disinformation to Guatemala, 'the climate for revolt had been created.'[4]

As for the propaganda and disinformation campaign accompanying the Bay of Pigs invasion, Phillips estimated that what took six weeks in Guatemala would take Radio Swan at least six months in Cuba.[5] He was, of course, spectacularly wrong, as Cubans declined emphatically this invitation to revolt. (Phillips simply packed his bags and went to Chile, where he organized a speaking tour by Castro's anti-Fidel sister, so that she could warn Chilean women if they voted for socialist candidate Salvador Allende they too would lose their children to Russia.)[6] But perhaps in his wrongness we can understand the escalation of covert action in the Cuban case. A year after Radio Swan began broadcasting the child-snatching rumours, in September 1961, Cuban authorities claimed they uncovered a spy ring operating in the town of Cienfuegos, complete with a printing press and copies of a false law, which provided details of how the newly opened *circulos infantiles*, daycare centres, were in reality permanent boarding houses for all children over the age of three. Rumours also circulated that the government planned a large census to amass information about all children under seven. State control of children would be achieved by revoking '*Patria Potestad*' – parental custody rights – essentially nationalizing children along with the nation's sugar mills and oil refineries.[7]

The extreme variant of this rumour, that children were to be shipped to the Soviet Union, turned into tinned meat, and shipped back to Cuba, dates from this era as well. The exact origins and trajectory of the tinned-meat rumour are, as rumours are wont to be, difficult to pin down, and there's no evidence that the CIA, even in its wildest dreams, came up with this one. It raises fascinating questions about how we interpret popular beliefs that are both widely held and as widely held to be false.[8] Today, everyone in Cuba I asked about it sees it as a Cold War relic, an example of how frightened people, especially parents, were in that era. The story does not appear in the written record until well into the 1970s and 1980s, where it starts to function as a measure of the paranoia of previous generations. The writer Gabriel García Márquez revived it in an article during the Elián crisis.[9] Cuban historian Ramón Torreira traces the rumour to the U.S. economic blockade, imposed in October 1960, and the increasing reliance on imported Russian and Chinese food supplies, including tinned meat, then a new product for Cuban consumers. Other Cubans I've interviewed recall the oddness of – and general distaste for – Russian tinned foods when they first arrived. Filmmaker Marina Ochoa, who produced the first Cuban documentary film on the story, told me she perceived a class and race hierarchy in the rumour campaign: the *Patria Potestad* story was directed at the urban, white, middle class, while peasants in the countryside, as well as those in Oriente (the area with the highest concentration of Afro-Cubans), were more likely to hear about their children disappearing and returning as tinned meat.[10] A generation earlier, rumours had circulated in Havana that Afro-Cubans kidnapped and killed white children for their blood or their organs, a not uncommon response to fears about growing Afro-Cuban attempts at religious and political autonomy in the early twentieth century.[11] Cuba's tinned-meat rumour also joins such legends as the vampire tales of colonial East and Central Africa, the '*chupacabras*' which stalked 1990s Puerto Rico, or the varieties of organ-theft rumours in 1980s and 1990s Guatemala, which I'll explore in a later chapter. We might, as many have, understand such rumours as the irrationality of the peasantry, or as straightforward metaphors for life under colonial or military rule. Or we might follow the advice of African historian Luis White and focus on what such stories articulate in a given time and place.[12] There's a world of baby-eating stories. To a Cuban population in the 1960s, reeling from the combined effects of the Revolution and the U.S. economic blockade, baby-eating was perhaps not such a stretch from baby-snatching; either way, the children were about to be devoured.

The Cuban government response to this escalating series of rumours in the early 1960s set a tone that lasted a number of years. An inventive balance was struck, in which both the perpetrators and the intended targets of the rumours were mocked. Initially, the Cuban government pointed to financial impossibility of such a project. Responding to the Radio Swan broadcast in December 1960, the revolutionary government declared that the *Patria Potestad* rumour was 'obviously too stupid for anyone with common sense,' for it would be impossible for the government to house and care for thousands of Cuban children.[13] Similarly, after the spy ring and printing press were exposed, Castro himself launched a long defence of *Patria Potestad*. Calling it 'the most absurd, ridiculous, shameless hoax the Counter-revolution has come up with,' Castro, with characteristic subtlety, laid the blame on both his opponents and the rumours' recipients. 'Those imbeciles,' he said, invented this story to 'trick the irrational people, because rational people would not allow themselves to be tricked.' Furthermore, he had a firm understanding of whom he believed the real target was. 'It is truly cruel,' he said, 'that they make a group of mothers the victims of their shameless actions, that a group of mothers has to suffer this fear ... they have planted a seed of doubt in the minds of Cuban mothers.'[14]

This link between the heinousness of the child-snatching rumours and the sheer stupidity of those who believed them continued during the rare occasions the story was discussed in public in Cuba – until recently. Those who sent their children away were acting 'in an idiotic manner, letting themselves be confused,' Castro declared in a speech in 1965. Later he called them 'naive people, cretins,' who 'believed the lies of the imperialists.' Discussing the false law rumour in an interview in 1987, Castro again revealed a specifically gendered understanding of this tale: 'A reasonable person,' he said, 'would never say that such a thing could be credible, but a mother who is told, "they're going to take your child away," may panic.'[15] Of course, this scenario makes huge assumptions about women's ability to make independent immigration decisions for their children; it is a view of the power politics of Cuban families in the early 1960s that is contradicted by immigration scholars and common sense.[16] It also provides a revealing glimpse into revolutionary sexual politics. Others have noted the same combination of blame and condescension in official state pronouncements on prostitution, an offshoot, perhaps, of the continued hyper-valorization of sentimental notions of mood in Cuban culture.[17] The Cuban Revolution demanded what Ruth Behar terms an 'ultra-virile sense of national identity,' an erotics of power which included women and feminist reforms, but obviously privileged charismatic revolutionary men. How else to confront the 'emasculating power' of U.S. imperialism?[18] In the home, women may ascend, as a Cuban journalist has put it, to 'a throne which no one disputes,' but as always the problem with moral pedestals is that it gives one further to fall. This disproportionate blame borne by Cuban mothers resurfaced during the González crisis, when Elián's mother was often depicted as a weak-minded dupe of her manipulative boyfriend.[19]

Socialist ideas about family life historically have been complicated and contradictory. In practice, the left has often been less radical and committed to changes in familial and gender relations than many feminists would have liked, and Cuba is no exception. From Operation Peter Pan to Elián González, all parties, in Cuba as much as in the United States, speak the language of blood ties, 'natural' families, and a relentless sentimentality about children. During the González saga, one commentator noted the 'absurdity' of Fidel Castro appealing to the preservation of the nuclear family as 'his "best means" of criticizing his opponents in the Cuban-American community and the U.S. government.'[20] As we'll see in the next chapters on adoption politics in North American Aboriginal communities and contemporary Guatemala, there's nothing like kidnap – real or imagined – to create essentialist counter-discourse. Symbolic National Babies are not the province of any particular political ideology. Yet socialist tenets about women's equality and children's political autonomy stand out, providing plenty of scope for anti-socialist attacks.[21] International outcries about communist baby-snatchers followed child relocation schemes by leftist forces during the Spanish Civil War in 1937, and again during the Greek Civil War in 1948, and the Soviet Union itself had a long and well-known history of pushing the limits of Western notions of childhood. [22] The Cuban government was well aware of this complicated history. 'This is not the first socialist revolution in the world,' Castro stated in 1961, and 'in no socialist country has there been made a law of parental authority which separates children from their parents.' Revolutionary publications dutifully reproduced the legal codes of the Soviet Union and Czechoslovakia, in an effort to calm baby-snatching rumours. Castro also reminded Cubans that 'revolutionaries also have children' and there was no contradiction between being both a communist and a 'faithful and loving parent.'[23]

But during these years there was no possibility for a 'loving parent' to make an immigration decision. Peter Pan parents (particularly those who were later able to rejoin their children in the United States) were understood in the familiar terms of all who departed from Cuba in these years, for, as de la Campa has put it, 'leaving the revolution was equivalent to leaving the nation, since they were meant to be one and the same.'[24] 'Imagine,' said Castro in 1971, speaking of the Peter Pan parents, 'all those undisciplined, anarchic worms, without a homeland, without principles, without anything.'[25] Consider the venal returning mother in Jesus Diaz's 1985 film *Lejania* (Distance), one of the first Cuban films to confront immigration and the tremendous tensions between 'los que van' and 'los que se quedan' (those who go and those who stay). Here the Peter Pan scenario is reversed; it's the mother who fled to Miami, leaving her teenage son in Havana. The end of upper-class autonomy – the same issue that created Peter Pan – provoked her departure. As she explained, 'They took over our schools and our world collapsed.' And when she returns some years later for a visit, her suitcases bulging with jeans, electronic equipment, and other spoils of capitalism, she was mocked at every turn. Ultimately her daughter-in-law voices what's on everyone's' mind: 'You should have stayed with your son. No one can understand what you did, lady.' Whether bamboozled by imperialist treachery or seduced by visions of shopping malls, we end up in the same place: weak-minded parents, always represented as mothers, whose immigration decisions have disastrous effects on their families and their nation. Particularly so when the fate of the children themselves was pondered. To the extent Peter Pan children themselves were discussed publicly in Cuba, they filled stereotypical roles in the Cuban imagination about life in the United States. 'What happened to these children?' Castro asked rhetorically in a speech in 1971. 'They were led into vices ... transformed into gangsters, put into prostitution.'[26]

The history of U.S. attempts to thwart Cuba's revolutionary government, by overt and covert means, is of course well known, but because of the centrality of children to the revolutionary enterprise, Operation Peter Pan occupies a special place in this history. Denouncing the false rumours about *Patria Potestad*, *Bohemia*, a popular weekly, declared that 'if the revolution has concerned itself with anyone, it has been with the children.'[27] It would be impossible to overstate the symbolic importance attached to early revolutionary reforms of the education system, literacy, and the creation of a public system of child welfare, including daycare, inside Cuba. Reviewing the national daycare system in the 1960s, U.S. visitor Marvin Leiner termed children the 'elite, the raison d'être of the Revolution,' who received better food than did their parents.[28] Healthy, educated, serious-minded children leap off the pages of early revolutionary publications, reinforcing one central message:

children were essential to the revolution, and vice versa. In this climate there was simply no sympathy for those parents who believed that the line between 'taking care of' and 'taking' was about to be breached.

Escape, Rescue, and Salvation: Peter Pan Flies to America

Cold War escape narratives were a popular feature in North American magazines of the 1940s and 1950s. According to historian Franca Iacovetta, these tales of escape from behind the Iron Curtain to freedom in North America featured handsome male masterminds of risky escapes, or sometimes couples who braved danger in their thirst for freedom.[29] Family reunification, generally between husbands and wives or boyfriends and girlfriends, lay at the heart of these heroic and uplifting stories, revealing how the Cold War touched insecurities from the abstract to the intimate. Political demonology is a complicated process, and during the Cold War enemies were created at levels simultaneously global and familial. By blurring fact and fiction and projecting collective fears, desires, and rumours, communist adversaries in foreign lands were transformed into a clear and present danger.[30] On the U.S. side of the divide, the Peter Pan story became a remarkably popular and powerful example of the escape narrative genre, and I think it suggests something important about what happens when *children* are added to this drama.

Invoking the language of the space race, the Miami Catholic clergy involved in the relocation and resettlement of Cuban refugee children referred to their project as 'a race between the two great powers of the world for the minds of children.'[31] By insisting that child-saving take its proper place alongside missile manufacture and rocket counting, the rescuers of course assumed for their project, and themselves, world historic importance. The most prominent of the churchmen, Irish-born Father Bryan Walsh, who became the public face of Operation Peter Pan, was the director of Miami's Catholic Welfare Bureau, a social service agency of the Catholic Diocese of Miami licensed by the state of Florida for child welfare programs. In October 1960, Walsh and his small staff were contemplating how they were going to continue their work in the face of a looming 30 per cent budget cut. (In this era, the state of Florida competed with Mississippi to see which could spend the least amount of money per capita on social welfare.) Two months later, he found himself at the Miami Airport waiting for the first planeload of Cuban children to arrive, having just received one million dollars authorized by President Eisenhower for their assistance. As he recalled, '… no longer were we simply a social agency concerned about a community problem. We were now sharing the worries of families we did not even know, hundreds of miles away in a life and death struggle in the Cold War.'[32] Given the extraordinary powers wielded by Walsh in this tale, he could be forgiven a bit of hubris. During the twenty-three months of Operation Peter Pan's existence, the Catholic Welfare Bureau's staff increased from fifteen to over three hundred, and Walsh oversaw a budget of several million dollars provided by the U.S. government for the care of Cuban children. More remarkably, Walsh himself acquired the power to direct immigration policy, for he was given authority to grant visa waivers to any Cuban child under the age of sixteen. As the best U.S. chronicler of this story, Maria de los Angeles Torres, has put it, with considerable understatement, this program created 'historically unprecedented relationships' between the government and private and religious refugee relief organizations.[33]

Of course, the U.S. government ran a parallel, generous, and overt refugee program for Cubans, and the first Peter Pan children joined a community of approximately 60,000 exiles in the United States by the end of 1960.[34] Operation Peter Pan, and the visa waiver program for minors, remained officially classified, and several decades later a lawsuit brought by scholar Maria Torres to open U.S. government archives pried loose a tiny portion of information.[35] U.S. government officials and Catholic Welfare Bureau staff worked very hard to keep this a clandestine operation, for, as the director of the Federal Children's Bureau explained, publicity 'would inhibit the 'endanger families and relatives.'[36] Secrecy is central to the escape narrative, and in this case it reinforced two key themes – the idea that Cuban children were in immanent danger, and that the U.S. population as a whole had a role to play in helping them. The role of spoiler was played by a reporter from the *Cleveland Plain Dealer*, who, over a year into the program, noticed the Cuban foster children in his neighbourhood and started asking questions. Unlike the dozens of other reporters who knew the story, this one decided to go public, and so Walsh, along with the U.S. government, did likewise, issuing their own press release and calling for foster parent volunteers. In a blaze of headlines, the dramatic story of the rescue of these 'political orphans,' saved from 'Castro's brainwashing,' was accompanied by self-congratulatory editorials of how the tale had been kept secret for so long.[37]

By this time, the program had moved far beyond Miami, and children had been taken in by fifty-six Catholic dioceses (as well as a handful of Protestant and Jewish organizations) in thirty states. Years later, a former editor at the *Miami Herald* recalled at a banquet honouring Walsh, one of many such affairs in the late 1970s and 1980s, that 'in this day and age, we would go to court to fight any attempt to gag us, but Walsh got voluntary compliance from all of us to keep quiet,' when he told them that to do otherwise would endanger the lives of the children.[38]

Even when the story broke, in March 1962, secrecy remained paradoxically an integral feature of the narrative. Heightening the drama, the Miami Diocese sent out an official photo of Walsh with a group of Peter Pan children who were photographed from behind, their faces obscured from the camera. The diocese officially requested that other media, pursuing local angles, never photograph the children's faces or publish their full names. And so, through the spring of 1962, daily newspapers and Catholic weeklies across the United States featured sentimental stories about how their communities had participated in the rescue of Cuban children from communism, complete with photos of children with black bars printed over their eyes. When this request for secrecy was ignored – which it was, more than once – Walsh's office took note: his voluminous archives of press clippings includes one story from a newspaper in Rockford, Illinois, on the margins of which an angry hand has scrawled in pencil, 'names and faces!'[39]

This on-going discourse of secrecy mixed culturally shared assumptions about the special vulnerability of children with garden-variety Cold War paranoia. Was it true? Were Peter Pan children, or their Cuban parents, ever in danger? This seems unlikely. 'That's Hollywood,' Peter Pan alumnus and spokesperson Elly Chovel told me, when I interviewed her in Miami and told her of the escape narratives I was finding in the press archives.[40] Departing children, like all Cubans, needed exit visas and vaccination confirmation from their government to leave. Furthermore, by 1960, the revolutionary government had effective intelligence operating in Miami.[41] But really all anyone had to do was open one's eyes. By all accounts, the departure lounge at Havana Airport (popularly known as the *pecera*, fish bowl, because of its glass walls) was, in this era, the site of massive, tearful departure scenes, packed with families that had chosen actual, rather than feared, separation. As a sorrowful middle-class Cuban explained to visiting U.S. journalist Warren Miller in 1961, 'You must go to the airport some time and see the children leaving this island. It is the saddest sight in the world, the tears of the parents and the tears of the children.'[42] (This image was later made famous in Tomás Gutiérrez Alea's 1968 film *Memorias del subdesarrollo* [Memories of Underdevelopment], which depicts many such tearful departing Cubans, including seemingly unaccompanied children, at the airport.) Escape narratives, however, have their own dynamic; dagger needs cloak. Accounts of children secretly whisked out 'right under Castro's nose' dominated the U.S. press in the early 1960s, even though a U.S. government representative was moved to declare such tales 'exaggerated.'[43]

This first flurry of U.S. media interest helped establish a lasting American framework for this story, featuring three essential components: escape, rescue, and salvation. More than one reporter used the term 'underground railway in the sky' to describe the story. Later, participants linked Operation Peter Pan with yet another iconic humanitarian rescue effort, the Kindertransport, which rescued Jewish children from Nazi Germany.[44] Headlines such as 'Displaced Tots Know Horror of Red Cuba' took common sense, Cold War anti-communism and wrapped it around the innocent, malleable child. 'They speak in adult terms about things with which no child should have to contend,' said the *Miami Daily News*, quoting four-year-old Consuelito, newly arrived from Cuba: 'Fidel kills children.'[45] To those across the narrow Straits of Florida, the range of dangers facing children in Cuba after the revolution was staggering. Reporting on the rumours that Castro was about to revoke *Patria Potestad* and send all Cuban children to full-time daycare centres, *Time Magazine* claimed that trucks were sweeping through the country picking up unaccompanied children. To those who found this surprising, *Time* reminded its readers that 'as Lenin himself said, revolution is impossible as long as the family exists.'[46] Another variant of this rumour was also popular: that children were being shipped – sometimes it was reported, *without passports* – to Russia for education and/or indoctrination. That Castro's own son was among those who had 'disappeared behind the Iron Curtain' moved this assertion quickly from rumour to fact.[47]

Another set of rumours concerned the changes the revolutionary government was making to the education system. One such change was the Literacy Campaign of 1961, during which all schools were temporarily closed, and thousands of young urban volunteers were encouraged to move to the countryside to teach literacy. While exiles, and the U.S. press, fumed about the highly politicized curriculum ('F' stood for 'Fidel' and 'R' for 'Raul'), to others it stood as a great and noble accomplishment. The campaign 'caught the attention of the world,' historian Richard Gott observed. Hugh Thomas declared it the 'last fling of the romantic side of the revolution.'[48] The Cuban visual record of the Literacy Campaign – preserved in such films as *La Brigadista* and *Batalla por un Idea*, and in a remarkable small museum in Havana – is one of wildly enthusiastic youth – many of them female, many of them black – cheering their role in eradicating Cuba's 40 per cent illiteracy rate. To some parents, however, the prospect of sending their middle-class teenagers to the countryside, long imagined as primitive and unsanitary, where they might encounter promiscuous mingling between the sexes (and even the races), was yet another example of the threat posed by the new social order. 'The literacy campaign,' writes Roman de la Campa, 'exposed Havana's white children to the rest of Cuba.' Former Peter Pan child Ileana Fuentes speculates that this lay at the heart of her parents' decision to send her away: '... perhaps,' she considered, in retrospect, 'it wasn't so much about political oppression as it was about premature personal freedom.'[49] Alarming (and often misleading) reports about revolutionary sexual politics (for example, that the new government discouraged marriage as simply a tax by the church) helped to fuel a small but significant migration of Jewish Peter Pan children as well.[50]

Even worse were the changes the revolutionary government instituted to right the lopsided balance of power and resources between the private and public education systems. The complex history of education in Cuba, the overwhelming inequalities between the private, religious system and the public system, internal rifts between Church and State, as well as among classes, races, and regions, were flattened into one seemingly inescapable fact: Castro was attempting to 'capture the minds' of Cuban children, who were forced to learn communism 'from Kindergarten up.' With no hint of irony, Father Walsh himself described Cuba's private Catholic schools as 'the last refuge from indoctrination' constantly threatened by the revolutionary government.[51] Cartoons which circulated in the U.S. media, depicting, for example, a wild-eyed Castro reading Marx to a group of schoolchildren, who themselves are frantically trying to swim away from Cuba, helped foster this one-dimensional understanding. Changes in the culture and politics of youth in Cuba after the revolution were indeed profound; Torres terms the changes a process of 'militarization' of youth. Others are more measured. 'They were teaching us Marxism in school,' remembers Eduardo Machado, who has written a play about his Peter Pan experience, 'but my parents treated it like they were gassing us.'[52] A fantastic example

¡CON LA "PESTE" EL ULTIMO..!   **Por Prohias**

'Last one in is the rotten egg!' This cartoon, by Antonio Prohías, of *Spy vs Spy*
fame, hung in the offices of Miami's Catholic Welfare Bureau.

of the horrors of the Cuban school system circulated in a *Miami Her-*
ald story titled 'African Savages Take Over Her School: A Cuban Girl
Flees in Terror,' which described how 'big black men with rings in their
noses,' exchange students from Congo, had 'invaded' thirteen-year-old
Anna Maria Delgado's school in Matanzas. 'I was terrified,' she said,
from the safety of Miami, 'they're savages; they wear short skirts and
eat wild fruits.'[53]

What made these stories believable? The long history of suspicion
concerning leftist ideas about the family is obvious here, and during the
Cold War, this met a set of new anxieties about youth. Where we 'educated,' communists 'brainwashed.' Like propaganda, brainwashing
was the sole province of communists: a scientific mechanism for repro-
gramming the minds of innocent victims. The concept was developed
by U.S. authorities during Stalin's 'show trials' in the 1930s, and was
useful again during the Korean War in the 1950s (to explain why such
a large number of U.S. soldiers in Korea appeared to be collaborating
with the communist enemy). It is striking, from the perspective of the

Cuban Revolution, that the concept moved into the U.S. mainstream in 1959, with the publication of the best-sellling *The Manchurian Candidate* (the less successful film was released in 1962).[54]

This coincided with an emerging set of concerns about young people's mental stability, particularly after the stresses of the Second World War. To some, such as psychologist Frederic Wertham, who published the inflammatory study *The Seduction of the Innocent* in 1954, even a quick peek at a comic book had mind-corrupting potential. The fragility of youthful mental and emotional development was a hallmark of psychiatry and social welfare of the era.[55] One story, which circulated in different versions in the United States through the early 1960s, revealed just how dangerous communist brainwashing methods were to youth. Cuban schoolteachers were reportedly telling their students to pray to God for ice cream. They close their eyes in prayer, nothing happens. Then they are told to pray to Fidel, and ice cream quickly appears on their desks. 'You see,' the communists tell the impressionable children, 'Castro is a bigger power than God, Castro can answer your prayers.'[56] In his recent autobiography, *Waiting for Snow in Havana*, Peter Pan child Carlos Eire captures magnificently how 'brainwashing' was understood in his upper-class Havana household:

> Fidel came down from the mountains ... swept down like an avenging angel burning with white-hot envy, frothing at the mouth. Beelzebub, Herod, and the Seven-Headed beast of the Apocalypse rolled into one, a big fat smoldering cigar wedged between his seething lips, hell-bent on imposing his will on everyone. Hell-bent on ensuring there would be no king but he, no thoughts but his. He wrecked Bethlehem, leveled it, slaughtered all its children or drove them away ... I was one of the lucky ones. Fidel couldn't obliterate me as he did all the other children, slicing off their heads ever so slowly, and replacing them with fearful, slavish copies of his own.[57]

Finally, to understand fully perceptions of the menace of the Cuban Revolution for young people, we have to remember that Americans have long had trouble granting Cubans – of any age – adult political subjectivity. The clearest answer to the question everyone asks now about Peter Pan – 'Why did their parents let them go?' – lays here. Most thought the United States would do what it had done in Cuba throughout the twentieth century: get rid of a government it didn't like. The revolution simply reinforced Washington's habit of representing

Cubans, as historian Louis Pérez describes it, 'as children incapable of understanding their best interests.' CIA director Allen Dulles, for example, advised that 'the new Cuban officials ought to be treated more or less like children,' and the metaphor of the wayward 'little brother' was invoked often.[58] The image of Third World leaders as volatile children was a constant motif for Eisenhower's administration, when a world of infantilized (sometimes feminized) decolonizing nations appeared vulnerable to subversive influences.[59]

Perhaps this helped Americans to understand – especially in light of the constant litany of horror stories – why the revolution attracted tremendous support from youth, at home and abroad. The virile young men who took the reigns of power in 1959 entered what one historian has called a 'geriatric' world stage: Dwight Eisenhower, Charles de Gaulle, Harold Macmillan, Nikita Krushchev, and Mao Tse-tung, all born in the nineteenth century, had been in power for years. [60] 'Everywhere,' wrote an enthusiastic Elizabeth Sutherland visiting in 1969, 'youth seems to be on the move ... Nobody is too young to be mobilized for anything.' Even Castro's opponents saw this. *Newsweek*, for example, opined in 1961 that youth were Fidel' s 'most fanatical followers.' Testifying to a U.S. government subcommittee studying Cuba in 1962, one adult refugee estimated that 70 per cent of his countrymen on the island opposed Castro, but among youth, his support was almost total.[61] Exiles claimed this was because children were being bribed – they were fed while their parents starved, flattered while their parents were terrorized. On the other hand, a generation of New Leftists in Europe and North America saw in the Cuban Revolution an inspiring illustration of youth culture in action. In any case, Fidel, like James Dean and the Beatles, was alarmingly hip. In the 1960s, declares Cuban writer Rafael Hernández, 'Cuba put Latin America in fashion.'[62] Growing up outside of all this, some Peter Pan children had the sense they missed a lot. Reflecting on her parents' decision decades later, an adult Peter Pan alumna said sadly, 'They sent us away from Cuba so that we would continue to be like them.'[63]

Both sides of this paradox – the revolution's sinister intentions, and young people's apparent receptivity to them – also help to explain the urgency of rescue. From the moment the story went public, when U.S. welfare secretary Abraham Ribicoff issued what was termed 'a national plea to American families to shelter the youngsters,' Operation Peter Pan invited widespread American participation.[64] One Christian publication put its pitch for foster parents in the familiar folk language metaphor of the 'Good Neighbours Policy,' which characterized Franklin D. Roosevelt's policy towards Latin America: 'Many U.S. citizens traveling through Latin America have received the gracious Spanish welcome "*Esta usted en su casa.*" Now several hundred American families can return the hospitality each month, saying to Cuban children bereft of parents, "Make yourself at home!" ... We can think of fewer better ways to "fight communism" than to care for the children who flee from it.'[65] In recent high-profile media campaigns, through donations and adoption, Americans had been encouraged to rescue Korean and Chinese children, thus personalizing U.S./Asian relations in terms of familial love and elevating adoption as an effective means to fight the Cold War.[66] After Ribicoff's appeal, hundreds of families came forward to help wage what some called 'a personal, everyday fight against communism.'[67] The small Jewish and Protestant contingent of Peter Pan children was eclipsed by the Catholic majority, as American Catholics were encouraged to recognize their personal stake in the contest. 'For the first time,' an Ohio priest explained, 'our American Catholic people are being given a taste of the communist hand reaching at us from only a few miles off our shores.'[68]

Peter Pan children came with a few liabilities. They were not cuddly babies, neither were they adoptable. The majority were older boys, perennial losers in the North American adoption and foster care system. Traditional prejudices against foster children were countered by a small army of local Catholic social welfare volunteers. As one woman in Rhode Island emphasized, 'These are not problem children, they have not been neglected, abandoned, nor were they delinquent. These children came from families who care what happens to them.'[69] To foster parents, the rewards for sheltering these 'little refugees from atheistic communism' were many. As one Illinois foster mother explained, 'Having Daniel in our home helps our own children realize how fortunate they are to be able to go to a Catholic school and the blessing it is to live in freedom.' Another agreed that 'Raimundo and Raul cause us to realize our own freedoms better now.'[70] A few foster parents saw in their Cuban guests an opportunity for cultural exchange. While the Miami Diocese made Spanish-speaking foster parents a priority, supply quickly swamped demand, particularly outside Miami. One Illinois couple actually prepared for their foster child by taking Spanish lessons, and noted that their children too enjoyed learning from their Cuban visitor, joking, 'The baby likes Lourdes so much that we thought she was going to learn to speak in Spanish.'[71] The foster parents of (future) Florida construction magnate Armando Codina enjoyed the lesson in Cuban cuisine their young charge provided; after a while, they said, 'We really got to like black beans.'[72] Far more common, however, were stories of triumphant transitions to American culture and values. 'If Cuban parents inside the tragic island are worried about their sons who came alone to America,' wrote a Miami journalist, 'they should have a look at the boys kneeling in the chapel or snitching sweet rolls from the dining room. On the basketball court, they looked and acted like American teenagers,' a picture made that much more poignant when he pointed out that 'these same arms could be carrying rifles in Cuba, and these legs would not know basketball courts.'[73]

Outside Florida, where Latin American immigrants themselves were rare, Peter Pan children were a curiosity, but also a heart-warming symbol of American generosity. Photo spreads from Birmingham, Alabama, Denver, Colorado, and Oswego, New York, for example, portrayed Cuban children 'enthralled' with their first snowfall, enjoying 'exotic' American foods like peanut butter, and defiantly learning Monopoly, 'a game of rampant capitalism.' One evocative photo, captioned 'God has not moved,' depicted a girl at her orphanage bedside praying.[74] Scenes like this, wrote a Virginia Catholic newspaper, 'filled the patriotic American with justifiable pride.'[75] Many of these human-interest stories about the lives of Cuban children in the United States included a remarkably un-ironic reference to the class inversion they were experiencing as refugees. Readers in Wisconsin, for example, were introduced to 'Pedro,' son of one of the wealthiest families in Havana, who grew up with his own servant. Now he bunked with four other boys, including the son of a labourer, who taught him, a reporter explained approvingly, how to make a bed. 'There was a time,' recalled another boy, between mopping and sweeping at the Miami boy's camp, 'when I didn't have to do anything but get out of bed, I had a maid and a pretty perfumed mother.'[76] 'Americanization' included a conversion to anti-aristocratic, egalitarian values – presumably some of the very forces they were fleeing in Cuba. Yet somehow this confirmed the superiority of the life the children would find in the United States. Out of this morass of contradiction and self-congratulation emerged this most chilling example of how Peter Pan children deflected glory back upon their American rescuers. Jean Wilson, a veteran Miami journalist, wrote, in a widely circulated Associated Press story, that the children 'arrived heartbroken, but hopeful that a life in freedom will make up for a life without parents.'[77]

Peter Pan Grows Up

The Bay of Pigs invasion in April 1961, combined with the Cuban missile crisis in October 1962, helped to determine that in fact many Peter Pan children would face 'a life without parents.' Commercial flights between Cuba and the United States ceased for several years after the missile crisis. An agreement between the two countries on family reunification was reached in the fall of 1965, and parents of unaccompanied children were given first priority on what were dubbed in the United States 'freedom flights.' Hundreds of Peter Pan families were reunited in this manner; however, exactly how many reunions took place – or failed to take place – is unknown.[78] Unlike their namesake, these children grew up, with or without their parents. The next chapter of their story takes place from the 1970s to the present, as the Peter Pan children evolved from mute icons into individuals who spoke in their own voice. As their symbolic meaning continued, even intensified, their collective fate remains open to question. To date the only empirical study of Peter Pan children, journalist Yvonne Conde's *Operation Pedro Pan*, is based on survey responses from a small group (442, about 3 per cent of the official figure of 14,048 child refugees), all drawn from the (then) thousand-name mailing list of a Peter Pan alumnae/alumni group active in South Florida.[79] Another Peter Pan chronicler, Victor Triay, based his tale of Peter Pan veterans on oral histories of a tiny (though moving) sample.[80] As the Peter Pan children grew up through the 1960s, the story receded from public view, in both countries. When the 'children' began, about a decade later, to narrate their own lives, a remarkable range of stories emerged.

Is Peter Pan a Marxist?

Despite their early symbolic value as miniature anti-communists, some Peter Pan children took their assimilation into American culture seriously, and, like many of their generation in the late 1960s and 1970s, became radicals. When they finally addressed their past in their own voice, 'recuerdos agridulces' (bittersweet memories) came flooding forth. A 1978 collective memoir, *Contra Viento y Marea* (Against Wind and Tide), speaks of the excitement of departure, mixed with vivid, sad memories of goodbyes at the airport. Most believed their stay would be short, and many were excited that they had the opportunity to study in the North, which had been a sign of status in Cuba for many generations. Almost all believed that their parents had been frightened by the *Patria Potestad* rumour into sending them away. Like immigrants the world over, they explain their subsequent radicalization in terms of the gap between what they'd been promised and what they encountered. Life in the Florida transit camps – which for some lasted years – evoked terrible memories. 'A microcosm of the social order of old Cuba,' recalled one. 'I was always in a state of alert,' remembered another. 'There were teams of kids who robbed each other, cut their hair, put snakes in their pockets. And to think our parents thought they were sending us to a good private school. The prehistory of radicalization, for many of us, began in the camps.'[81] As they moved through the foster care or orphanage system, they encountered humiliation, racism, and numbing homesickness. 'We weren't allowed to complain,' recalled one woman, 'because after all they had saved us from Communism.'[82] A few remembered excursions to local American Legions, where they were expected to narrate their story as an anti-communist parable. Despite all this, some of them, at least, proved remarkably ungrateful. By the early 1970s, Young Cuban Socialist Groups began appearing in Florida university campuses, and many joined with other Latinos in the cause of civil rights, Puerto Rican independence, and anti-imperialism. Taking their symbolic currency into their hands, Peter Pan radicals appeared in demonstrations marching under banners that read, 'No Todos Los Cubanos Son Gusanos' (Not All Cubans Are Worms).[83] Even more remarkably, a group of them, dubbed the Antonio Maceo Brigade, returned to Cuba in 1978. A Cuban-made documentary, *55 Hermanos* (Fifty- five Brothers), told their story to a mass audience in Cuba as a tale of prodigal children returning to correct the errors of their parents. 'The Cuban-American community thinks we are victims of mind-control techniques,' says one, smiling to the camera, 'but we decided we wanted to come to Cuba to see for ourselves.' As the visitors symbolically and literally construct socialism by volunteering with a 'micro brigade' (volunteer construction groups which attempted to extend Cuba's housing stock in the 1970s), one of the Cubans with whom they are working declares, 'It's important for them to be here to see how badly mistaken their parents were to abandon the revolution.' The highlight of the film is an emotional meeting between the visitors and Fidel Castro. This is first time, as film scholar Marta Díaz notes, that pejoratives were *not* used in official discourse to describe Cuban immigrants. Instead, as victims of their parents (and obviously enthusiastic supporters of the revolution), they were embraced.[84] Cuban writer

Teresa de Jesús Fernández recalls watching the documentary as a teenager growing up in Havana, and her astonishment that the return of child migrants indicated 'the tiniest opening that went beyond dogmas and preconceptions.'[85] Castro discourages them from moving back to Cuba, as some of them wanted to do, and asks instead that they return and 'enlighten' the United States about life in Cuba. 'We consider you part of the family,' he tells them, to tears and applause. 'I believe our homeland has grown.' A year later, a Miami-based anti-Castro group assassinated travel agent Carlos Muniz Varela, a Maceo Brigade member and organizer of several such trips for returning Cuban exiles.[86]

Is Peter Pan a Republican?

By far the loudest and most public voice belonged to those Peter Pan children who told their story as one of success, pure and simple. The success narrative positions Peter Pan children as the ultimate rags-to-riches immigrants: from child refugee to secure, well-off American in little more than a decade. 'Where else,' Jeb Bush's former business partner, construction entrepreneur Armando Codina, inquires in *Readers Digest*, 'could a young kid go alone, with nothing, and grow up to do the things I have done?'[87] The achievements of the children reflect the wisdom, indeed heroism, of those who organized the Operation, and thus another part of this story is the elevation of its protagonists, especially Father Walsh, to the status of sainthood. Finally, there can be no question that Operation Peter Pan was simply the right thing to do, that personally and politically the premises of the rescue mission were accurate. To hold all this together, of course, the handprints of the CIA are erased; rather than a Cold War plot, Peter Pan is remembered as a moving tale of immigration under trying circumstances.

Cynical observers might be forgiven for thinking that the success narrative was predetermined – that just as the Cubans believe all Peter Pan children grew up to become prostitutes and drug addicts, Americans have been encouraged to believe they are all construction magnates and real estate agents. Occasionally the U.S. press peeked in on the children as they were growing up, and always offered reassurances about their well-being. The children have adjusted 'remarkably well,' the *Miami Herald* reported in 1969, indicating that fewer than one hundred of them required psychological treatment. On many occasions Father Walsh, like a doting father, pointed to the high numbers of professionals – including several dozen ordained priests – and the low level of delinquency among Peter Pan youth. 'They all grew up pretty much unscathed,' seemed the happy consensus, and thus for decades, Operation Peter Pan has basked in the warm glow of several of its most successful participants.[88]

The list of professionally and economically successful Peter Pan alumni/alumnae is well known in South Florida. Among them are Codina, singers Willy Chirino and Lysette Alvarez, and numerous Miami politicians. In 2007 a fictional character was added to this illustrious list, when CBS television introduced a new series, *Cane*, in which Jimmy Smits portrayed a former Peter Pan child adopted into a wealthy Cuban-American family. In the 1990s, Peter Pan alumni could brag that they were running Miami, but a decade later their political influence extended much further, as George Bush appointed two high-profile Peter Pan alumni, Eduardo Aguirre and Mel Martínez, to political posts in Washington. Martínez, probably the most famous Peter Pan alumnus outside Florida, was elected to the U.S. Senate in 2004, the first Cuban-American to hold this position. His Peter Pan credentials became strong assets during his campaign, as what he referred to as 'my incredible life story' became part of virtually every speech he made. By highlighting his own dramatic escape from communism – claiming, for example, that as a child he hid from photographers when they visited his Florida boy's camp, fearing for his parents' safety in Cuba – he effectively (if inaccurately) used his childhood to bridge the Cold War and the War on Terror. 'Mel Martínez knows what it's like to live in a world without freedom' (next to an image of the World Trade Center ruins in New York) became a key campaign message.[89]

These success stories confirm the appropriateness of the mission, and they tell the same tale, writ small, of which Cuban Americans are so proud: meteoric economic and political success within one generation. Just as the escape narratives proved exciting at the height of the Cold War, the Peter Pan story continued, over the decades, to confer greatness on some of its protagonists. Since the beginning, Father Bryan Walsh occupied centre stage, but Peter Pan created two other Cuban heroes, Ramón (Mongo) and Polita Grau. The Graus, brother and sister, were descendants of an illustrious family; their uncle Ramón Grau San Martin was a former Cuban president. Turning against the revolution early on, the Graus were both arrested in 1965 as CIA agents. Both did long prison stints in Cuba, and both were received as heroes by the exile community in Miami upon their release, she in 1978, he in 1986. Maria Torres has noted the presence of large numbers of women in the

Peter Pan underground in Cuba. Yet an excessive number of 'fathers' dominate the public record, Polita (dubbed the 'godmother' of the operation by the Miami press) is a significant exception. While Mongo and Polita both admitted proudly to years of activities against the revolution – including assassination attempts against Castro – it was their work as Cuban intermediaries of Peter Pan that garnered them the most praise, and ensured their heroic status. On many different occasions, both told this story (each one claiming it happened to them): upon their arrest, Cuban police told them directly that their Peter Pan activities were much worse than their attempts on Castro's life, for through Peter Pan, they 'robbed Cuba of its future.'[90] So, while Peter Pan was, for the Graus, a highly selective part of their heroic self-fashioning in exile (much more than, for example, their abortive attempts to poison Fidel Castro), it is also true that, from the Cuban perspective, the Graus link to Peter Pan earned them a special enmity. Upon learning that they were to be honoured in Miami after Ramón's release from jail in 1986, *Granma* published a rare story on Peter Pan, reminding Cubans of the 'imperialist propaganda' which circulated after the revolution (including the Russian tinned-meat rumour, which rarely appears in print), and calling the celebration of the Graus a 'glorification of a crime.'[91]

The real hero of this story, however, remains Father Bryan Walsh. Endlessly described in the media in sentimental, familial terms ('Father, they call him as in Dad,' declared a typical headline in 1985), Walsh clearly inspired affection from a great many of his fourteen thousand 'children'; even his spankings are recalled fondly.[92] His archives bulge not only with his own press clippings, but also with Father's Day cards and photos of 'grandchildren' (children of Peter Pan alumnae/alumni), more than one bearing the name 'Bryan. His death, in December 2001, was the occasion for massive tributes from civic, political, and religious leaders in South Florida (including former U.S. attorney general Janet Reno), as well as hundreds of Peter Pan alumni/alumnae (one of whom placed his Visa waiver in Walsh's casket during his funeral).[93] Walsh is remembered as a 'father in exile' to his Peter Pan children, but also more generally as 'the conscience of the community' – a friend to Haitian immigrants, African Americans, and others at the margins of Florida society. To be sure, Walsh endorsed some positions which remain politically unpopular in South Florida: he believed the U.S. economic blockade against Cuba, for example, was a 'violation of international morality'; he supported those Cuban Americans who advocated dialogue with Castro's government; and he opposed U.S. military aid to El Salvador.[94] He referred to himself as an advocate for 'social justice,' crediting his suffragist mother in Ireland for instilling his social conscience. Over time, he explained his involvement in Peter Pan less in the cataclysmic terms of Cold War anti-communism, and more as an issue of human rights. Towards the end of his life, he was more likely to dwell on the rights of Cuban parents over the horrors faced by Cuban children. A month before his death, for example, he addressed a Barry University convocation – home of the Peter Pan archives – explaining his motivation for organizing Operation Peter Pan: 'Who was I to deny Cuban parents one of the most fundamental human rights, the right to decide how their children would be educated?'[95]

So while the ground upon which Walsh made his reputation has shifted, he provided the main conduit for the ongoing memorialization of Peter Pan in the United States for several decades. This began in 1978, when five hundred Peter Pan alumnae/alumni, including developer Armando Codina, honoured Walsh, to much media fanfare, at a dinner at a swanky Miami hotel. Ostensibly raising funds to help unspecified 'needy children,' this event established a pattern which would be repeated many times over the next decades; banquets like this were held occasionally through the 1980s (once timed to coincide with Father's Day) and annually in the 1990s. The success narrative is confirmed at such events through their exclusive location: hotel banquet rooms, with plenty of photos of wealthy revellers in Miami newspapers the next day. This allowed for the continued circulation of the Peter Pan story through the 1980s and 1990s, when it might have otherwise disappeared from public view. Peter Pan events were also always tied to children's fundraising efforts, casting the Operation in the warm glow of humanitarian child rescue. Recently, the Operation Pedro Pan Group – the organization of alumni/alumnae headed by Miami realtor Ellie Chovel – led a successful campaign to turn one of the original camps which held newly arrived children, Matecumbe, into a combined museum, park, and nature preserve. 'This is like my Ellis Island,' declared one Peter Pan alumna, perhaps an indication of how the story is likely to be told in the planned museum.[96]

Of course, all historical memory is selective, but in this case it is staggeringly so. The public cracks in the rescue narrative – and there have been a few – disappear quickly, leaving almost no trace. In 1990, for example, when Ramón Grau admitted to a Miami journalist that the U.S. government had indeed manufactured and spread false rumours concerning *Patria Potestad*, the *Miami Herald* called Operation Peter Pan 'a massive form of child abuse perpetrated by the U.S. government' and insisted, 'It's time to stop idealizing this horrible chapter of Cuban American history.'[97] A flurry of letters from grateful Peter Pan alumnae/alumni refuted this, as did others when Maria Torres launched her well-publicized lawsuit against the CIA to try to force open their archives. 'The CIA's role, no matter how crafty or embarrassing, will have sowed a noble and justified undertaking,' one wrote.[98]

The painful, familial intimacies of this story – Cold War dramas played out in thousands of Peter Pan families – further complicate the creation of historical memory. To acknowledge the role of the U.S. government in creating a climate of fear in 1960s Cuba is, in a sense, to erase Peter Pan parents, or, perhaps worse, to render them in the same terms as Castro's early speeches on the topic – stooges who permitted themselves to be hoodwinked by the Yankees. So when some middle-aged Peter Pan veterans opted for denial, declaring that 'no level of Cold War misinformation from the CIA or anyone else could foster such a momentous decision' – a theme repeated by many – we should remember the intimate familial, as well as the abstract ideological, perspective: these were their own (by now aging) parents they were talking about.

Yet abstract ideology continues to find its way into this tale, and nowhere more so than with the recent involvement of high-profile Republican senator Mel Martínez. Martínez, who has clearly learned the value of a good origins story, often lent his name to the ongoing memorialization of Operation Peter Pan, which ensured that its most prominent, public face would be its happy one and that its Cold War origins and premises remained valid. And this is not just about the past. Martínez, for one, is motivated by contemporary as well as historical political concerns. He considers Operation Peter Pan a precursor of the faith-based initiatives promoted by George W. Bush.[99]

Peter Pan Returns: Elián González

Four decades of frayed U.S.-Cuba relations have done little to dislodge the kidnap narrative as the primary lens through which Operation Peter Pan is publicly remembered in Cuba. As we've seen, Cuban understandings have dwelt upon the weak-mindedness of the Peter Pan parents, who allowed themselves to be hoodwinked by imperialist treachery. For decades, Operation Peter Pan presented a vexed problem in Cuba: in a country in which everyone, including schoolchildren, was encouraged to take to the streets to denounce departing fellow citizens as *traidores* (traitors), how might one interpret the politics of *child* migration? As a (fictional) Cuban explains to a visiting Cuban American (who departed the country at a young age) in Achy Obejas's novel *Days of Awe*, 'You are absolved, my friend, you may live guilt free among the bourgeoisie, the enemy, because you had no say in your predicament. You can come back and we will help you cry about your lost, lost Cuba, because none of this is your fault.'[100] The relative silence about Operation Peter Pan in Cuba, for the first few decades of its history, may well reflect exactly this ambivalence: Who did it? Who is the agent, who is to blame?

At the end of the 1990s, however, this silence was abruptly broken. Torres's lawsuit against the CIA awarded the Cuban version of the kidnap narrative some external credibility. The Cuban press reported that even the *New York Times* was finally acknowledging CIA involvement.[101] Shortly after this, in March 2000, the first Cuban study of Operation Peter Pan appeared, amidst the ongoing custody battle over Elián González. This proved an extraordinary powerful combination, and brought renewed attention to national babies, old and new.

Operación Peter Pan: Un Caso de Guerra Psicológica contra Cuba refocuses the story from bamboozled parents, locating culpability squarely in Washington. Ramón Torreira and his co-author José Buajasan Marrawi highlight not just U.S. government involvement but U.S. financial interests as well. The start-up funds for Peter Pan, well before the U.S. government kicked in, came from recently nationalized U.S. oil companies, as well as the American Chamber of Commerce.[102] Their main argument is that Peter Pan was not a spontaneous flight but a well and consciously organized campaign to instill panic, uncertainty, and rebellion in Cuban parents. 'My hypothesis,' Torreira told me during our first of many interviews in 2004, 'is that the children were held hostage in the U.S. so that their parents in Cuba would become counter-revolutionaries.'[103]

This understanding has now found its way into Cuban official discourse, as *Granma*, for example, recently explained that Peter Pan had 'the concealed intention of overthrowing the Revolution.'[104] *Operación Peter Pan* locates the story squarely (and solely) in the context of the ongoing campaign of intervention, 'dirty tricks,' and terrorism directed at Cuba by Washington, and documents the extensive underground activity – in Catholic private schools, embassies, and elsewhere – which facilitated the rumour-mill inside the country. In this way, the authors removed some of the lustre from the heroic rescue narrative building in

Miami. 'With this book,' Buajasan told a Cuban journalist, 'we are trying to prevent every CIA agent from entering Heaven ... during these
forty years in banquets and self- tributes they have elevated an aggres-
sion to charitable work.'[105] In this account, the children's parents fade
from view; the real motor of the story is the counter-revolution. 'The
paradox is,' they write, 'that the same persons who said they had humanitarian motives were the material or intellectual authors of multiple criminal actions ... which resulted in the death and mutilations of
children and youth.'[106] Virtually all of those involved in Cuba in Operation Peter Pan, according to Torreira and Buajasan, were also participants in a host of other more sinister and violent counter-revolutionary
activities; the line separating 'humanitarian' child rescue is inseparable
from assassinations, bombings, and other forms of terror. While Torreira, a specialist in the history of religion in Cuba, had spent many
years researching and writing the book, the fact that it was released at
the height of the Elián González saga (by 'happy coincidence,' Torreira
explained to me) helped to cement the symbolic ties between these two
sets of National Babies. 'La historia de 14 mil Eliáns,' reads the cover
jacket. The parallels between the two stories 'jump out at you,' declared
Granma. 'Yesterday it was Radio Swan that spread false news to plant
terror; today it is the (Miami) Hispanic channels and the columnists at
the *Nuevo Herald* ... The CIA and its internal acolytes tried during the
60s to destroy the Cuban family; the Cuban-American National Foundation takes their turn with the true family of Elián.'[107] So, while those
selfsame columnists at Miami's *Nuevo Herald* accused Cuba of 'trying to
dust off Operation Peter Pan to use it as a strategic blow' in their campaign to repatriate González, the links between the two stories certainly
brought the past to the present with rapid and unusual speed. Inside
Cuba, the book sold 'como pan calient' (like hotcakes) in two large print
runs. Throughout the Elián saga, Torreira and Buajasan toured the island giving numerous presentations on their work.[108]

During my research time in Cuba, several years after González's return, many of my Cuban friends had grown weary of both Elián and
Peter Pan. González and various members of his family continue to
grace the stage during many government functions in Cuba, and while
I have heard of no one in Cuba who didn't support his return to his father, there are those who grumble that there's been too much celebrity
culture around Elián since his return. Some of this may have rubbed off
on the Peter Pan story as well: when I told one especially acerbic Cuban
friend that the historian Torreira was granting me considerable inter-

view time, he replied: 'You need to understand that there are only two people in Cuba who care anymore about Operation Peter Pan, and one of them is you.' Yet when I accompanied Torreira to the 'Elián Museum' in Cardenas, where we both addressed an audience of children from Elián's school on the topic of Operation Peter Pan, and international adoption, I witnessed what for me were several historic firsts: a room full of ten-year-olds as conversant with history, global politics, and international relations as many of the Canadian undergraduates I teach. When I told them that I had learned what people think *about* Cuban children, but I wanted to know what Cuban children think themselves, they told me, standing up and giving rapid-fire political testimony. They especially wanted me to know that Fidel Castro is *not* their father. I also watched people line up – in one case even stop him on the street – to tell Torreira their tearful story of family members whom they had 'lost to Peter Pan' (a common, and deeply telling, way of expressing this in Cuba.) 'I didn't realize you are so famous, you are a star,' I joked to him later. 'More like a therapist,' he replied.

The intrusive public discussion of painful familial intimacies that accompanied the González saga – a level of personal politics foreign to Cuban political culture – helped create a new idiom for speaking of the past as well as the present. American scholars termed the González story a 'magnifying glass' for immigration tensions in Miami, and a host of commentators have seen in it a potent symbol for Cuban/U.S. foreign policy, the U.S. economic embargo, immigration policy, religion, and the self-presentation of Miami's Cuban-American community, to name several examples.[109]

It is notable that on this rare occasion when a child entered the lexicon of international politics, few analysts have focused on Elián as a *child*. I think the story caught fire on both sides of the divide because of the ways it symbolized, in the body of one photogenic boy, the tensions, fractures, and separations experienced by Cuban children over decades of U.S./Cuban hostilities. Operation Peter Pan was clearly part of this history, but so too are the countless stories of Cuban families separated by immigration. Indeed, 10 per cent of the Cuban population has relocated since the early 1960s. The ongoing Elián González saga did more than bring the Peter Pan story back into the limelight, it also added a new layer of meaning to the place of the National Baby in U.S. and Cuban historical memory. 'I was an Elián of the 1960s' was how one Peter Pan alumna described herself, as many related their stories – almost always remembering its painful dimensions – and weighed in on the proper fate of González. There was certainly no consensus of Peter Pan alumni/alumnae in the United States on this. For some, the distance between the early 1960s and the early 1990s was but a heartbeat, and the same rescue narrative served González as it had in the past. 'Clinton's government will give the child back not to Juan Miguel González but to Castro,' declared one Peter Pan alumnus in Miami. Others compared Elián's flight to young women fleeing genital mutilation or those escaping Nazi Germany.[110] Old clichés about the status of children in Cuba surfaced with a vengeance: Cuban children, according to a Miami-made documentary (a selection of the 2001 Miami International Film Festival), learn they must denounce each other to achieve success, and that loyalty to Castro is more important than familial relationships. In other words, four decades later, some believe that *Patria Potestad* has, in effect, been abrogated.[111]

Yet other Peter Pan alumnae/alumni supported his return and, as is fitting, perhaps, for those now experiencing middle age, found the language of therapy, forgiveness, and familial reconciliation more compelling than the Manichean discourse of the Cold War. Elly Chovel decided, after meeting with Elián in Miami, that he was better off with his father in Cuba. For her, as for many Peter Pan alumni/alumnae, the story raised painful memories; after her meeting with Elián, she was shocked to find that 'nothing had changed.' Even Father Walsh refused to jump on the Elián bandwagon; he declined to reveal his views on the subject other than to note his alarm at the evidence of what he termed 'an emotionally disturbed child' in Miami.[112] Speaking of the attempts of adult Peter Pan alumnae/alumni to understand their peculiar and painful childhood, U.S. academic Flora González notes the difficulties of analysing individual traumas in a climate of ongoing political tensions.[113] Indeed, not many of us have two governments' foreign policies deeply invested in our childhood memories. Nevertheless, for several, a combination of middle-age self-reflection and the sharply drawn debate about Elián created new space for thinking about the past.[114]

The González saga also brought to Cuban official discourse a new subtlety about Peter Pan parents. When Castro told the Peter Pan story to Elián-era audiences, he stated simply that parents had been 'taken in by a carefully crafted and deliberately fabricated rumour ... spread by the U.S. intelligence service.' 'It is always hard when a child leaves,' Castro told a group of children during the Elián crisis, 'but we respect the rights of parents.'[115] Of course, Elián's story unfolded in a vastly changed Cuba, after the catastrophic economic effects of the demise of the Soviet Union (the so-called 'Special Period') set Cuba on a path of partial 'dollarization,' new patterns of immigration, and new relationships – economic and cultural – between Cubans and their immigrant families abroad. Last decade's *gusanos* became this decade's 'Cubans living abroad,' most of whom, far less ideologically driven than earlier generations, support relatives in Cuba financially and return for visits (despite U.S. policies which discourage this).[116]

González's story was popular because, despite its particular – and profound – tragedies, it reflected widespread social experiences, and this vast public conversation authorized a popular rethinking of child immigration conflicts in Cuba. In the González era, migration issues – always sensitive in Cuba– emerged with a vengeance in cinema, painting, fiction, and theatre. While Peter Pan has yet to be explored – or even mentioned – on the screen, child migration and family separation have.[117] Humberto Solas's popular film *Miel para Oshun* (2000) follows an adult child exile on his return through Cuba during the González saga. The parallels between the adult child émigré and González are established as the protagonist, Roberto, looks out from his window at the Hotel Nacional on the crowd gathered in the plaza outside the U.S. Interests Section. In the background, we hear the voice of Juan Miguel González demanding his son's return. Roberto's quest is for his lost childhood as well as for his mother, portrayed sympathetically (if one-dimensionally) as a woman mad with grief when her son left. Themes of forgiveness and reconciliation are pervasive. Juan Carlos Cremata Malberti's *Viva Cuba* (2005) is the first Cuban film that tries to narrate child migration conflicts from the point of view of a child, rather than a retrospective adult. Focusing on the impending separation of two best friends, Jorgito and Malu, as Malu's mother has decided to leave, *Viva Cuba* is a unique attempt to imagine immigration conflicts not over the bodies of, but rather through the eyes of, children. In music, the left-wing British rock band Manic Street Preachers became one of the first Western bands to perform in Cuba, largely because of their song 'Baby Elián,' which tied Elián, Peter Pan, and anti-imperialism together:

> Kidnapped to the promised land
> The Bay of Pigs
> Or baby Elián
> Operation Peter Pan
> America, The Devil's playground.[118]

'They wanted to derail the roller coaster / With the slander of *Patria Potestad* / And later, my friend's father took him / To a little boat, and he never returned.' Carlos Varela, 'Jalisco Park' (1989). (Photo by author)

More elegantly, in 'Jalisco Park' (1989), Cuban singer/songwriter Carlos Varela uses the imagery of an empty playground to lament the loss of childhood playmates, vanished thanks to the 'slander of *Patria Potestad*.' Yet in his recent elegy for the Cuban Revolution – his 2009 album *No es el fin* – Varela sings, more angrily, 'I'm not your Peter Pan / Don't tell me what I have to do' ('La Comedia Silente').

González himself has faded from view. He pops up in the U.S. press occasionally, in the same sort of 'where-are-they-now' tone used for the formerly famous.[119] In Cuba he, or a family member, occasionally graces the stage at a state function. He's still the most famous boy in the country, but he's hardly a media star (a far cry from his treatment by the U.S. press during his stay in Miami). Yet his saga will not fade, because it has been enshrined. As there were two Elián narratives – encompassing kidnap and rescue – now there are two Elián museums. One is in his hometown of Cardenas, in a beautiful building that was once a fire station. The museum has a similarly imposing official name, the 'Museum of the Battle of Ideas.' The other is in Miami's Little Havana neighbourhood, 'Unidos en Casa Elián' (United in Elián's House), where a tribute to Elián's five months in the United States has been created in the front rooms of his uncle's small home (an ingenious use of space, ironically similar to that in Havana, where Cubans squish together in backrooms in order to turn the front of their homes into apartments or restaurants). The Miami museum is a tribute to religion and abundance. To the Peter Pan–era list of the advantages of a North American childhood, one more has been added: consumption. I counted five bicycles in the front porch alone. Pristine toy trucks glisten behind glass cases, his bed is hidden under a jumble of stuffed animals, and his closet overflows with clothes, including a prominent Spiderman costume. Amidst the toys are religious icons: plenty of Christ and Mary figures, but also the Cuban saint Caridad and Mexico's Lady of Guadelupe. The famous photo of a frightened boy being taken by force by armed federal agents hangs prominently in the room in which the capture occurred, displayed next to the inner tube on which he was found. Interspersed throughout are political messages: a bumper sticker from a local radio station which exhorts 'Remember Elián When You Vote,' and a large poster which depicts Castro and Elián next to a line of other leaders posed with children: Hitler and Stalin.

Like the war of symbols outside the U.S. Interests Section in Havana, the warring Elián museums answer each other with breathtaking precision. Prominent in the Cardenas museum is a statue of a young boy in the act of throwing something. It's a toy, a superhero doll. A rejection of American children's consumer culture is also on display in a collage of cartoons, including a ball and chain depicted with Mickey Mouse ears (Cuba's answer to González's famous visit to Disneyworld) and a play on his name: 'Gon$ales.' The overt political message here is provided by images and quotes from various Cuban revolutionary heroes – including Conrado Benitez, a teacher who was killed by opponents of the Literacy Campaign.

'The Museum of the Battle of Ideas' is more than a typically pedantic title bestowed by the Cuban government. It comprises part of a massive attempt to maintain the momentum generated by the widespread domestic support for Elián's return, not to mention the joy in this unusual recent success in staring down the *Yanquis*. Many commentators on the Elián saga noted its legacy of generational renewal in Cuba. Veteran British political commentator Robin Blackburn, for example, put it this way: 'The hopes of the sixties may have crumbled like so many of the buildings in old Havana, but something has lodged in the people that will not be easily rooted out. Young people can be heard saying that for the first time they have a sense of something like the historic confrontations of their parent's generation.'[120] If the Elián victory was a tonic after the devastating post-Soviet Special Period, the 'Battle of Ideas' attempted to harness this – using the popular Literacy Campaign Brigade model to educate and then hire thousands of youth, *trabajadores sociales* (social workers), to work in anti-corruption and other social welfare capacities.[121]

Conclusion

Maria Torres argues that Peter Pan 'manipulated' children's needs to suit competing political ideologies. 'The exodus,' she argues, 'was not a contest over protecting children, but, rather, about competing state building projects.'[122] My argument emphasizes the centrality of children *to* state building projects. In this history, Cuban children were indeed manipulated; so, too, were their parents and their country. But children specifically were canonized, rendered mute symbols of an especially stark contrast between kidnap and rescue. Foreign encounters always shape domestic identities, and U.S/Cuban conflicts have produced extraordinarily durable national self-perceptions. What could be more suited to the benevolent supremacy of Cold War America than the story of thousands of its citizens providing refuge for young victims of communism? What could provide better anti-imperialist inspiration in Cuba than the revelation that, along with profits, resources, and the national treasury, the children too had been stolen? In her short story 'Miami Relatives,' the writer Ana Menéndez describes tensions in a Cuban family between the old uncle in Havana and the rest of the family in Miami. 'He is crazy because of us,' she writes, 'and we are crazy because of him.'[123]

In the following chapters, I'll tell other tales of kidnap and rescue, drawn from political contexts that differ, in some ways, from the mind-boggling world of U.S./Cuban relations, especially after 1959. One final sad story – of many – highlights just how selective this rescue narrative is. I've mentioned already that in 1937, during the Spanish Civil

War, nearly twenty thousand children were evacuated after the intense bombings of the cities of Durango and Guernica by Franco's Nationalist forces. Thousands of civilians lost their lives. In Spain, the evacuations were organized by the left, predominantly by the trade union movement, and in the host countries their stay was sponsored by coalitions of church groups, leftist parties, and trade unions. The largest number, fifteen thousand, went to France, but Spanish children were also sent to Britain, Belgium, the Soviet Union, Mexico, Switzerland, and Denmark, but not to the United States. Despite a campaign to admit Spanish refugee children, supported by high-profile humanitarians such as Albert Einstein and Eleanor Roosevelt, as well as by almost three thousand U.S. families who volunteered to be sponsors, only a handful of Spanish children were permitted into the United States – those with family there. Intense opposition to these refugees emanated from none other than the U.S. Catholic Church, which believed the evacuation to be an 'unholy exploitation of children for Communist propaganda purposes.' 'It is quite evident,' explained *America*, a major Catholic weekly, 'that the purpose was not merely the safety of the children. The aim quite apparently seems to be to put Franco and the Nationalist cause in the light of a ruthless aggressor.'[124]

CHAPTER THREE

The Hybrid Baby: Domestic Interracial Adoption since the 1950s

An efficient combination of U.S. government money, church social welfare systems, and an army of committed volunteers met most of the problems faced by Cuban refugee children. Yet despite the ideological enthusiasm for their presence in the United States, the 8,331 (documented) Peter Pan children who were not immediately taken in by families or friends taxed even this impressive effort. Church officials took shortcuts and ignored established child-welfare practices. For example, they crossed denominational lines when placing children in foster care, and, more tragically, they separated siblings. Many Peter Pan children went to orphanages. In North America, the pendulum had swung against the institutionalization of children, in favour of family-style foster care. Recently cleared of American kids, orphanage beds were waiting.

But some Cuban children brought with them a problem no one in America quite knew how to solve. In May 1962, Margaret Harnett from Miami's Children's Service Bureau, the group responsible for the care of Protestant Cuban children, met with representatives of non-denominational child welfare organizations at the offices of the Child Welfare League of America in New York. Harnett was probably disappointed to see fewer than ten agency representatives at the meeting; she had invited forty. Social workers from across the country were in New York that week for the National Conference on Social Welfare, and Margaret Harnett badly needed the help of her colleagues. Even though only 4 per cent of Cuban children had found their way to her agency, she was swamped and needed to unload some of her caseload on agencies outside Florida. To her fellow social workers, she was honest about the characteristics of the children. By the spring of 1962, her charges were not the children of the upper class who left immediately after the revolution. The new arrivals, she explained, 'represent a lower socio-economic group.' Some were malnourished. Complicating their desirability as foster children even more, some were what she termed 'Negro,' but not the kind to which most at that meeting would have been accustomed. 'They have not,' she told the group,

> lived as Negroes in Cuba but have been integrated into the community. Therefore, if they are placed in a Negro foster home in the south, where Negroes are rather highly segregated, this becomes rather frightening to them. Also, the placement of certain sibling groups in the Miami or Southern area is impossible because within a family there will be many different shades of children.[1]

I don't know how, or if, Mrs Harnett's racial problem was solved. Like many aspects of this story, the numbers are vague, but there were not many Afro-Cuban Peter Pan children. This incident is an illuminating reminder, of course, that racial boundaries are porous; secure notions of who is a 'Negro' don't necessarily travel well. But because Mrs Harnett presented the racial ambiguities of Cuban children to her colleagues as a 'problem' – a hindrance to finding them immediate care – the issue underlies the importance of racial categories and race-matching practices in the U.S. child welfare system.

Had they been having this conversation in Canada at this time, it might have been posed differently. While Americans were being encouraged to think about Cuban children as small vessels of Cold War political ideology, just across the border to the north, Canadians were also finding a new meaning for certain children. Starting in the late 1950s, a group in Montreal began to push against racially restrictive child welfare practices, mounting a strong and high-profile campaign to encourage the adoption of black children by white parents. Through these efforts, the political meaning borne by such children – Hybrid Babies – became symbolic of Canadian racial liberalism. 'Mississippi,' declared Malcolm X, 'is anywhere south of the Canadian border.' Ironically, this comment on the breadth of U.S. racism worked, unintentionally, perhaps, to flatter Canada. Malcolm joined a long list of those who, as George Elliott Clarke puts it, 'exempt Canada from racism.'[2] The adoption of black children by white parents bolstered this colour-blind image, and helped put Canadians in the forefront of an international discourse of integration and civil rights. Yet, at the same time, the adoption of First Nations children by white parents in Canada acquired the opposite meaning; it was a shameful illustration that the colonial past lived on. Things seemed better in the United States, which acted before Canada did to cease cross-racial adoptions of Native children.

I spent months working in the archives of transracial adoption in Canada. I was, luckily, granted permission to read one thousand sad stories – the files of black children adopted by whites through an agency in Montreal, and Native children adopted by whites through a Winnipeg agency. As we'll see, there were differences in adoption practice between these two agencies, which help to account, in some measure, for the different reputation of transracial adoption in different communities. I am certainly not contrasting the private stories found in those files with public perceptions or common-sense understanding.[3] It would be simplistic indeed to suggest that the adoption of black children by whites was inherently progressive, while the adoption of First Nations children by whites was wholly reactionary. Relations between birth parents, adoptive parents, and social workers narrated through the framework of 'the case file' – the official dossier of adoption – confirm and depart from these public narratives. Just as there are plenty of reasons to be skeptical of Canada's discourse of national self-congratulation about race relations, it would also be naive to believe everything I read in an adoption file. In the era of closed adoption, social workers were like directors in a strange drama in which the actors were unseen by each other. The historical traces left in the case file are, mostly, told to and through the social worker. The first interview I had for this research was with a group of retired social workers in a Canadian city, former employees of an agency I ended up not using for this book. They spoke of the overwhelming difficulties they faced finding adoptive homes for children in the 1950s and 1960s, and I was amazed at their candour. They laughed as they remembered how they would embellish or hide unseemly circumstances of birth parents, so as not to scare off adoptive parents. A prostitute, for example, might be described as someone who 'enjoyed walking outside,' one recalled. The conversation quickly turned towards how stressful they found working in child welfare, and how they had preferred other aspects of social work. Naively, I asked them why. Classic withering looks all round: 'Because it's the pits!' one replied. 'No one *wants* to take a child from their mother.'

This truthfulness was conveyed in another conversation, one I wasn't supposed to hear. One afternoon, at another agency, two employees didn't notice me taking notes, tucked in a corner of a huge file storage room. As they searched for a particular file, one of them said to the other, 'God, think of all the history in this room. Think of all the people we've screwed over.' 'I don't want to know,' said the other.

When the perspective offered by adoption's private, official record seems out of synch with adoption's public profile, the issue isn't which story is wrong. Rather, I want to explore why such different ranges of understandings and beliefs about interracial adoption emerged at all. Despite the universality of the concept, the symbolic child in the case file had many faces. Just as the Afro-Cuban child was transformed in the movement from Havana to Arkansas – or Boston – so too the Canadian black child in Montreal meant something very different than the Aboriginal child in Northern Manitoba.

Canada's Ambassadors for Peace?

In September 1961, Canada's *Star Weekly* published a heart-tugging story about adoption. 'The Children Nobody Wants' painted a sorry portrait of daily life for parentless multiracial children in Canada. 'Some are infants, others have waited (in foster care or institutions) twelve years. It is the same story across Canada, nobody wants them. Red skinned, brown or yellow, they have committed the unforgivable sin of having one parent who wasn't white. Because of this they'll never know security, never be part of a family.' Abruptly, the story moved from the child to the nation: 'For years we've been told Canada is the bridge between Old world and New. Couldn't we build another bridge? In a fast changing world, new Afro-Asian nations are being born. The white Anglo Saxon has lost supremacy. Couldn't our future citizens of mixed race brought up in white homes, knowing the best of both backgrounds instead of the worst, be Canada's ambassadors for peace? In a country that's gone on record against apartheid, its worth considering.' The story ends on an upbeat note, introducing the Open Door Society, a group of white Montreal parents who have made a project of adopting non-white children, or, in the words of this journalist, 'Canadian parents putting Christianity quietly to work and delivering their own smashing blow against prejudice.'[4]

A version of this tale, featuring identical dramatis personae, leaping from the fate of individual babies to the tribulations of nations, appeared in just about every newspaper and magazine in North America through the late 1950s and 1960s. The practices of interracial adoption, and the activism of parent groups such as the Open Door Society, helped to create a public persona for the transracial adopted child, a figure I'm calling the Hybrid Baby. 'Hybridity' has a long and complex cultural meaning, and has travelled some distance from its origins in what Robert Young termed 'the vocabulary of the Victorian extreme right.'[5] I am drawn to the term – which in this context can signify the multiracial origins of adopted children as well as children of one race (black, Native, or Asian) raised by parents of another (almost always white) – because it can accommodate relations of hierarchy and power as well as cultural exchange, *and* because, quoting Young again, 'wherever it emerges it suggests the impossibility of essentialism.'[6] Of course, this is hardly the first time in history racial lines were crossed in the raising of girls and boys – white children have been cared for by brown and black women around the globe for generations. But the adopted Hybrid Baby acquired a specific configuration and social meaning in 1960s North America, and came to signify a spectrum of interracial understandings, politics, and conflicts.

To Margaret Edgar and the handful of others parents who organized themselves into the Open Door Society in Montreal in the late 1950s, racial boundary-crossing occurred in the most intimate setting imaginable: their own families. While black children had been cared for in white foster homes in Montreal since the 1920s, the Edgars became, in 1958, among the first white parents to adopt legally non-white children in North America (some versions of the story say they were the first). They, along with the two other sets of adoptive parents, organized the Open Door Society (ODS), which was intended initially as a small support group, but very quickly became involved in advocating for interracial adoption, mixed-race families, and the integration model of civil rights. They attracted enormous media attention, and they helped to spark similar organizations across the United States and Canada.[7] Over the next twenty years, Montreal's ODS maintained an extensive international communications network, lobbied governments to change antiquated adoption laws, worked with Montreal's black community to promote civil rights and teach black history and culture to adopted children, held workshops in black beauty salons to learn how to do their black daughters' hair, swapped tips with each other about where to buy black dolls or Christmas cards with black Santas, organized international conferences, and prompted the first stirrings of academic research on race and adoption, all the while searching for a politics of transracial adoption which was unifying, not colonizing.

If Margaret Edgar is the founding mother of interracial adoption, Muriel McCrea was the midwife. McCrea was the executive director of

the Children's Service Centre (CSC), one of Montreal's oldest welfare organizations (an incarnation of the Protestant Infants Home, established
in the early nineteenth century). McCrea, seemingly single-handedly,
and alone in North America, overturned decades of adoption practice
by facilitating, in fact, encouraging, cross-racial placements in the late
1950s. This defied the common custom of scrupulously matching parent
with child, the paradigmatic feature of modern adoption. 'Successful
matching,' according to historian Ellen Herman, 'erased itself, making
the social design of adoption invisible.'[8] It also made adoption's ugly
stepsisters, illegitimacy and infertility, easier to hide. For the first half
of the twentieth century, needy children were divided into two categories: adoptable and non-adoptable. While never exact, 'non-adoptability' fused the racial, the social, and the moral to render certain kinds,
and colours, of children permanently non-adoptable. One (rare) study
of 'non-adoptable' children in the 1940s defined them as follows: they
were of 'unknown paternity' or their mothers were of 'low mentality'
or promiscuous, or they had undesirable features such as 'asthma, TB,
epilepsy or Negroid blood.'[9] Of course, 'blood' itself was hardly a stable
category. In Alberta, for example, it was Ukrainian and Métis children
who were defined out of the domestic adoption system. Instead, they
were allegedly trafficked to unsuspecting adoptive parents in the United States and Central America, a remarkable turnabout, as we'll see, on
the baby-selling scandals that haunt contemporary Guatemala[10]

So when Muriel McCrea announced to the annual general meeting of
the CSC in 1955 'the wonderful fact is that when we began looking we
found that there were many people who could take some chances, so
that this year we were able to place Brian with a club foot, Joyce with a
cleft palate, Nadia with Central European ancestry, and even Paul who
had some coloured blood,' she was both challenging and confirming
the social hierarchies which informed adoption practice in the twentieth century.[11] In fact, according to the CSC, 75 per cent of the 'Negro or
partly Negro' children in orphanages or foster care in 1950s Montreal,
over one hundred children in total, were legally adoptable. McCrea's
willingness to break adoption's colour bar brought black children into
the adoption system. A publicity campaign targeted first black and then
white parents for these newly categorized 'adoptable' children. Enter
Margaret Edgar and the ODS, which was formed in November 1959.

Despite what I'm going to argue about the cultural importance of the
Hybrid Baby and the influence of the Open Door Society, the numbers
of such children in Anglo Montreal were, in fact, very small. Montreal,

like the rest of Quebec, was of course a majority French-speaking city, though it was also home to the vast majority of the province's anglophones and immigrants. Child welfare services were, on the whole, divided on religious and linguistic lines, particularly so for adoption agencies since religious matching laws were in force at this time.[12] The statistical landscape for interracial adoption in the past is complicated and, like racial classification schemes everywhere, capricious and unreliable. However, my best estimate is that there were about 350 children who were labelled non-white placed for adoption by the CSC in Montreal between 1955 and 1969 (the last year for which I have found statistics), 300 of whom were adopted by whites. This represents about 25 to 30 per year, when the total number of adoptions this agency dealt with ranged from approximately 400 to 600 annually. These are figures from one agency in one city, although as Montreal's Children's Service Centre was widely recognized as an interracial adoption pioneer, these figures probably represent the apex of black placements in Canada. Even the province of Nova Scotia, home to a sizable black community, placed adoption ads in Montreal newspapers.[13] Black children made up the vast majority of these children, followed by a small number of Asian and Native children.[14] So the Hybrid Baby was definitely more powerful than numbers alone would suggest, for it carried huge cultural weight. As popular culture heralded its birth – even TV's *The Brady Bunch* featured an episode on interracial adoption – many looked *through*, not at, these children, and saw in the Hybrid Baby the promise of racial reconciliation. The processes of adoption, of course, denaturalize the family in basic and fundamental ways. Adoption exposes how family relationships are no more real or pre-given than any other sort of human relationship. Such ties are socially negotiated, not biologically ordained. All adoptive parents in this era were in the curious position of reconciling essentialist notions of blood, heredity, and familial sameness and security – mainstays of North American culture in the mid-twentieth century – with the practice of introducing complete genetic strangers into their lives forever. What happened when adoption began to breach the apparently secure biological borders of race as well? Through the stories of transracial adoption, we can hear an extended conversation about the social meaning of race, which took place mostly among white people, a group not accustomed to such exchanges. Whether they invested race and racial difference with enormous social meaning, or downplayed its significance entirely, or whether they feared it, ignored it, attempted to cure it, or embraced it, all of these discussions began from the premise that the racial identity of *children* was something quite distinct.

White parents who adopted across racial lines in Montreal were not, demographically speaking, hugely different from other adoptive parents. They were a little older, a little richer, and a lot more educated.[15] But this generation of adoptive parents *felt* themselves to be different. They described themselves as 'liberal thinkers,' 'freethinkers,' 'internationalists,' 'rebels at heart.' As one social worker delicately described a potential adoptive mother, 'She gains a certain amount of security from being different from the run of the mill.' Another was described, somewhat less delicately as 'inclined to get on a soapbox.'[16] Adoptive parents and social workers alike constantly denied explicitly political motives while speaking publicly. 'We're not tilting at windmills,' one adoptive mother told *Maclean's*. 'Don't make us out to be do-gooders,' another told *Good Housekeeping*. Even the U.S. black magazine *Ebony* assured its readers in 1961 that 'mother love provides the only motivating force' for many white adopters of black children.[17] Yet privately, social workers looked for signs – generally expressed in what we might now call the language of therapy or personal growth – that potential parents understood interracial adoptions were different. 'I went into their attitudes towards Negroes quite fully with them and found they did not have the strength,' wrote one social worker in 1960. 'They feel quite guilty about this.'[18] 'They have the necessary streak of independence and unorthodoxy,' wrote a social worker of another couple enthusiastically. 'They are not concerned about what other people think.'[19] Qualities such as 'strength,' 'independence,' and the ability to 'handle risk' were endorsed approvingly by social workers examining potential parents. Many decades later, former social worker Grace Gallay told me that part of her effort in recruiting white parents for interracial adoption involved 'seeing how far I could stretch them.'[20] Thus the explicitly political discourse of interracial cooperation and civil rights was muted, but not erased, in the language of the helping professions, and race remained, like epilepsy or blindness, one more 'risk' which not everyone could 'handle.' 'She will be the kind of mother who will help her children fight their own battles,' wrote one social worker of a new applicant, a suburban housewife, giving a keen endorsement of her parenting potential *and* acknowledging that all the 'mother love' in the world would not inoculate black children from future conflicts.[21]

Why would self-described 'freethinkers' and 'rebels' – most drawn from the cozy confines of Montreal's West Island suburbs or stately

Mr. and Mrs. Edward Henderson of Roxboro pose with their two adopted children Tommy and Suzanne. The Hendersons are members of the "Open Door Society," a group that is trying to find places for "Unadoptable" children, the ones that are too old, or problem children or children of mixed race.
—Spencer photo.

Open Door children

The Hendersons. (Pointe Claire, Quebec, *News and Chronicle*, 28 December 1967)

downtown Westmount – choose interracial adoption to express their independence? The majority were convinced by the international publicity, much of it generated by the CSC and ODS, about the grave problems facing 'hard to place' non-white children. As one Westmount adoptive father explained – one of many featured in flattering stories in the media in and beyond Montreal – 'Interracial understanding and communication was one of the greatest needs in today's world, and since we wanted another child anyway, we felt that this was a way in which we could do our part.'[22] The use of media by both the adoption agency and, later, the parents' group was extremely effective; forty adoptions of non-white children occurred in the first two years of the ODS's existence directly because of publicity.[23] While these stories were almost always accompanied by photos of adorable babies, the ODS was not naive about the potential for visual sentimentality when it came to children. They complained, for example, about the 'Wednesday's Child' column in the *Montreal Star*, which profiled individual children needing adoptive homes. They objected to its 'syrupy' and 'pitying' tone, and also noted that Montreal's black community hated such advertising. They also decided against inviting journalist Doris Giller, who had just published a long and flattering feature on interracial adoption, to cover the annual ODS / Negro Community Centre picnic, worrying that this would look like a 'publicity stunt' and antagonize their friends in the black community. Yet they were also adamant that interracial families needed to show the public they were functioning in what they termed 'a very ordinary manner' and thus needed to 'offer themselves as subjects for questioning and photographing.' Such stories, they insisted, 'produce more adoption applications, which is the sole reason we do them.'[24] And so the 'we adopted a Negro' narrative became a quintessential feel-good story of the times. Most people who came to the CSC willing to adopt mixed-race children said they were inspired by interviews with multiracial adopting parents.

Many were convinced by a popular left/liberal rescue narrative: that it was selfish to reproduce when the world had so many needy children. Would-be adoptive parents voiced concerns about the so-called 'population explosion,' itself a highly racialized notion.[25] It followed that the more needy children were, the more good one was doing by adopting them. Like burnings one's draft card, coming out of the closet, or tallying who did the dishes, adopting a 'hard to place' child made the personal political, and vice versa. 'The premise of inter-racial adoption,' declared adoption activist Clayton Hagen at an ODS conference, 'is consistent with how it seems we must live in our world. We must come to see ourselves as individuals separate from our biological families and biological races, and to see other people in the same way.'[26]

So by the time Prime Minister Lester Pearson posed for the national media with a multiracial adoptive family to proclaim Brotherhood Week in 1966, the Hybrid Baby had become symbolic of hope, optimism, and good. Pearson urged Canadians to continue to their 'inherent revulsion' to racial and religious discrimination, framing the story in familiar national terms.[27] (At the same moment in Sweden, some of the first formal mechanisms of international adoption were created, which also confirmed, to their proponents, Sweden's egalitarian ideology.)[28] While groups like the Open Door Society soon emerged in many cities across North America, Montrealers were never permitted to forget that theirs had been the first, that Montreal was, as one parent put it, 'the mecca for multi and interracial adoption.' As the U.S. magazine *Coronet* declared in 1964, 'Only in Montreal are mixed race adoptions an honor, not a stigma.'[29] In answering the hundreds of requests for information from researchers and child welfare agencies throughout North America, ODS parents found themselves in the unusual position of advising nervous Americans about which U.S. hotels and restaurants might welcome mixed-race families, and even which U.S. cities had integrated neighbourhoods. In 1965 the group was contacted by a desperate family in Florida who were trying to adopt a Cuban child against the will of local authorities. Whether this was a Peter Pan child or not is unknown, but we've seen how Cuban children confused the racial categories of the U.S. child welfare system. In this case, Florida authorities claimed, in the absence of 'test cases,' interracial adoption was 'doomed to fail.' The ODS quickly supplied the family's lawyer with studies and advice on how to fight for permanent custody of the child.[30]

Montreal's position in the vanguard of interracial adoption reinforced several long-standing Canadianisms: that it was a land of much greater racial tolerance and liberalism – always positioned against the United States – and that Montreal edged out Toronto as Canada's most sophisticated city. Interracial adoption reflected the worldliness of Montreal's citizens. 'Montreal has been quietly demonstrating the message of Man and His World for eight years through the activities of our Open Door Society,' proclaimed a parent during Expo '67, the World's Fair held in Montreal. When a similar project was launched in Toronto in 1962, the Committee for the Adoption of Negro Children found Montreal's example 'encouraging' but constantly worried that Toronto lagged far behind.[31] The hegemonic goodness of Montreal's mixed-race adopting parents was also evident in the comments of those who considered but declined the attempts made by the CSC to find homes for non-white children, most of whom refused because, as one typical couple told the agency, they 'admired people who could do this but were simply not big enough people.'[32]

'It's Hard to Hold a Grudge against a Baby': Children and Racialization

Yet a willingness to cross one racial boundary in no way suggested that white adoptive parents had divested themselves of *all* of their culture's tropes of race. This first generation of white adoptive parents faced a myriad of uncertainties and anxieties about the cultural meaning of race within their families and communities. A clear pattern of racial preference emerged, in which 'full Negro' children were at the bottom, and mixed-race (always imaged in white/non-white groupings) Asian or Native children were at the top' though details of this hierarchy varied by region. Montreal social workers believed, for example, that Native children were difficult to place for adoption in the Prairie provinces, black children were hard to place in Halifax and through most of the United States, and Asian, especially Eurasian, children were always relatively easy placements.[33] One Montreal woman, the wife of a clergyman, told her social worker in 1959 that 'she was ashamed to admit it but she had difficulties with Negroes, though she thought Orientals were fine.'[34] Another set of parents worried that their small town was 'too sticky' for black children, but part Native children would be welcome. A white foster mother declared that she would welcome a 'coloured' child in her home and neighbourhood, but she feared her country club would not; 'Orientals,' however, would be no problem.[35]

Many adopting parents imagined race as a kind of disability that could be overcome, perhaps even be made to disappear, with the love and care of a good family. This way of thinking located race in children's bodies, but it opened the possibility of transcendence. Some parents attempted to depoliticize and forgive their black children's bodies, suggesting, for example, that one son's black skin was the same as another biological son's birthmark, or comparing a black daughter's 'kinky' hair to a white son's 'big ears.' Another suggested that their black daughter got teased just as much as a neighbour's red-haired freckled daughter. More than one likened their child's complexion to a tan, which most people 'have to sit in the sun and suffer for.'[36] This disability/transcendence model of racial identity seemed especially appropriate for children. For several centuries, adults in the West have imagined childhood as the site of their innocent, natural selves, seemingly unmarked by identities like race.[37] Hybrid Babies became symbolic of racial harmony and integration, in large part by imagining children as the ultimate race liberals. 'Children have no prejudice,' announced one headline, a theme repeated in countless stories (and, later, numerous Benetton ads).[38] From this perspective, it was not difficult to separate race from bodies altogether, and re-imagine adopted children as virtually raceless. 'What does color matter when a child strokes your cheek and tells you she loves you?' declared one anonymous adoptive mother to the *Toronto Star* in 1962. Another parent told *Parents* magazine how their newly adopted child finally won the hearts of her disapproving grandparents: 'It's hard to hold a grudge against a baby.'[39] As children grew up, some parents continued to work to contain racial difference. An ODS membership canvass in the early 1970s, for example, revealed a wide array of perspectives about the racial identity of adopted children, including one white father who declared he 'believed black people should take on Canadian culture and is bringing up his girl to be a Canadian first.'[40]

The flip side of transcendence model was the tendency to exoticise, another common feature of press commentary. References to 'dark skinned Tahitian princesses,' and 'tiny Oriental pixies,' filled pages of testimonials from new parents. And as historian Veronica Strong-Boag has explored, adoption advertising of the era relied on finding a positive new spin for old racialized tropes – describing, for example, boys who possessed 'the typical Indian child's gentle disposition.' Adoptive parents continually complained about what they called the 'overbearing attention' their non-white children received from strangers, and ODS activist Irene Henderson recalled with chagrin regular encounters with prospective parents who 'couldn't stop talking about how cute Negro children were.'[41]

Black children provided great scope for white parents to ponder the minutiae and quotidian meaning of racial difference. Following the logic of help for the 'hard to place' child, a few parents preferred to adopt 'full Negro' children. As well as satisfying the greatest need, they also believed that racial ambiguity created by adopting light-skinned children would make their lives even more complicated. As an ODS parent explained, it was easier to cope with 'obvious' children, who could 'not escape the reality of difference.'[42] While this was almost always discussed from the perspective of children, clearly the appearance of children reflected back on parents as well. Rarely were undertones of cross-racial sexuality acknowledged publicly. A typically forthright Margaret Edgar once told a reporter about the 'sensation' caused when she and another adoptive mother strolled through a small resort town with their eight children, including two 'part Negro babies.' 'The natives are still wondering what we'd been up to,' she declared.[43] Edgar laughed this off, but others pondered the appearance of black children quite gravely. Other parents believed light-skinned black children would be 'easier,' in predominantly white neighbourhoods, for example, or to introduce to recalcitrant grandparents. Even those convinced that 'the lighter the easier' had questions about the possibility of 'Negro blood' emerging in grandchildren; indeed, U.S. social workers told *Newsweek* in 1969 that many adoptive parents considering mixed-race children were scared off when asked to consider the possibility of 'even blacker grandchildren.'[44] One Montreal father wondered if his mixed race son might 'assert his Negro race aggressively' in the future.[45] Social workers almost always accepted such preferences – though one interracial couple was finally rejected after they declined three successive black children they deemed too dark and lacking 'good hair.' Generally, however, the CSC facilitated these hierarchies, taking scrupulous physical descriptions of the birth mother and father (if possible) and examining newborns closely to see whether they 'showed their colour.' 'Watch for colour in this baby,' read a typical file notation in 1960, 'there is coloured blood in the putative father's family.'[46] Rae Rambally, one of the few black social workers employed in Montreal during this era, remembers the regular adoption placement meetings she attended at the CSC, during which the skin colour and hair texture of black children were detailed with precision.[47] When a white birth mother did not divulge paternity, doctors were called into the hospital at birth to pronounce the race of the child. Ambiguous or absent racial signifiers – understood generally as complexion and hair type – were generally seen to work in the baby's favour, making him or her more 'adoptable' (particularly since in such cases even this groundbreaking agency occasionally declined to disclose the whole truth about a child's racial origins to adoptive parents).[48]

Birth-Parent Stories

All of this helps to explain the paradoxical treatment of white and black birth mothers. One of the long-standing, and highly romantic, beliefs about the Hybrid Baby in this era is that most of the 'black' adopted children in Montreal were mixed-race, the offspring of liaisons between whites and blacks. This narrative of cross-racial adoption depends upon and helps to sustain a host of other fictions: that most such liaisons involved unmarried white women and black men, and that these relationships, and especially the children they produced, were doomed, victims of still rampant social intolerance. When unmarried black mothers do enter this story, they, and their offspring, quickly disappear into the great void known as 'black culture' – a monolithic, classless, and genderless block which, in this instance, holds that unwed black women reject adoption in favour of extended family networks. A corollary of this is that black families were unmotivated to adopt through the child welfare system – why should they, when they were perfectly able to 'take care of their own.'

This narrative of doomed interracial romance certainly fuelled media interest in and public representations of needy black children, especially as interracial dating was emerging as an issue of civil rights. To the press, mixed-race children were 'unwanted victims of racial discrimination' or 'strange, contemptible victims in no man's land.' Yet this was also their potential; through interracial adoption, they became, as one Christian periodical put it, 'innocent bearers of racial reconciliation.'[49] Hybrid Babies, the offspring of various interracial encounters, had for generations challenged one of the central fictions of colonial hierarchy: that the boundaries separating the colonizer from the colonized were self-evident, easily drawn, and maintained. Mixed-race children (perhaps the ultimate child standard bearers) symbolized the contagion of indigenous (black, brown) women and the susceptibility of white men, and threatened almost all of the classification schemas upon which racism rests.[50] As global movements for decolonization were re-charting domestic racial identities and relationships in 1960s North America, perceptions of interracial romance and adoption ran parallel. Interracial love became, as historian Renee Romano termed it, 'a metaphor for the possibilities of racial equality.'[51] When the public face of interracial adoption was the mixed-race child, white adoptive parents found another claim upon which to base their parenthood. Some might think it was 'wrong to take the child out of his milieu,' Margaret Edgar told a reporter in 1962, 'but what is the child's milieu? If he's half coloured and half white, does he belong in the coloured milieu or the white milieu? The fact is he doesn't belong in either.'[52]

This origin story is true to a point. In my sample of one hundred non-white children whose births attracted the attention of the CSC, almost one-third were the offspring of white women and non-white (mostly black) men. The vast majority, almost 90 per cent, relinquished their children. The mixed-race origins of these children joined a long list of factors shaping unmarried white mothers' choices. The almost complete lack of social, familial, psychological, and economic support for single motherhood was not *caused* by having a mixed-race baby, though such progeny might make unmarried white women feel their ostracism and isolation more acutely. Even as adopting a black child was becoming an act of goodwill, giving birth to one signified immorality.[53] Thus adoption provided, as it did for almost all white unmarried mothers in this era, what U.S. historian Barbara Melosh has termed 'the best solution,' so long as they played by the rules. Shame and remorse, and seclusion during pregnancy (preferably in either an unwed mothers' home or doing domestic labour for middle-class women), followed by instant relinquishment of the baby and a willingness to convince at least their social workers of their unshaken belief in the moral rightness of their culture (as the CSC social workers put it, to 'profit by experience' or 'mature through mistakes'), offered redemption for countless white women, in Montreal and throughout North America. The adoption records, and everyone's lips, were sealed, until this punitive model of single motherhood and adoption began to crumble, and birth mothers asserted themselves in their own histories.[54]

Yet there is another origin story for Montreal's black adopted children, one which relies less on Hollywood-esque stories of thwarted interracial love, and more on black women's limited labour and migration options. This story starts with the Domestic Immigration Program of 1955, which partially relaxed Canada's immigration colour bar and recruited almost three thousand English-speaking black West Indian women to work as domestic servants in middle-class homes. Their story is often told – at the time and by subsequent historians – as a tale of loneliness and rejection; they were scorned as housemaids by both whites and established Canadian blacks, and rendered almost freakishly lonesome by the absence of black male company here – the only sexual interest publicly imagined for these women. Watching a West Indian community dance one evening in Montreal in 1961, a reporter noted the 'sad excess' of women, mostly domestics, who outnumbered the men five to one. 'Women like mangoes in this place,' claimed a black West Indian student, 'abundant and at low price.' (This same reporter also learned that students at an unnamed Montreal university forbade domestics from attending West Indian social events).[55] Given the extent of such musings about the sexual and moral perils posed by – as well as to – single black women in Canada's cities, it would have come as no surprise to anyone at the time that West Indian immigrant unmarried mothers soon began to turn up at the doorstep of the CSC. And then, like all unwed mothers in this era, these immigrant black birth mothers promptly disappeared from public view. Of course, the very existence of a global black underclass in Canada complicates the beloved national narrative of anti-conquest. No wonder, then, their tale has been eclipsed by feel-good stories about the rescue of their children.

There were twice as many black women as white in my sample of the birth mothers of non-white children. Of these women, 80 per cent were pregnant by black men, and almost half of them decided against adoption and chose to keep their 'illegitimate' children. Given that, overall, approximately 30 per cent of women seen by the CSC decided against relinquishing their babies through the 1960s (peaking at 43 per cent by 1969), this definitely seems to confirm the common-sense view, expressed in the social welfare literature and anecdotally for decades, that 'black women keep their children' – at least more than white women tended to.[56] The lengths unmarried black mothers went to in order to hold on to their children were remarkable. Typically, they took advantage of the agency's provision for four months of postnatal foster care – paid for by the mothers themselves – in order to cobble something together. Between working long shifts, usually in Montreal's garment or service industries, they cajoled extended family members in the West Indies to move to Canada to help with child care, they made private arrangements with foster mothers for extended care, and they even found friends willing to become roommates and raise children together. Occasionally they returned home with the child, intending to leave it with a relative and return to work in Canada; even more occasionally, they convinced the birth father to support them. Not surprisingly, sometimes such plans, conceived in desperation with meagre resources, failed, and children were returned to agency care, causing social workers to grumble about women who 'produce coloured children, leaving the upbringing for society.'[57]

Yet despite what CSC staff once described as a 'strong cultural need' for West Indian women to keep their children – ironically, in this instance, when the unmarried mother in question arrived at the agency having survived a botched abortion – half of them didn't. Furthermore, black birth mothers were generally encouraged by social workers to plan to keep their child, advice rarely dispensed to white women in this era. Usually, this took the form of repeatedly warning them that their child – particularly 'full Negro' children – would fare poorly in the adoption system and may stay in the foster system indefinitely. Pregnant black women considering adoption were told, for example, 'the hard reality that to give up her child for adoption could not be considered until she had given birth, then the full force of her emotional feelings will have a different meaning to her.'[58] Hundreds of case files later, I simply cannot imagine a white woman hearing this. Black women, such as one twenty-two-year-old Barbadian immigrant who arrived in

Canada pregnant and wanted neither single parenthood nor even marriage because, as she said, 'people in the West Indies get married too early,' often had to fight their way into the adoption system.[59] In their way stood agency staff who treated them alternately like children ('a good deal of firmness is required with this one') or, as the decade progressed, with a great deal of fear. Encounters between blacks and white social workers speak volumes about changing racial politics in 1960s Canada. In the early years, a social worker congratulated himself for using the washroom in a black client's home, imagining this as an act of tolerance which helped to win the trust of the potential foster parents he was investigating.[60] Slowly social workers began to note a new restiveness on the part of their black clientele; as one wrote of an unmarried mother in 1965, 'I suspect she's not quite so servile as she appears on the surface.'[61] By the end of the decade, social workers were perplexed: black women, even the young, pregnant, and vulnerable ones, had changed. They were 'stubborn,' 'aggressive,' 'challenging,' full of 'pride.' They felt 'society owed them something,' and worst still, they had become 'color conscious' and began to complain about 'discrimination.'[62] This powerful combination, then, of fearful, often hostile responses to black female clientele, and a lingering rebuff of 'full Negro' children due to their 'hard to place' status, helped to create a different experience for unmarried black birth mothers. The boundaries here, between distinctive black culture and racism, are difficult to untangle. Historian Barbara Melosh calls adoption 'a strategy of upward mobility that, in practice, benefited whites almost exclusively.'[63] I've come to believe that rather than assuming blacks' disinterest in adoption – as adoptive parents or as birth parents – it might be more accurate to say that blacks mistrust the adoption *system,* mostly because historically it has treated them poorly.[64] Adoption case files tell a complicated story, including the shamed white birth mother who redeemed herself through adoption, but also a variety of racial and ethnic combinations, for whom the redemption narrative was far less available.

Black Children and the Politics of Transracial Adoption

Interracial adoption produced another discourse of racial difference, which neither exaggerated nor denied its existence, and this is the integrationist civil rights philosophy espoused by the ODS.[65] There was certainly a range of people attracted to this group. A few were liberals or leftists who had given issues of racism and civil rights some thought before they decided to adopt. But most ODS activists were politicized *because* they parented black children, not before they did. The experience of raising black children in a racist society politicized them. As one black social worker observed to me recently, 'Those parents had never encountered racism, and they simply walked around in shock for a few years.'[66] 'I think I know how a black mother must feel, at least some of the time,' a white adoptive mother told *Parents* magazine. 'Whenever there's any kind of trouble on our block, no matter what it is, my son seems to be the first child people suspect.' There's nothing like having your black child – possibly the only one in his class – offered the role of dog in the school play to make white adoptive parents realize, as Margaret Edgar explained, 'love is not enough.'[67] This stands in stark contrast to the U.S. experience at the same time, when, according to historian Ellen Herman, agencies turned to white families only grudgingly, and actively discouraged politicization, or what we would today call anti-racism, on the part of white adoptive families.[68]

At the same time, Montreal's black communities were experiencing the vast demographic and political changes of African diasporas in the 1960s and 1970s.[69] Just what kind of 'black' child was waiting at the adoption agency? West Indian? Canadian? Was 'black' a racial, social, or political designation? The combination of watching their children move from cute 'raceless' babies to youngsters exposed to adult-size racism, as well as the changing demographics and politics of the black community, had huge reverberations for transracial adoption.

Issues of reproduction and child-rearing have been complicated and explosive within black communities in North America. Legacies of slavery, exclusionary immigration laws, discriminatory welfare regulations, and forced sterilization mean that, for women of colour, the politics of *having or keeping* children runs a parallel course with the right to *not have* children. For these reasons, pronatalism has strong roots in black nationalism, and American Black Power organizations of this era emphasized childbearing and nation-building as the domain of revolutionary black women. Women of colour who refused to separate civil from reproductive rights, and instead demanded control over fertility, constantly countered this – as well as the hegemonic raceblindness of white feminism.[70] Added to this was the historic alienation of African Americans and African Canadians from child welfare and adoption systems. Thus we can understand the context for the commotion caused when, in 1972, the Association of Black Social Workers (NABSW) in the United States famously condemned the Hybrid Baby, claiming that interracial adoption distorted and undermined African-American racial identity. White parents, they argued, could never teach black children how to survive in a racist world. They also repeated the charge they had been making for some years, that the child welfare system discriminated against black adoptive families. While a few scholars have recently argued that this should be seen as an attempt to de-pathologize black families and wrest some control from a white-dominated social welfare system, the NABSW statement is commonly read as a kidnap narrative, and the death knell for the liberal integrationist era in transracial adoption.[71]

It surely was a polarizing moment. White adoptive parents groups on both sides of the border believed that racialized conflicts about adoption were more profound in the United States. Certainly in Montreal, the ODS had enjoyed a long history of cordial and I think meaningful relations with local and national black community leaders and organizations. They raised funds for black community initiatives and held regular speaking events, inviting black activists to speak about racism in the school system or the Canadian workforce. They supported social justice causes of the day, such as the California grape boycott. The guest speaker at the first Open Door Society conference on transracial adoption in 1970 was Howard McCurdy, long-time black activist in Canada and then chair of the Canadian Conference Committee on Black Organizations. He welcomed the opportunity to speak to a room full of white parents of black children, noting that 'those of us who are totally from the black community have something extremely fundamental in common with those of you who have come to join us by choice.' But he also turned immediately to a denunciation of Canadian 'arrogant self righteousness' about race relations and spent most of his talk explaining the concept of 'black power' to his audience.[72] The politicization of Montreal's white adoptive parents – at least the open-minded of them – reshaped their notions of race, citizenship, and parenthood. As Irene Henderson, a white adoptive mother of three black children, told me, the weekend she spent as one of the only white delegates at the National Black Coalition founding conference was a personal turning point, for 'it helped me see what my kids live every day.'[73] Another white adoptive parent activist, Lawrence Scyner, acknowledged the criticisms from some parts of Montreal's black community that white parents alone cannot provide 'support, stability and identification' for their black children, and agreed that black homes were preferable. 'Adoptive parents must effectively become black,' he argued, even though they've only experienced racism 'second hand.' He urged parents not to 'play down' the blackness of their children and to acknowledge the realities of racism, at the same time as celebrating the 'idealism typified by our own families.'[74] Many decades later, philosophers, sociologists, and anthropologists have begun to research and theorize how transracial adoptive parenthood can refigure the racial identities of white parents, as well as black children.[75] This process began, tentatively and often awkwardly, with the experiences of this first generation of activist parents.

Critics rightly point out that predominant rescue narratives privilege adoption as the only way to help or support marginalized black families – a 'particularly selfish approach to child welfare,' as Dorothy Roberts puts it.[76] In this early chapter of adoption's history, the activism of the Open Door Society stands as an important and rare example that the individual act of adoption is not irreconcilable with community-mindedness. Yet as the decade progressed, Christmas parties and children's picnics at the Negro Community Centre, or hairstyling lessons from community leader Daisy Sweeny (Oscar Peterson's activist sister), were not sufficient to address the changes in North American race politics. Like interracial marriage, adoptions across the colour line began to look less like a gesture of solidarity and more like cultural annihilation. I have found no Canadian equivalent to the statement of the U.S. black social workers. When the Congress of Black Women of Canada was organized, in 1973, a resolution was passed encouraging black women to 'open our minds and assess our values concerning marriage, illegitimacy, adoption and foster care.' Aside from this cryptic statement, transracial adoption was neither blessed nor cursed by this group.[77] Disinterest may well have been the fallback position among blacks in this country. One long-time black community worker in Montreal told me that 'we hardly noticed' the activities of the ODS.[78] In 1972, Margaret Edgar expressed privately that 'the flak which we received from black groups in Montreal against trans-racial adoption seems to be diminishing,' though she noted that the 'heavy guns are only just beginning to be felt in the U.S.A.' Perhaps revealing the real motor of adoption activism – past and present – she continued, 'Parents are rallying their defences, while social workers are inevitably retreating!'[79]

But, despite the force of adoptive parent activism, there were moments in Canada when African Canadians viewed interracial adoption through nationalist tropes of family. The Afro-centric Montreal newspaper *UHURU*, for example, labelled interracially adopted children 'misfits' in 1970 and called for a black CSC.[80] In this story, headlined 'Do Black Parents Care?' the Hybrid Baby was both a social embarrassment (blacks were not doing their part for needy children) and a symptom of the racism of the child welfare system (blacks were shut out of the foster and adoption system). *UHURU* described those black activists who cooperated with the ODS 'black liberals' and chided them for their too-cozy relationship with whites. While *UHURU* urged Montreal's black community to step forward as adoptive or foster parents, they were no less punitive than the worst white social worker in their condemnation of birth parents 'who refuse the responsibility of raising' their children. There was also a now legendary meeting between black Sir George Williams University students and ODS parents, which exists vividly in the memories of everyone who was there, for at one point one of the black students stood up and demanded that the white parents 'give us back our children' (the line everyone remembers).[81]

The Hybrid Baby left its infancy behind in the turbulent late 1960s, yet in some quarters it remained symbolic of optimism, a site of cross-racial solidarity. ODS parents cooperated with black community leaders in the early 1970s to create a Black Studies Centre, staffed and run by black volunteer teachers, which provided, among other things, instruction in black history and culture to interracially adopted children and their white siblings. This was accompanied by the creation of a 900-title lending library of books on black history and culture, including children's titles, maintained by the ODS. And so, for several years through the 1970s, every Saturday morning white parents brought their children, white and black, downtown for classes, music, and other activities. Occasionally, the parents themselves would meet to discuss the ideas of Frantz Fanon, Richard Wright, Ralph Ellison, and other black thinkers of the day.

So in these various ways, something like a community of interracial adoption was created in and around Montreal. This community believed the families they had created through adoption embodied the possibility of racial equality. The social meaning of 'blackness' and 'race' were fluid and certainly not unanimously understood, but notions such as race pride, respect for black knowledge, history, and culture, and the importance of relations with other black people were paramount. The force, and uniqueness, of this community of interracial adoption was obvious, especially compared to other communities with other politics. For example, in the early 1970s, a black social work consultant from Missouri approached the group, offering his services to educate white adoptive parents. He was politely rebuffed, as the ODS noted they had already had such an education program in place for several years, and had no trouble finding speakers from Montreal's black community. They encouraged him 'to continue to offer services to parent groups in the U.S.'[82] On the rare occasion that a kidnap narrative was voiced by a Canadian black organization (an article critical of transracial adoption from the *Village Voice*, reprinted in *Contrast* in 1972), the Open Door Society's letter to the editor extolling the virtues of how transracial adoption was practised in Canada was printed with a polite note: 'Your points are sincerely well taken.'[83] Again the United States functioned as Canada's racial foil, to reflect multicultural tolerance back.

'Love, Lies and Ideology':
Aboriginal Adoptions and the Limits of 'Integration'

> In some totalitarian regimes, people disappear because death squads take them away. In Canada, young Native people disappear into the dominant society through love, lies and ideology.
>
> Shandra Spears[84]

The story of the adoption of Aboriginal children by white parents in Canada is quite different. It is widely perceived in Canada that this has been an almost unmitigated disaster. Individual horror stories, of Native kids 'gone wrong,' abused, addicted, and 'acting out' circulate widely. One of these horror stories involves the extremely troubled son of former prime minister Jean Chrétien, adopted from an Inuvik orphanage in 1970 when Chrétien was minister for Indian affairs. This has become the elephant in the room in the production of common-sense knowledge of Native adoption in Canada. The adoption of Aboriginal children is popularly known as the 'sixties scoop': the timing is a bit off, but the politics are clear.[85] 'Cultural genocide' is another common term, given mainstream legitimacy by a Manitoba government inquiry into Native adoptions led by Justice Edwin Kimelman in 1983.[86] The adoption of Aboriginal children by whites is now invoked, constantly and almost automatically, by Aboriginal and non-Aboriginal writers and scholars alike, as an instrument of colonization. To activist and writer Winona LaDuke, for example, adoption joins eugenics and blood quantum as 'the new mechanisms to cause the elimination of nations of indigenous peoples.'[87] Social workers and other adoption professionals acknowledge the profound lack of empirical research on the lives of cross-culturally adopted Aboriginal children. Yet anecdotal evidence and practical experience lead many, if not most, Aboriginal adoption professionals to oppose cross-race placements. For Kenn Richard, social-work professor and director of Toronto's Native Child and Family Services Centre, 'far too many Aboriginal to non-Aboriginal adoptions break down ... and cultural dynamics must play a significant role in this process.'[88]

Reflecting on his troubled adopted son, former prime minister Chrétien told his biographer, 'Nobody told us there was a big problem to take Indians, that their record was not good.'[89] Another white adoptive parent of a Native son gone terribly wrong, sadly recalled the words of her father when she announced her adoption: 'You can't make a white man out of an Indian.'[90] In stark contrast to the discourse of black adopted child as harbinger of racial peace, the Aboriginal adopted child seems, to some, almost freakish. 'By treating him white, [they] rubbed away his native soul,' is how one reporter explained the unfortunate Chrétien family.[91] The public conversation about Aboriginal adoption begins and ends here: with a static, essential notion of 'Native identity,' irrevocably 'lost' in adoption. As adoption researcher Raven Sinclair has recently argued, almost all commentators on the topic proceed as though at birth 'adopted children had their native identity intact and dropped it by the wayside.'[92] Rather than locate the problem in the lost identity of individual children, Sinclair encourages us to widen our thinking about Aboriginal adoption. 'The lost identity paradigm,' she argues, 'does not hold the system accountable.'[93] Following her advice, I want to move from the symbolic language of 'scoop' and instead consider how racism and poverty created a set of adoption experiences for Aboriginal children which were often profoundly different from those of Montreal's black children. There are plenty of Hybrid Babies in North America; how do we account for the different symbolic meanings of adoption among different racialized groups at different moments? Today, to adoptive parents and adoption professionals alike, Chinese girls seem infinitely preferable and certainly more 'rescuable' compared to the abjectness and general hopelessness of domestic American black children. Sara Dorow asks why it is easier to imagine the former being absorbed into white kinship.[94] What makes one group a 'model minority' – and hence a good 'bet' for adoption – and another a 'risk'? What do these hierarchies of preference in adoption tell us about the varying symbolic function of children in different communities?

The most obvious difference between the adoption of First Nations and black children in Canada is numbers; there were many more Native transracial adoptions. The statistical picture for Aboriginal adoption is complicated, but by whatever measure, Native children have been vastly overrepresented in the child welfare system since the 1950s. Native children have been placed into state care at a rate as high as four-and-a-half times that of other Canadian children; in the four western provinces, they represent at least 40 per cent of the children 'in care.' Thus, here, we are speaking of thousands, not hundreds, of adoption placements. The province of Manitoba recorded the highest number of adoptions in the country. An internal file review conducted by the Manitoba Department of Family Services in 2004 calculated that between 1960 and 1980, almost five thousand children were placed outside Manitoba, two-thirds within Canada, the rest to the United States.[95] Encounters between Native children and child welfare systems mushroomed during the 1960s, when Aboriginal social welfare was transferred from the federal to the provincial government.[96]

Thus it is in no way surprising to discover a wealth of stories of apprehension in the case files. Children took many routes into the world of child welfare, for First Nations families imploded in ways that ranged from the dramatic to the mundane. Fathers shot mothers and/or themselves. Fathers abandoned families. Fathers lost their jobs. Mothers went to jail. Parents responded to the pressures of dislocation, poverty, and violence by neglecting or bullying their children; they beat them, they abandoned them, they didn't feed or clothe them or keep them warm in winter. Once, parents locked their children in a car overnight because they couldn't stand their crying. Children responded to such dysfunctional and abusive behaviour in kind. 'By the time I was born,' explains First Nations writer (and former foster child) Richard Wagamese, 'our tribal life had mutated into something ugly, and we kids were neglected, abandoned and abused. The great spiritual way of the Ojibway had been expunged by the nuns and the priests, and in its place was terrible hurt vented on those closest to you.'[97]

In approximately half of my sample of two hundred files, direct intervention and apprehension by social workers is discernible. What makes these stories different from other encounters between the poor, their children, and the state?[98] Numbers provide part of the answer: overrepresentation is simply the racialization of poverty. But so, too, are the historical interactions of colonialism, which have consistently produced infantilized relations between Aboriginals and the Canadian state. These infantilized relations, enacted in encounters between social workers and Aboriginal families (as they were in other realms with police, doctors, and teachers, to name a few) worked to undermine one of the mainstays of our culture: that the family takes care of its own. 'Children have historically been the battleground on which the struggle between Indigenous People and newcomers has been waged,' declared the Union of B.C. Indian Chiefs in 2002. The child welfare system simply replaced residential schools as a mechanism for removing and assimilating Native children.[99] In what other circumstances can we imagine children living with their grandparents being described as 'deserted'? What is necessarily 'irresponsible' about leaving one's children with one's own parents? Why was it not even possible to redeem good parent status when children were in the care of grandparents while parents were away working?[100] That in such situations some grandparents turned to the state for assistance was not necessarily a referendum on permanent custody. In a perceptive study on shared parenthood among the Brazilian poor, Claudia Fonseca asks whether the basic premises of legal adoption are intelligible to those who are most involved: 'the poverty-stricken families from which adoptable children are drawn.' Are 'abandonment,' 'foster care,' and 'adoption' – presented as obvious in the offices and courtrooms of the child welfare system – understood in the same terms by all?[101] Did the widowed birth father who requested temporary care for his son while he spent a summer looking for work expect to lose permanent custody? Even the potentially more ambiguous tales from the social work archive, such as the parents who, according to caseworkers, 'would simply drop the children off with anyone who would look after them,' appear startling when the trajectory leads from this to legal apprehension, sibling separation, and adoption to families in Minnesota and Pennsylvania.[102]

It is a truism that child welfare systems normalize and promote a universal definition of parenthood and family life, in which the experiences and cultures of the Anglo middle class are privileged. Nothing explained this better to me than a jolting personal/archival moment as I was doing this research. During my research time in Winnipeg, at the offices of the Department of Family Services, I began my day, as was customary, by opening an adoption case file from a large pile. This birth mother, described, incidentally, as 'an unkempt woman who presents herself as being quite dull and confused, and looks like she has just come off a binge,' seemed to 'require time out from parenting, so would leave the children with whomever would look after them.'[103] An hour earlier, I had left my then three-year-old son, who accompanied me on this research trip, at a new daycare. Sure, he was in the company of the child of the friends with whom we were staying, in a perfectly reputable, state-licensed daycare, to which I paid a lot of money. But these truths did not change the fact that I too needed 'time out from parenting,' and had just left my child with someone who 'would look after him.' (As I read the file, I realized I could not remember the name of his new caregiver at the daycare that morning.)

The contradictions in (and profound racialization of) the production of normative parenthood leaps from the social work archive. Consider this description of a birth family in the malevolent terms it was intended to invoke: 'a large collection of extended family living in one house.'[104] What did it mean to describe Aboriginal parents who consistently 'drifted,' 'wandered,' 'rambled from one place to another,' and how might this contrast to other parents – like me, perhaps – who 'travel'? In cases of severe family implosion, such as the deaths of birth parents, why were extended family deemed 'inappropriate,' their motives for wanting custody, 'questionable'? (A particularly tragic example because, in one such case, children were given instead to an adoptive family that used torture, sexual and physical, as discipline.)[105] Indeed, why were extended family not contacted at all, in some cases learning about parentless children only after adoptions had been finalized? When social workers described someone who had a 'higher degree of responsibility to their children than most Métis,' or warned potential adoptive parents that Métis children have a 'lower mental potential' because it was usually 'a low class white man who would rely on Indian women for his sexual gratification,' or dismissed the repeated and increasingly hostile attempts of a birth father to regain custody of his children as 'more than an ego blow than anything else,' the compelling force of the kidnap narrative comes into view.[106] 'Cradle snatchers. That's the whole long and short of it, nothing more than common kidnappers!' declares a character in Drew Hayden Taylor's play *Someday*, describing her experience as a mother whose child was apprehended in the 1960s. Children were taken simply 'cuz we were Indians. Things were different way back then.'[107]

At the same time, Native women were, in some areas in North America, subject to forced sterilization at rates twice as high as poor white women; it is not surprising that the politics of reproductive rights looked different in these communities.[108] No wonder, then, adoption as a form of colonial kidnap came to dominate the discourse of Native activism in the 1970s. The full story of the First Nations response to adoption and child welfare issues has yet to be fully told. Unlike the narrative of black opposition to transracial adoption, which (allegedly) rises and falls with the single statement of the National Association of Black Social Workers in 1972, there is no simplified origin story for Native opposition. Certainly within the child welfare system, some social workers, at least, were aware of Native opposition since the early 1970s, and some took pains to appear, at least, sensitive to Aboriginal concerns.[109] First Nations women voiced their public opposition to transracial adoption placements in various national and provincial women's organizations in 1974. The same year the North American Council on Adoptable Children, a lobby group, approved a Native initiated resolution which asked agencies to work WITH (sic) Native communities to strengthen families, find Native adoptive homes, or, in the last resort, 'find good people' to care for Native children.[110] First Nations communities, especially women, also worked locally to provide shelters and other forms of housing for Native women with children, in order to keep their children out of the child welfare system.[111] Aboriginal publications constantly stressed the need for Aboriginal adoptive and foster homes, and many published lengthy stories, complete with photos, of children in need of adoptive homes.[112]

Aboriginal politics, particularly the 'Red Power' variant, drew inspiration from global movements for decolonization during this time, and, as we've seen, children have can be stark and powerful symbols of anticolonial solidarity.[113] A cartoon in *Akwesasne Notes* in 1975 told the story of the 'rescue' of Vietnamese children from the perspective of those on the losing end: it featured a white couple pointing at a showroom display of children, labelled 'Vietnamese Orphan Souvenirs: Remember Your Stay in Vietnam Forever.' 'This would look nice in the den,' the wife is saying. The real punchline, though, is the headline: 'Another Native People Lose Their Children.'[114] Such transnational consciousness of and solidarity around adoption politics explains, perhaps, why the so-called 'export' of Native children to adoptive homes in the United States seemed to sharpen the pain of child apprehension. Almost all political interventions by activists on child welfare issues highlighted the 'exportation' issue. In March 1976, for example, fifty First Nations and Métis people occupied the office of the deputy minister of social services in Saskatoon. Their general concern, about what they termed the 'rapid increase in the intrusion of social workers into Native family life,' was triggered by one especially high-profile case of Native children recently sent from Native foster parents in Saskatchewan to adoptive parents in

Michigan.[115] The forced removal of Aboriginal children for adoption to the United States was cited as an example of imperialism and colonialism when Montreal's Black Power student leader Rosie Douglas toured Indian reserves across Canada in the summer of 1975.[116] One Aboriginal publication, *New Breed*, even featured an Aboriginal cartoon superhero who rescued Native children from U.S. adoptive parents.[117]

Virtually the same conditions applied in the United States: high rates of Aboriginal children in state care; the popularization of transracial placements through an active promotion program by the Child Welfare League of America; horror stories of unjust apprehensions which occasionally made the papers; and Aboriginal organizations increasingly committed to resisting what they saw as the incursions of the child welfare system. This resistance caught the attention of James Abourezk, senator from 'Indian Country,' South Dakota. Abourezk, the first Arab-American elected to the U.S. Senate, had an affinity for unpopular causes – he left politics after one term to found the American Arab Anti-Discrimination League. But he did some remarkable things in office, including helping to organize Senate hearings on Aboriginal child welfare in 1974, in which dozens of Aboriginal people told their stories of forced removal of their children. In 1978 the Indian Child Welfare Act, which made the adoption of Aboriginal children by those without tribal affiliations extremely difficult, became law.[118]

This legislation, clearly a political victory for Indian tribes in the United States, had immediate reverberations. Researcher Patrick Johnston stressed the enormous symbolic importance of ICWA, the very existence of which, he argued, 'increased the demands made on the Canadian government to find solutions.' Canadian commentators and activists cited the U.S. precedent approvingly and enviously. At the same time as Canada appeared as a bastion of multicultural harmony for encouraging cross-racial adoptions of black children, the United States appeared as the more progressive place for prohibiting the same thing for Aboriginal children.[119]

The high point of the kidnap narrative was the multi-year Kimelman Commission in Manitoba, appointed in 1982. Justice Edwin C. Kimelman and his committee spent many months touring the province, and issued an exhaustive and hard-hitting final report – termed by historian Veronica Strong-Boag a 'wake-up call' – in 1985.[120] The commission provided a forum for a steady stream of Aboriginal people from across the province to speak publicly, and often bitterly and sadly, of their experiences with the child welfare system. Isaac Beaulieu of

Brandon spoke for many when he declared, 'In the eyes of our people, the agencies that care for children are looked upon as policemen, not a helping agency.'[121] Here, too, the pain of losing children to *American* adoptive homes dominated. Peter Kelly, veteran First Nations activist from Northern Ontario, was blunt:

> What is objectionable is to take some dried up old prune in a suburb of Philadelphia who couldn't bear a child and take an Indian child from Canada and place them with that prune in Philadelphia. That kind of trafficking is what is objectionable.[122]

While Kelly harnessed sexism to buttress his point, a particular form of anti-imperialism fuelled this issue. 'Big shiny American cars would come onto the reserve, followed by the social worker's car,' a Native social worker in Manitoba recalled, 'when they left, there'd be a little Indian child sitting in the back of the American car bawling their eyes out.'[123] It's possible to argue – as the *Winnipeg Free Press* did – that it was this trope of adoption that created the Kimelman Commission itself. In March of 1982, the newspaper published a series of sensational stories about 'child export' to the United States. They found a voluble foil in the form of Richard Zellinger, a former Ontario child-care worker turned director of a private adoption agency in Louisiana. Zellinger claimed to have a long waiting list of Americans who wanted what he termed 'those beautiful Canadian children,' most of whom, he went on, 'take to their new homes like a duck to water.' The press dutifully reported that such talk 'riled' and 'stirred up' local Native leaders and quoted a chief who 'condemned Zellinger and said he should be "hanged."' A week later, out-of-province placements were banned, and Kimelman's commission was convened.[124]

Yet we need to make room in this discussion for the less straightforward tales, for which 'kidnap' – always an abstraction – is also a distortion. Of the almost hundred life stories of adopted Aboriginal adults gathered by researchers in recent years, a small minority – 8 per cent – believe their adoptions were illegal or improper. The vast majority were either relinquished or apprehended as a result of neglect, abuse, or some form of family dysfunction.[125] These stories, of course, represent a tiny fraction of the total, and, in making the argument for a more complicated understanding than the discourse of 'scoop' provides, I in no way diminish or disbelieve the pain of those who had horrific experiences. But 'scoop' is heavy-handed and leaves out a lot.

Birth parents tend to disappear when adoption is narrated in the abstract terms of either cultural genocide or humanitarian rescue, and none more so than the Aboriginal birth mothers who requested adoption for their children. A relatively unambiguous request for adoption is discernible from about a quarter of my sample. Birth mothers of Aboriginal children had some of the same reasons for requesting adoption as did other women of the era. Their boyfriends – Native and non-Native – abandoned them. They had affairs with married men. They were raped. They had several children and couldn't cope with more. 'She is not content being a single parent on welfare,' noted the social worker's report of one women, who had two children and a dysfunctional husband. 'She would like to improve her conditions by furthering her education. Her family is not in favour of the relinquishment.' Adoption promised secrecy, even from immediate family, who, as one single woman explained, 'would put considerable pressure on her to keep the child.'[126] Some were white woman with Native boyfriends and furious, racist parents. Here, too, the secrecy promised by adoption in this era was paramount.

Historian Veronica Strong-Boag warns us not to glamorize what she terms the 'classical family of Native nostalgia,' which can of course both inspire but also homogenize.[127] To some young women, the bonds of Aboriginal community felt closed and restrictive. One woman entered a maternity home in order to hide her pregnancy, and refused to register her child as 'Indian' in order to leave no trace for her reserve. Some were students who didn't want to interrupt their studies. 'This is the most heart-breaking decision I have had to make,' explained one such young woman, surprised by a pregnancy as she was about to enter nursing school.[128] 'As she is Indian I feel she is showing a great deal of initiative in choosing adoption and should be encouraged to continue her education,' wrote a social worker of another such woman in 1966, a rare indication that adoption as a strategy of upward mobility – common for single white girls of the era – was occasionally seized by others.[129] Others relinquished their children after trying, and failing, to raise them on their own. One such mother said she wanted adoption but also feared that her child, being Native, would never find a secure adoptive family (a fear echoed by many Montreal mothers of black children as well). In all such examples, the circumstances that produced such narrow choices should not be conflated with the absence of adult subjectivity itself.

Women reflect on their experiences as birth mothers differently with the passage of time. The archive of Native adoption often brings the story forward, as parties attempted to find each other later in life. In a trove of remarkable stories, these offer a kaleidoscope of emotions – among them chiefly grief and forgiveness – and testify to the immense continuing damage this era of adoption inflicted. But here, too, the lines between kidnap and rescue are sometimes difficult to see precisely. Fifteen years after her children were apprehended by the state, one mother wrote what she titled 'A Mother's Anguish' and asked the Children's Aid Society to send it to her sons. In it she recounted her story, of severe abuse by her husband, divorce, poverty, and serious alcoholism. 'I had no right to drag my beautiful babies to my level, so I got up the last bit of decency in me and took them to the CAS and left them there to be put up for adoption ... All the people I knew told me what a horrible person I was, even drunken women threw it in my face: "at least they kept their kids." But for what? Those kids with the drunken mothers turned out to be hoodlums and prostitutes, which I had not wanted for my boys ... I know in my heart that I made the right decision at the time.'[130] That even a handful of Native women narrated their stories of relinquishment like this, as *decency*, obliges historians not to let such voices disappear.

These varied experiences of birth mothers point towards some fundamental distinctions in the discourses of adoption in different communities. These differences include vastly contrasting circumstances of adoption, differently motivated adoptive parents, and different agency practices.

Most Aboriginal children experienced the ragged edges of adoption practice: multiple placements, at an older age. In my sample, two or three placements in foster care was average, and as many as six was in no way unusual. The high number of apprehensions, of course, also determined a very different pattern of adoption: adopted Native children were older; and often more than one child was involved, and many siblings were separated. As one frustrated social worker noted, speaking of a poorly functioning teenage boy who had survived physical abuse in multiple foster and adoption placements, 'Ironically the social services establishment usually throws up its hands in awed amazement when it is not understood "why this boy isn't gratefully happy to have such a loving mother?!"'[131] Montreal's black children were spared most of these problems; most were adopted as infants.

There were also some fundamental differences in the demographic profile, motivation, and politics of adoptive parents, all of which produced different cultural milieus for adopted children. As we've seen, the typical destination for Montreal's black adopted children – to simplify – was a 'freethinking' middle-class family, headed by a teacher or an engineer in the West Island suburbs. Native kids were adopted – also to simplify – by electricians in small-town Ontario or small business-men in rural Minnesota. While religion was hardly absent in the Mon-treal case, secular humanism was the dominant idiom of Montreal's adoptive parents. In the case of Aboriginal adopting parents, religious motivations were paramount. Adopting an Indian child, explained a Presbyterian couple from West Virginia, was possible only because they had attained sufficient 'faith.' They could not imagine a 'Negro' child in their family, but, having visited what they called 'the wilderness' to witness the 'plight of the Indian child,' their conscience, they explained, would not rest. 'I have my heart set on a little Indian girl,' explained the mother. A Baptist couple in North Carolina had recently undergone a religious conversion, which, as they described it, saved their mar-riage and started them thinking about adoption. 'Their recent success in business and recent discovery of Christ made them feel strongly that they need to share what they have with an Indian child,' their social worker explained, approvingly. 'It is difficult to describe the adoptive parents on paper, as one only has to be in their presence a short time to begin to feel the "good" which emanates from this couple,' wrote an-other especially enthralled social worker in a 1977 report.[132] 'I have at times believed my parents adopted me for the purpose of adding bonus points to their heavenly tally,' writes Korean adoptee Jae Ran Kim, a sentiment with which many Aboriginal adoptees might agree.[133]

Perhaps most importantly there was little sense of a community cre-ated around Manitoba's adopted Native children. They were widely disbursed geographically, often in rural areas and small towns. While individual families may have aligned themselves with adoption advo-cacy groups, there was no equivalent to the Open Door Society operat-ing in Manitoba. Project Opikihiwawin, a group of adoptive parents of Aboriginal children, started in Winnipeg in 1979. Adoptive parents never spoke with one voice (in Montreal or in Manitoba). Of course, there were adoptive parents of Aboriginal children who voiced, how-ever awkwardly, sentiments of cultural respect and race pride. One adoptive couple, who lived near a reserve, were described as having an 'interest in and a social commitment to the Indian population ... they believe in imparting as much pride in the child's racial group as possible.' In another case, it was noted that the prospective adoptive mother had 'taken a course in Indian Studies and seems very aware of the problems and background Indian children can come with.' (On the other hand, it was noted that this adoptive mother was 'admittedly very moralistic' and was disapproving of the birth mother's status as an unwed mother.) In a handful of cases, white adoptive parents emerged from – and intended to stay in – an Aboriginal community; they were typically teachers on reserves.[134]

Yet overall the defensiveness of some white parents of Aboriginal children is striking. A Brandon-based group of adoptive parents testifying at the Kimelman Commission in 1985, for example, rebuffed the concerns of Aboriginal spokespeople as 'making the issue into a racial confrontation.'[135] In the case files, 'Indianness' often became a kind of a diagnosis, an easy way to explain the tremendous difficulties endured by children who lived complicated, often tragic lives. 'As an Indian, she doesn't fit in with her peers,' wrote one distraught adoptive mother to the agency, about her suicidal daughter. 'She didn't want to be part of the American upper middle class,' wrote her psychiatrist. Speaking of a child who experienced seven foster home placements in the first five years of her life, he continued: 'She should be returned to her own culture.'[136] 'They want to go back to Canada and live like Indians,' wrote an adoptive mother from Pennsylvania of her two teenage sons, apprehended from their widowed birth father and adopted when they were ten years old.[137] This obvious gap between adoptive parents and Aboriginal communities might have been a result of the recruiting practices of adoption agencies, which were at times scandalous. Older couples (those over forty) were told they were only eligible to adopt a (less marketable) Native child. Others were clearly pushed where they didn't want to go. 'They do not feel comfortable about a child of Indian background but I feel further group discussions would help them explore this a bit more,' read one file notation. 'I believe they understand the child is full-blooded Indian,' read another.[138] Not surprisingly, then, social workers rarely engaged prospective parents in extended discussions on racial identity or racism. Indeed, in many case files, race was barely mentioned, and when it was, it was simply another way of saying 'appearance.' Parents might explain, for example, that that they were willing to adopt an Aboriginal child because others in the family had dark hair or a 'swarthy' complexion, and thus the child would not feel 'different.' Another couple decided to adopt an Aboriginal child after they had observed 'Eskimo' children on a trip to Denmark. 'They thought Indian children to be similar to Eskimo in appearance and were very much taken with them,' explained their social worker approvingly.[139] One couple went public with their story, that their six-year-old daughter was traumatized when she learned they were about to sign the official adoption papers. 'But I'm Indian,' she finally told them, 'I didn't want you to find out.' Written to draw attention to a government program in 1968 to promote Aboriginal adoption, this story was framed to highlight the goodness of the adoptive white parents, who of course knew of their child's origins but adopted her regardless. But missing in this narrative was the profound strangeness of the fact that Aboriginality had gone unmentioned in this household. This was exactly what the social welfare system, in this instance, encouraged. 'There's no Indian orientation in these children,' announced the director of the Adopt Indian and Métis program. 'The only difference when they grow older will be the skin pigmentation.[140]

The language of interracial adoption in Montreal was that the parents should stretch; in Manitoba the favoured phrase was that the children should fit in. An adoptive father declared his intention to send his son to Boy Scouts and Sunday school in order to 'learn to mix with white children at a young age, so he could function effectively in white society.'[141] Another would-be adoptive father commented to his social worker in 1969 that, despite the opposition from his extended family, he felt that he and his wife were 'strong enough' to handle an Aboriginal child, as long as they received a girl, who would 'fit in' more easily.[142] 'They have been in a white environment (a foster home) for three years and have adjusted well to white standards,' wrote another social worker in 1975. In this climate, it is not surprising that discussions of race pride and consciousness could take superficial forms. Were the parents who dressed their child in an Indian chief costume for a party and explained this to their social worker as an example of pride in heritage typical? It's difficult to know for the discussion of this topic, among my sample of social workers and adoptive parents, at least, was barely audible.

A 1979 survey of adoptive parents of Aboriginal children in Manitoba revealed a similar pattern: only one-quarter of parents reported 'ongoing' discussions with their children about their background, or had 'significant' contact with Aboriginal people or culture.[143] But perhaps the issue went beyond the number of times they were taken to powwows. As Sinclair argues, idealized versions of Aboriginal culture like powwows do not square with the rest of life, for anyone. 'What the adoptee may not know,' she writes, 'is that they are not seeing Aboriginal culture; they are seeing the vestiges of colonization and a neo-colonial society's construction of Aboriginal culture.'[144] But who was going to explain that?

Canadians are fond of the high moral ground, but these different moments of adoption politics in this country suggest that *how* one imagines children, race, and racial hierarchies is more significant than *where*. The differences in perceptions of black and Aboriginal transracial adoptions cannot be accounted for solely by a 'progressive' record, on the one hand, and a 'failure,'on the other. How can black children in white families be bearers of reconciliation, but Aboriginal children in white families be monuments to colonialism? How can transracial adoption come to mean such different things in Canada and the United States? 'Perhaps nothing was sadder in the early 1970s,' writes U.S. historian Steven Unger, 'than the feeling of hopelessness coming from so much of Indian country regarding not being able to keep their children after so many experiences, over generations, of having them taken away.'[145] In this sense, the victory represented by the passage of the American Indian Child Welfare Act in 1978 was simultaneously huge and narrow. It did nothing to address the impoverished conditions of Aboriginal families, for example, which gave force to the rescue narrative. In Canada, decades after the 'sixties scoop,' Aboriginal children remain hugely overrepresented in the child welfare system. One recent study estimates that there are three times more Aboriginal children in the child welfare system now than in residential schools at their height in the 1940s.[146] The practices are more accountable than in the past, yet, as Sinclair suggests, 'now it is Aboriginal social workers ... operating under the umbrellas of First Nation Child and Family service agencies who are doing the "scooping."'[147] Perhaps the problem lies in the inherent instabilities of using symbolic children to solve adult social problems.[148]

CHAPTER FOUR

The Missing Baby: Transnational Adoption and the Vanishing Children of Guatemala

The controversies created when children moved across the boundaries of race within *one* country shaped the cultural and political ground on which transnational adoption takes place. Opening adoption's domestic closet logically was necessary before adoption across national borders could begin to enjoy visibility and cultural support. After the 1960s, as Ellen Herman has observed, matching looked 'more like a lie than the truth.'[1] The white suburban couples posed shyly with their black babies in 1960s newspaper features – always written as tributes to the inherent oddity of such a grouping – gave way, a few decades later, to the near ubiquitous photos of white celebrities with black or Asian adopted children. But, emerging from the contested politics of domestic Hybrid Babies in the 1960s and 1970s, transnational adoptees also inherited similarly narrow political frameworks: were such families heroes or villains?

Transnational Adoption: A Preliminary History

While children have migrated without parents for centuries, it's common to date the emergence of modern transnational adoption to the post–Second World War era, a 'philanthropic response' to the devastation of Europe.[2] Once established as a solution for war orphans in Germany and Greece, adoption simply followed the path of other orphan-producing wars, such as Korea in the 1950s and Vietnam in the 1960s and 1970s. From the 1970s to the present, a wider array of Third World countries – with the notable exception of those in Africa – entered this circulation. The exact processes by which transnational adoption spread in this era are, at this point, insufficiently understood.

Historian Karen Balcom recently completed a mammoth study of the flow of babies across the Canada-U.S. border throughout the twentieth century, uncovering a complicated history of personal and professional ties between social workers, as well as recurring baby-selling scandals.[3] There's no equivalent study of other border crossings. Researchers Alstein and Simon say transnational adoption required several preconditions: a civil or international war, an imbalance in socio-economic conditions between sending and receiving countries, and the sorts of cooperative links between child-welfare agencies which Balcom has examined.[4] To this list, other researchers have added such considerations as the condition of health and social welfare systems in 'sending' countries and the cultural glorification of 'family' – and concomitant devaluation of childlessness – in Western countries.[5] Tobias Hubinette makes two other trenchant observations about the spread of transnational adoption in the post–Second World War era: it reminds us, he argues, of the 'astronomical power imbalance between the West and its former colonies.' It's also not a coincidence that most of the countries supplying children have been exposed to American military intervention, presence, or occupation.[6]

While the exact mechanisms of a nation's entry into – or exit from – adoption systems vary, the practice was popularized and sometimes actually created by a number of high-profile individuals. This is not to overlook the important role of long-standing child welfare and refugee aid organizations, such as the Geneva-based International Social Service, which facilitated most of the adoptions from Europe immediately after the Second World War. But transnational adoption grew in the 1950s thanks to the sheer personal will of grassroots activists, most of them adoptive parents, many of them with staggering numbers of adopted children. These are the people I think of (with profound curiosity) as 'adoption saints,' as most, though not all, were religiously motivated. American businessman Henry Holt is one example. Holt and his wife, Bertha, adopted eight mixed-race children from Korea and founded their own adoption agency. Holt is sometimes said to have 'invented' transnational adoption single-handedly. This overstates the case, but Holt (and his eponymous agency) definitely became synonymous with Korean adoption; his agency placed half of all Korean children adopted since 1956.[7] American author Pearl S. Buck also fits this category. Buck was the adoptive mother of seven mixed-race Chinese children, and also founded an agency for Chinese, Japanese, and Korean children. Lesser known, but no less committed, adoption links were created by countless others. Grassroots international child rescue initiatives did not emerge in Canada until the late 1960s. Only a small number of Koreans were adopted through the 1950s and 1960s, and to my knowledge no Cuban Peter Pan children were sent to Canada. This proved an embarrassment to social welfare officials, who occasionally declared that Canada lagged behind the United States in 'humanitarian' assistance. It was another war, in Vietnam, which encouraged Canadians towards transnational adoption. Families for Children, a group of adoptive mothers (all of them with enormous adoptive families), began in Montreal in 1969 and waged a high-profile child rescue campaign, first in Vietnam and later in Bangladesh.[8]

The United States receives the majority of such children, more than all other countries combined. Transnational adoptions account for approximately 20 per cent of all adoptions there.[9] While the numbers are smaller, in some Northern European countries, with a tiny domestic adoption rate, transnational adoption is essentially the only form of adoption.[10] Other countries, such as Canada and Spain, are in the peculiar position of moving quite recently from sending to receiving status. As we've seen, in the 1960s and 1970s Canada was both 'sender' (of Aboriginal children) and receiver (of Vietnamese children) at once, and the United States is also a sender, particularly of African-American children.[11] Yet, whatever the numbers, like transracial adoptees before them, when babies cross national borders, their visual and cultural power far outstrips statistics. As Briggs explores, since the 1950s two images have come to represent 'need': the mother-with-child, and the imploring waif.[12] These visual tropes indeed draw attention away from structural explanations of poverty (or war, or other disasters) in favour of ideologies of rescue. These ideologies and images of rescue are the foundation for today's global system of adoption. Those who created the international institutions of adoption, especially activist adoptive parents and private adoption agencies, have had their way illuminated by the near universal beacon of the needy child.

The Cold War helped too. While noting the role of activist adoptive parents in pushing the practice forward, immigration scholar Kirsten Lovelock cautions against treating the concerns of prospective parents as 'somehow outside of or separate from the needs and concerns of the nation.'[13] It made sense, during the Cold War, that from a world of possible choices, needy children from hot spots such as Cuba, Korea, or Vietnam would become the most visible to North Americans. Yet despite the obvious convergence between familial and national interests, when it came to the international transfer of children for adoption, formidable obstacles loomed; for example, a century of racist, exclusionary immigration laws. 'Sure, they're cute when they're young,' a friend recently overhead someone remark, speaking of his two Vietnamese adopted daughters. Embedded within this crude – perhaps even antiquated – racism are exactly the issues adoption advocates had to confront several decades ago. In countries such as Canada and the United States, with a history of hostility towards Asian immigration, the 'innocent victim of Communism' was not a shoo-in. An effective discourse of pity had to create foreign children not just as needy, but also non-threatening, race-less. That this worked is evident in the popular status of Chinese adoptions in North America, which began to top the lists in the 1990s. As Chinese immigrants in North America changed from sources of peril to 'model minorities,' adopted Chinese daughters were marked, as Sara Dorow puts it, by their 'rescuability.'[14]

Along with changing immigration laws and pushing state bureaucracies to facilitate transnational adoption flows, zealous parent activists also occasionally clashed with established child welfare professionals. We've seen that Cuban Peter Pan children broke several rules of what was then deemed good child welfare practice, including taking up residence in orphanages, institutions all but forgotten by social workers of the era. Private international agencies such as Henry Holt's ran afoul of established domestic social work practice in countless ways; by all accounts, Holt's single-minded evangelical child-saving approach upset child welfare professionals.[15] Mainstream child welfare opinion about transnational adoption remains mixed, to this day, and groups such as the International Social Service, as well as domestic authorities in Canada and the United States, voiced private and public reservations throughout the 1970s as the practice picked up steam.

Creating a Climate of Rescue

Rescue, however, was such a compelling story. This was so, in part, because in the early years, as governments were pushed and prodded to facilitate international adoption procedures, adoption advocates often stressed the dangers of *not* adopting. Legal reform was, to adoption advocates, a 'life or death' situation. One passionate Canadian adoptive mother, Helke Ferrie, went on a hunger strike in 1972 to highlight the plight of Bangladeshi orphans and her frustration at a slow-moving Canadian bureaucracy.[16] In this era, some agencies privileged sickly children, those who they felt would not survive in their own country. Thus the risk, rather than the safety, of the process was its *raison d'etre*. As Ferrie told a Canadian reporter in 1972, 'When you adopt from a foreign and war-torn country, the babies are not lovable when they come. They're cranky. They stink. They have worms and scabies ... It's a fantastic experience to watch them become fat and happy.'[17] While adoption agencies now stress the health, not the illness, of foreign babies, the dangers of non-adoption remain an important part of the rescue narrative. The visual trope of 'need' has occasionally been ramped up by Western investigations of foreign orphanages.

One such milestone was the Romanian orphan scandal of 1990. After the execution of former leader Nicolae Ceausescu, architect of a brutally pro-natalist regime, a number of Western journalists filed stories about the quantity and quality of orphanages in that country. The effect of the display of deprivation after the American ABC news show *20/20* aired footage of malnourished, despondent institutionalized children was enormous. Prospective adoptive parents booked their air tickets to Romania almost before the news story was over, and adoptions from Romania to Canada and the United States sky-rocketed. Lisa Cartwright calls this a 'transnational politics of pity,' which seemed to bridge, at a level both intimate and immediate, the distance between spectators and subjects.[18] This was repeated a few years later when a BBC news crew snuck a hidden camera into a Chinese orphanage and then broadcast a report, 'The Dying Room,' which paradoxically demonized and popularized adoptions from China at the same time.[19] Images of suffering Third World children jarred the Western psychic economy of childhood, which stresses innocence, sentiment, and dependence. Western aid agencies long have recognized the visual power of children in distress. Disaster relief campaigns, for example, almost always feature children, whether or not the campaign is focused specifically on the young. The submissive appeal of children, according to Erica Burman, 'protects our compassion and enables us to give.'[20] Or take.

Rescue narratives also circulated in voluminous 'human interest' stories about transnational adoption that have been a staple feature of mainstream journalism for at least two decades. 'Families Give Globalization Added Meaning,' read a recent *Globe and Mail* headline on the topic, capturing perfectly the up-beat tone and sentiment of these tales, which are inevitably accompanied by photos of smiling babies and deliriously happy parents.[21]

Sara Dorow's observations about media depictions of Chinese adoptions can be extended to transnational adoption in general: they stand as 'the shining exemplar of all that is good about transnationalism.'[22] Transnational adoption is, as Briggs puts it, a 'surprisingly literary affair,' and many adoptive parents have taken to print to make sense of their unusual experiences.[23] Like any birth, transnational adoption has its own rhythms and milestones, and adoptive parent accounts generally move through the complications of bureaucracy, the thrill of a first photograph, the fears of unknown health or other risks, the anticipation of the green-light telephone call, preparation for the voyage (which always involves shopping), and, finally, the disorienting but intensely joyful moment of meeting one's pre-existing 'kin' in a foreign hotel room or orphanage.[24] Occasionally, the story is complicated, and the drama heightened, by an unforeseen illness or a missing document, anything that threatens, but does not destroy, the happy ending. I suggested in the introduction that adoptive parents hardly speak with one voice, and first-person accounts vary widely. The self-congratulatory blindness of some is simply staggering. 'We thought it would be neat to have our own multi-ethnic family,' wrote CNN journalist John Towriss. 'I travel around the world and experience different cultures ... and I thought, what better way than to just establish that kind of diversity in my family.'[25] For others, adoption works to challenge, and channel, the privilege of ignorance. A powerful example in this genre is Lea Marenn's *Salvador's Children*. Marenn adopted her daughter at the age of eight, at the height of El Salvador's civil war. Deciding to listen to her traumatized child, rather than 'cure' her, Marenn and Maria embark on a joint journey to learn the circumstances of her family and her country, a candid combination of naivety and tenacity.[26] Yet even when they are thoughtful about the conditions that produced their children, adoptive parents accounts – similar to the narratives of Western tourists – often remain partial and one-sided. Returning from his trip to China in 1993, journalist and adoptive father Bruce Porter declared exuberantly, 'We had walked off with something of incalculable value – a baby – with the approval of everyone involved. What a coup, what a blessing, what a relief!'[27]

Perhaps the most influential transnational adoptive parent advocate in North America is Harvard law professor Elizabeth Bartholet. Bartholet wrote the popular book *Family Bonds* in 1993 and has contributed voluminous other writing in defence of transnational and transracial adoption in law journals and other scholarly venues. Her own story, recounted in *Family Bonds*, of adopting two boys from Peru is riveting, filled with all the drama and emotion of the transnational adoption genre. She is perhaps particularly appealing to those (like me – Bartholet's was the first book I read on the topic) who are sympathetic to feminist critiques of the normative nuclear family. Adoptive families, she insists, are not only 'real,' they are transformative. Furthermore, she argues, the fetishism of blood ties and essentialist understandings of family has unfairly privileged 'child production' through reproductive technology over adoption. 'A sane and humane society,' she writes, 'should encourage people to provide for existing children rather than bring more children into the world.' [28] Yet birth parents, not to mention the power relations produced by global political economy, lay outside Bartholet's story.[29] As Claudia Castañeda notes, Bartholet offers great freedom of choice to consumers in the adoption market; namely, to prospective white parents (hence, perhaps, her popularity). But in attempting to direct the conversation away from the notion that people 'belong' to racial groups of origin, Bartholet individualizes race, making it a property of individuals, rather than communities. It is important, she insists, for people to learn how to love those who are not biologically and racially similar. I cannot disagree. But by framing the movement of children across racial and national lines in adoption as solely cause for celebration, unequal relations, between races, nations, as well as adults and children, all but disappear.[30]

Through the 1990s, a generally supportive climate for transnational adoption was also built and sustained by banks that initiated low-interest adoption loans, airlines that offered special rates for adoption-related travel, and a handful of private companies that created 'adoption assistance plans' to reimburse expenses.[31] Durable and active communities of transnational adoptive families now exist electronically, in the hundreds of 'cybercommunities' created by adoptive parents on the Internet, as well as in real life, in 'culture camps' devoted to teaching adopted children their heritage, in language classes aimed specifically at adoptive parents and their children, in 'roots visits' undertaken by adoptive families to visit their children's countries of origin, and in play groups and support groups which can now be found in virtually every city in North America.[32] Of course, no recounting of the creation of a transnational adoption rescue narrative would be complete without mentioning the influence of celebrity culture, and the flood of images of foreign-baby–toting Hollywood mothers.

Yet perhaps this is also its undoing. When Madonna went on *Oprah* to defend her controversial adoption from Malawi in October 2006 and uttered the fateful words 'If everybody went there [Africa], they'd want to bring one of those children home with them and give them a better life,' the world shifted, a little bit, and 'rescue' slowly began its cultural descent.[33] I don't think it's a coincidence that, exactly a year after the firestorm over Madonna's adoption, another act of child rescue from Africa, an attempt by the newly minted French charity Arche de Zoe to bring 103 orphans from the Darfur region of Sudan to France (via Chad), ended in the arrest of nine French nationals on kidnapping charges. This rescue operation, it seemed, was built on enormously flimsy premises: the Sudanese war orphans were, rather, children from Chad, relinquished by parents who'd been promised boarding-school education in the next town, not adoption in France. That their rescuers were caught on film applying bandages and iodine to make them look like war orphans was, perhaps, just as amazing as the comments from Chad's President Idriss Deby, who claimed that the plan was to 'kidnap and steal these kids from their parents, and sell them to pedophile organizations in Europe, or kill them and sell their organs.'[34] Yet what I also find stunning in this tale is that, as a historically minded journalist from the *Toronto Star* also noted, a few decades ago 'we wouldn't have batted an eyelash if someone tried to spirit orphaned or underprivileged children out of a war-ravaged country into the waiting arms of prosperous Europeans.'[35] Instead, this time, activists in Canada organized a public march from Parliament Hill to the French embassy, to protest 'the atrocity of mass child kidnapping' in Chad.[36] How did rescue beget kidnap, so quickly?

Of course there are a range of criticisms of transnational adoption, and not all of them fall strictly into kidnap. Social welfare professionals have not only criticized the practices of such evangelical adoption advocates as Henry Holt, but they have also raised concerns about the process in general. Individual social workers, as well as such major social welfare organizations as International Social Service and Save the Children, have argued since at least the 1970s that transnational adoption hinders the development of a domestic social welfare system, and encourages child abandonment in favour of an imagined 'better life' elsewhere.[37]

Adoption's 'Dark Side': A History of the Scandalous

Professional concerns about adoption practice are voiced in the relative obscurity of social work journals. Adoption's public face is more easily, and frequently, seen in magazines, newspapers, and television and on the Internet. Running parallel to the public celebration of child rescue is a more uneasy and sinister discussion of what is often called 'the dark side' of transnational adoption. Scandalous readings of adoption – stories of abduction, theft, or purchase – can be narrated dispassionately, as aberrations, bad apples, exceptions. Other times the volume is high, the language heated, and political or moral conclusions drawn from particular incidents sweeping.

What do we learn when our knowledge of transnational adoption comes from scandal? Here's what English-language readers in the West might have learned in the past couple of decades:

In Mexico, hospitals on the U.S. border sell newborns to Americans, along with the documents necessary to register their births in the United States. In one case, an employee of an adoption agency in Texas was charged with transporting pregnant Mexican women across the border, in order to buy their newborns in the United States.[38] The circulation of children from Brazil to Italy came under fire in 1990 amidst allegations that the children were sold and killed in Europe for their organs.[39] In 1980 in Colombia, the country with the second highest adoption rate in the world, the practice came to a halt after a scandal involving the kidnapping and switching of newborns with deceased babies, masterminded by a lawyer formerly on the staff of the Colombian welfare department.[40] In Ecuador, a study of adoption irregularities by an international NGO in 1989 found stories of children kidnapped from public markets – having accompanied their market-vendor mothers to work – and disappearing from hospitals.[41] Rosario Godoy, director of the Honduran Office for Protection of Minors, tells stories of children stolen and smuggled out of hospitals in laundry sacks. One inventive kidnap ring in Honduras involved a man who dressed in a clown suit, in order to snatch infants out of the arms of distracted mothers.[42] In Paraguay, according to an investigation by a judicial research office, strangers posed as evangelists and offered to pay the medical expenses of pregnant women. They then took the baby as payment.[43] In the aftermath of enormous floods in Venezuela in 1999, which killed twenty-five thousand people, a community alleged that a group of 120 children had been saved and immediately sold to a trafficking ring.[44] Missing babies abounded during the civil war in El Salvador. One organization, Pro-Busqueda, organized a massive hunt for the estimated six thousand children who, through whatever means (abduction, baby-selling, theft, or being 'legitimately' orphaned), were sent to Europe or the United States for adoption, or adopted by military families in El

Salvador. Eight hundred families have requested help locating missing children, and two hundred reunions have occurred.[45]

In Vietnam, several different smuggling rings have been prosecuted, resulting in the conviction and imprisonment of over twenty people. In all cases, children were bought from poor parents and sold for adoption. The same story has been repeated in Cambodia. Licadho, Cambodia's largest human rights organization, alleges that recruiters on retainer from orphanages prey on poor mothers, and that government bureaucrats are paid to create fictitious identities for babies, essentially laundering them once they land in the orphanage. More recently, baby-selling rings with a similar modus operandi have been arrested in China.[46] In Sri Lanka, police raided a seaside hotel in 1991, which housed not tourists but young Sri Lankan women, together with their newborns. *Time* magazine called it a baby farm, 'where foreigners looking for children to adopt could come to browse.' A similar set-up was discovered in Malaysia, where pregnant Indonesian migrant workers were housed together by a gang that then sold their newborns.[47]

Western parents who flocked to Romania in the early 1990s, responding to those horrific images of orphanages, instead encountered, reports said, 'greedy hustlers' selling babies on the black market. A British couple spent several months in prison after a five-months-old baby was discovered in a cardboard box on the floor of their car as they crossed the border from Romania into Hungary.[48] In the chaos of Russian economic changes of the early 1990s, when adoption restrictions loosened, reports circulated immediately of couples who bartered their babies for food vouchers, or placed their unborn children in want ads. A few years later, a Russian woman was charged with masterminding an illegal adoption network between Russia and Italy, which allegedly falsified the identities of at least six hundred babies.[49] At the same time, a Canadian lawyer was charged for his role in a baby-selling ring in Poland. In Ukraine, employees of a maternity home were charged with stealing newborns and selling them to foreigners. The exact same allegation was made about a maternity home in Georgia a few years later.[50] A doctor in Hungary was convicted, along with eight co-defendants, in an illegal adoption ring in which pregnant Hungarian women were offered a trip to the United States in order to have, and leave, their babies there.[51]

Three nurses were among those charged in 2002 in Pakistan with taking babies from hospitals and selling them for adoption.[52] In Andhra Pradesh, India, a babies-for-sale scandal developed around a few orphanages, which allegedly bought infants from 'scouts' and sold them to adoptive parents. This tale was remarkable because it was on-going and consecutive; one orphanage would be implicated, close, and re-open, while similar charges would emerge about other institutions in the same region.[53]

Over 40 per cent of the top forty sending nations over the last fifteen years are effectively closed to transnational adoption, due to concerns about corruption, child trafficking, or abduction.[54] A few years ago, I was giving a talk at a Canadian university about the research for this book. I had just made the difficult (for an academic) decision that I would place myself in my investigation, and so I prepared a talk on the history and politics of transnational adoption that circulated through this research and my own story. In the audience there was a woman, white, with a newly adopted brown (and remarkably quiet) baby in her lap. After I finished, she was the first person to ask a question. 'I hope you don't think this is prying,' she said, 'but really, why on earth did you choose Guatemala?'

Guatemala and Cultural History of Missingness

These headlines could be taken as an indictment of modern transnational adoption in general. Clearly I think this would be shortsighted, and certainly a-historical, because baby-selling scandals, both domestic and transnational, have been part of adoption's history for a century.[55] Rather than magnify these stories, one could, alternatively, try to minimize them by invoking the mathematics of suffering: how many scandals, involving how many children? After all, there are a lot of orphans in the world. Some might even ask, how *much* bribery? As an American would-be adoptive mother, stalled in Cambodia while the U.S. government investigated a baby-selling scandal, declared to the *New York Times*, 'The government is holding up my adoption because maybe somebody gave the birth mother $25?'[56]

I don't believe scandal and kidnap represent adoption as a whole. Nor will I engage in a sordid calculus of commodity chains. I'll ask other questions: What knowledge is created – not only about adoption but also about children, families, and nations – through contested transnational adoption stories? Taking my cue from historians of sexuality – another realm in which binary understandings of human relations (pleasure/danger) dominate, and 'normal' slips easily into 'scandal' – I wonder about the effect of scandal on consciousness and cultural understanding. Kidnap stories, as we've seen, are fleeting; as do other culturally distasteful practices, they throw certain stories into relief, leaving others invisible.[57] Most transnational adoption kidnap stories move through print journalism or the Internet with the incredible speed of our age, and rarely do we learn about investigations, outcomes, or complications. This invariably leads to hasty conclusions and reinforces superficial or stereotypical understandings of adoption in general.[58] When adoption scandals occur in 'far off' parts of the world, such as Latin America, the Western imagination can run wild. 'Contemporary knowledge of Latin American children,' writes Tobias Hecht, is limited to the 'murdered and the murderous.'[59] So to look more deeply at adoption's contested trajectory over recent decades, I'll focus on one sending country, Guatemala.

As we'll see, virtually every scenario of illegality about transnational adoption I listed above has appeared, in rumour and in print, in Guatemala over the past several decades. The most comparable scenario is that of neighbouring El Salvador, in that Guatemala's adoption origin story also lies in brutal civil war. The circulation of children for adoption is a tale that is at once local, regional, and global; the fact that Latin America surpassed Asia and became, in 1975, the main source of adoptable children in the world should point us in the direction of that region's violent recent history.[60] Since the end of the Second World War, in the name of containing communism, the United States aided local allies to overthrow governments in Brazil, Dominican Republic, Chile, Uruguay, Guatemala, Cuba, and Argentina. Such interventions led to civil wars and internal repression throughout South and Central America. As historian Greg Grandin has described it, by the end of the Cold War 'Latin American security forces trained, funded, equipped and incited by Washington had executed a reign of bloody terror – hundreds of thousands killed, an equal number tortured, millions driven into exile – from which the region has yet to fully recover.'[61]

The CIA-orchestrated coup that deposed Guatemala's reform-minded elected president, Jacobo Arbenz, in 1954 provided, as we saw in chapter 2, the template for the psychological side of military intervention, in which the manipulation of parental anxieties about children figures prominently. Indeed, during Arbenz's successful election campaign, opponents of his plans for agrarian reform warned that an Arbenz government was bent on taking children away from their parents.[62] Arbenz's overthrow ushered in a period of political instability, repression, and war, which turned such anxieties into terrifying daily realities. Commonly dated from 1963 (when army officials attempted a rebellion against the U.S.-installed regime) to the signing of peace accords in 1996, the Guatemalan Civil War accounts for almost as many killed by war and repression as throughout the entire remainder of the Western Hemisphere.[63] How the world could pay such scant attention to what was happening in Guatemala, writes George Lovell, 'has yet to be satisfactorily explained.' Two hundred thousand people were killed or disappeared, 93 per cent at the hands of the Guatemalan army. Massacres occurred in 626 villages, and one and a half million people became refugees.[64] The height of the repression was during the period from 1981 through 1984, when a 'scorched earth policy' unleashed waves of terror. Half of the massacres took place in those years alone. The goal, according to General Efraín Rios Montt, was to 'drain the water from the fish,' to demolish the civilian support base of the guerillas. Thus, through burnings, massacres of entire villages, and massive forced relocations, the northern Mayan regions were vanquished. Of the war's victims, 83 per cent were Maya; as Grandin puts it, 'Anticommunist zeal and racist hatred were refracted through counterinsurgent exactitude.'[65]

'When people become only numbers, their stories can be lost,' writes anthropologist Victoria Sanford, whose work with massacre survivors and mass grave exhumations in Guatemala has recovered and publicized inconceivable tragedies.[66] Recently, the work of recalling the stories of dead and disappeared children has begun. Survivors' testimonies, in truth commission reports and in the work of a dedicated group of anthropologists and human rights workers, recount gut-wrenching stories of the army's attempt to 'destroy the seed.' Children were subject to everything: torture, kidnapping, forced recruitment to the armed forces, murder, and collective massacres. In Guatemala City, street children were subjected to a parallel campaign of terror. Several especially grotesque cases of everyday violence against street children were publicized, starting in 1989, by Amnesty International and other Guatemalan organizations, revealing a pattern of torture and murder carried out by police and private security forces. Guatemala, writes Guatemalan-American journalist Victor Perera, is one of the few countries in the world with death squads that 'specialize in torturing and killing children.'[67]

Violence against children reverberates on a different register, and never more so than during war. Threatening and torturing children was an effective means of torturing families, forcing collaboration, and destroying community, killing bodies and spirit at once. Further, Guatemalan soldiers admitted that they killed children in the belief that this would settle accounts for generations to come: as one put it, 'Those wretches are going to come some day and screw us over.'[68] There are now volumes of haunting testimony – 'things too sickening to relate,' wrote normally pacific folksinger Bruce Cockburn in *If I Had a Rocket Launcher*, penned after his visit to Guatemalan refugee camps in Mexico in 1983. One of these stories, one that won't leave me, seems the perfect, perverse example of the particular powers of children I'm trying to explain in this book. In 1984 the Guatemalan army captured nine-year-old Baudillo Monzon when he became separated from his family as they fled an attack on their village. His family and community hid in the relative safety of nearby mountains. Two months later, an army helicopter flew past and scattered hundreds of leaflets, bearing a photo of Baudillo lying in a hospital bed, reading. 'Thanks to God I am healing,' read the caption; on the opposite side was text blaming the guerillas for causing hunger and displacement. 'The soldiers won't harm us,' it continued, and encouraged them to go to Xalbal, one of the 'model villages' set up by the army to contain and control the indigenous population during this period. This tactic flushed communities out of their hiding places; their captured children were never seen again.[69]

Testimony from Baudillo Monzon's mother recounts her initial joy at being told her captured son was alive. And to add to the perversity, he might be. Over four hundred children were adopted in the United States during these years, and others were sent, through the 1980s, to European countries.[70] Children, orphaned and/or stolen, were also taken and adopted by armed forces personnel inside the country. The illegal adoption networks created in Guatemala in these years also facilitated the movement of children from other countries, notably neighbouring El Salvador.[71] The most recent attempt to document and trace Guatemala's missing children, *Demos a la niñez un futuro de paz* (Give children a future of peace), published in 2006, lists 3,465 names, victims of massacres, executions, torture, and disappearances.[72] (Of course, these figures don't include those who died 'regular' deaths, from malnutrition and disease.) A search movement has begun in Guatemala, and there are several high-profile stories of reunions. *Discovering Dominga*, a documentary made in 2003, tells the story of Denese Becker, who, when she was nine years old, survived a massacre in Rio Negro and was placed in a Guatemalan orphanage. Shortly after, she was adopted by an American Baptist minister and grew up in Iowa.[73]

Children's toys uncovered by the exhumation of one of hundreds of mass graves in Guatemala. (Photo by Rene Calderon)

The legacy of such a history is devastating. Peace accords, signed in 1996, did little to change the staggering inequalities of resources that drove the war. Accounts of post-war Guatemala – even the phrase 'post-war' seems inappropriate – all stress ongoing conditions of poverty, racism, and extraordinary levels of crime and violence, experienced especially severely by the marginal: women and poor children. 'What we are living with in Guatemala City today is just as dangerous as it was in the rural areas during the war,' Norma Cruz told me when I interviewed her in 2005. Cruz is the director of the Asociación Sobrevivientes (Survivors Association), a group that formed in 2001 to publicize the escalating murder rates of women – a phenomenon some call femicide. More recently, Cruz has been organizing the mothers of stolen children.[74] I recall the disorienting sense I had, leaving her house in Guatemala City at dusk, after hearing several hours of stories of kidnapping, murder, and other acts of violence in today's Guatemala. I felt jolted when I stepped outside and saw a normal, busy, poor Third World city. Norma's stories had turned the city into a war zone, which it is, but my imagination for war zones is shaped and limited by Western media. Bombed buildings do not lay in a crumpled heap in Guatemala City, but the war is tangible in countless other ways.[75]

An enduring and extraordinarily strong culture of what I think of (ungrammatically) as 'missingness' about children in Guatemala is one such legacy. It is impossible to narrate the history of, and responses to, transnational adoption from Guatemala without appreciating this. In a sense, the psychic space occupied by the war orphan has been filled by adoption; the fact of missing children did not go away when the war ended. After the peace accords of 1996, Guatemala's documented participation in transnational adoption systems almost doubled, from 731 children in 1996 to 1,278 in 1997, and climbed steadily every year thereafter. By 2006, 4,918 children were adopted internationally, making Guatemala the country with the highest per capita transnational adoption rate in the world. One hundred and sixty adoption agencies have ties to Guatemalan adoption programs; in 2005 adoption was the fourth-highest earner of foreign currency.[76] 'If they shut down the adoption system,' an American who runs a bed and breakfast for visiting adoptive families told me, 'it will be like closing an auto plant.' Until the law was reformed in December 2007, the Guatemalan system permitted lawyers to receive children relinquished by birth mothers, and then prepare the documentation for approval by a government ministry. This gave lawyers greater involvement, and potentially more money, than in the regular state-run systems. By 2007 there were reports that U.S. adoptive parents were paying up to $40,000; a coalition of NGOs in Guatemala reported that the actual cost of processing foreign adoptions in Guatemala was $4,000.[77] The United States has always been the largest recipient of Guatemalan children; by 2002, when Canada and most European countries ceased accepting children from Guatemala as a result of Guatemala's failure to endorse an international adoption convention (the Hague Convention), the United States became essentially the only destination.

The trends these figures represent have been mobilized to make powerful claims about the practice and meaning of adoption in Guatemala. These controversies have their own peculiar inner dynamics; all the world's corruption and kidnap stories are told in and about Guatemala, with a few fresh angles to boot. There has been an extensive debate about adoption reform, inside and outside the country. Yet the question of whether Guatemalan adoptions are 'dirty' or 'clean,' child-stealing or child-saving, has tended to remain in an ahistorical bubble, divorced from this memory of war and displacement. 'Wars don't end simply, and wars don't simply end,' writes Cynthia Enloe.[78] In Guatemala, the conditions that created missing children in the war years continue to create missing children in the post-conflict years. Legacies of war such as racialized economic inequalities, corruption, a military system which has simply morphed into organized crime, a culture of impunity about crime from the mundane to the catastrophic, a breakdown of community and trust – all foster the conditions which create missing children. To many, this also renders their 'missingness' completely believable. The children taken by force from their parents during the war were also given for adoption by 'honorable lawyers,' wrote one correspondent during the long adoption debate in the Guatemalan media in 2007, invoking the history of adoption's past, and suspicions about its present, at once.[79]

So it does not come as a surprise that when we turn the tables on transnational adoption discourses, and train our ear to the conversation in sending countries, the voice of kidnap roars. The history of kidnap narratives in Guatemala begins in earnest in the 1980s, when organ theft rumours, pertaining specifically to children, swept several Central and South American countries. Like Operation Peter Pan, the waves of organ theft narratives in Latin American break on a Cold War fault line; there is no ground for such stories apart from this political context. Tales of stolen children kept in Third World *casas de engorde* (fattening houses), then transferred to the First World, not for adoption but for organ harvesting, moved rapidly from word-of-mouth, to local media, to foreign media, to non-governmental and human rights organizations, and, ultimately, global government attention. In 1988 the European Parliament, pushed by leftist deputies, condemned U.S. and Israeli families for buying Honduran and Guatemalan children for organ transplants. The Soviet newspaper *Izvestia* was flatly unsurprised by the allegations: 'There is only one step from America's arrogance and its racist contempt for the Latin-American peoples to complete cannibalistic license.'[80] For its part, fully nine U.S. government agencies, including the Ministry of Justice, the FBI, and the Immigration and Naturalization Service, were kept busy in 1988 denying allegations that they participated in baby-stealing and organ theft, and the U.S. Information Agency (USIA) worked hard to blame the circulation of the rumour on Russia's KGB. A few years later, a USIA report blamed deliberate Soviet and Cuban disinformation, as well as 'Soviet front groups' such as an international association of lawyers, for the continued circulation of the rumour. An angry *Newsweek* magazine complained that 'pushed by Cuba, the World Health Organization drafted transplant guidelines that made the phony problem an official UN concern.'[81]

We've seen that, when it comes to conflicts about children, great global conflagrations can spring from thin evidence. Medical, legal, and political authorities constantly denied Latin American organ theft rumours. Yet the manner in which such denials were made helps us understand their plausibility in the first place. At one point in the child organ theft controversy, U.S. ambassador to Guatemala Thomas Stroock felt compelled to address the Guatemalan Rotary Club on the issue. After lunch at the Hotel Conquistador Ramada, Stroock red-baited the stories, blaming both the KGB and the Cuban government for their continued resonance in Guatemala. But he also made a personal plea, noting that the rumour campaign had caused much heartache to the entire U.S. diplomatic mission, because 'most of us are parents.' 'I have sixty-nine grandchildren,' he continued, 'these accusations are cruel and inhuman.'[82] A couple of years before this public appeal to common humanity, Stroock had actively discredited Sister Dianna Ortiz, a U.S. nun kidnapped and brutally tortured in Guatemala, claiming that her story (and, presumably, the 111 cigarette burns on her back) could be a hoax to end U.S. military aid.[83] Perhaps this was not the man, or the embassy, to dispatch humanitarian reassurances. This is but one example of a more general global pattern of claims and refutations about child organ theft, and perhaps helps to explain why these rumours seem to pop up seemingly randomly around the world. Denials rely on a trust in systems of regulation that not everyone shares.[84]

One of the most commented-upon tragedies of the kidnap narrative in recent Guatemalan history is the assault of U.S. traveller June Weinstock, Easter weekend 1994. A fifty-one-year-old environmentalist from Alaska, travelling by herself, Weinstock spent a couple of days in a small village, San Cristóbal Verapaz. When a child went temporarily missing at a market she was visiting, she was accused of baby-snatching. (The child reappeared an hour later, and the child's mother tried unsuccessfully to stop the attack.) Weinstock was yanked off a bus as she was set to leave town, and her bag was searched. The crowd grew; eventually an American missionary, as well as a local judge, tried to intervene, to no avail. Weinstock and the U.S. missionary, Mike Lewis, took refuge in the one-room courthouse, but the crowd broke in and grabbed them both. Lewis was released; Weinstock was beaten (with sticks and machetes), stoned, raped, and stabbed. For three hours. The courthouse was torched. She survived, in a coma for several months, and was returned to her home in Fairbanks, Alaska, where she lives, with greatly reduced mental and physical capacities, in an assisted-care facility to this day.[85]

Just before Weinstock came to Guatemala, a now infamous, widely circulated chart was published in *La Prensa*, illustrating and detailing the price of stolen children's organs on the international market. The chart had been posted in a store in San Cristóbal.[86] Weinstock's ordeal was both especially horrible and unusually famous; it was captured on film, shown on Guatemalan television, and featured in a string of media investigations in the United States and Europe. In the aftermath of this event, authorities worked overtime to restore 'calm.' But in this story – an attack on a lone middle-aged U.S. woman, in the midst of a child-theft panic, towards the end of one of the most brutal wars in the hemisphere, itself the legacy of decades of U.S. intervention – what was 'calm'? A week after the attack on Weinstock, the U.S. embassy in Guatemala organized a televised panel, featuring American doctors and social workers, who attempted to explain the processes of adoption and organ donation to Guatemalans.[87] For its part, the 'normal' that Guatemalan authorities tried to restore emerged at a widely publicized meeting of doctors, convened by Guatemala's Ministry of the Interior. One by one the doctors took the floor to explain that organ theft was impossible in Guatemala because the country simply did not have the medical equipment, resources, or personnel to perform organ transplants. The minister of the interior hoped that these testimonials to poverty and backwardness would put an end to the bad international image generated by the Weinstock crisis, and especially that tourism (which had plummeted) would return.[88]

This is a remarkable reminder that child organ-theft rumours originate in Latin American experiences, not Soviet ministries.[89] Anthropologist Nancy Scheper-Hughes, who has done the most sophisticated work on global organ-theft rumours, concludes that such reports have their basis 'in poor people's perceptions, grounded in a social and biomedical reality, that their bodies and those of their children might be worth more dead than alive to the rich and powerful.'[90] I think we can extend this analysis, formulated to explain how the violent everyday encounters of the poor turn the metaphor of body-snatching into believable realities, to the belief that healthy, intact, living children have, in certain circumstances, a value beyond measure. 'Guatemalans believe the stories that children are being sold to rich foreigners,' writes journalist Stephen Fraser, 'and in a sense, that is what's taking place.'[91]

The kidnap narratives that circulated in the Guatemalan press through the 1980s and 1990s predate the steady climb of adoption rates, but gave shape to a story that had developed over several decades. Stories of babies stolen from hospitals (occasionally by hospital employees) vie for space with tales of babies snatched from mothers' arms, or children who failed to return from school or play. Newspapers featured elaborate maps of the maternity hospital in Guatemala City in which 'robochicos' – child-snatchers – were especially active.[92] Parks and markets were also identified as dangerous places for children. Stories of the discovery of 'casa cunas clandestinas' – unregistered foster homes – in which babies in the adoption process were cared for by foster mothers, were also prominently featured in the media. Colloquially, and occasionally publicly, known as 'fattening houses,' where children are 'prepared' for adoption, the discovery of unregistered *casa cunas* always reads as a kidnap narrative; babies are 'rescued,' or 'saved,' and the stories are almost always accompanied by photos of middle-aged foster mothers, eyes downcast. Further suspicion was cast on *casa cunas* by reports that they were occasionally disguised as medical clinics, to throw off suspicious neighbours.[93]

Claims that such practices have turned adoption from a 'noble institution' to a lucrative business have been the defining feature of the adoption reform debate for at least two decades. Almost every single person I interviewed – those in and outside the adoption system – told me this. Some version of the phrase 'es un negocio, nada mas' ('it's a business, nothing more') appears in all of my interview notes, with the sole exception of the adoption lawyer I spoke to. This reached a crescendo as the long-debated reform bill edged closer to reality. 'We think the lawyers are planning their retirement fund,' child welfare activist Hector Dionisio joked to me, speaking of the escalating adoption rate in 2006, as the United States announced it too would cease adoptions from Guatemala unless the Hague treaty was ratified. But this sentiment has long roots, and it predates the rise of adoption rates. 'Se venden niños, bonitos y baratos' ('children for sale, beautiful and cheap') read one headline from 1992. Using the damning language of the market, Guatemala's place in global political economy is here figured to produce or reinforce anxieties about children:

Products for export have sustained the Guatemalan economy since forever. The circumstances of the international market determine the commercialization of the product and the price. However, the transactions have taken a grotesque turn in the last fifteen years. Now they are our children.[94]

Through the 1990s, in editorial cartoons and feature stories, the language of the market was matched with imagery: babies in export containers, babies on an assembly line, babies being weighed and measured on industrial scales, to name a few examples drawn from the Guatemalan press. Guatemalans – like others in developing countries – have been told repeatedly that 'export-led growth,' one of the hallmarks of neo-liberal economics, and in particular 'non-traditional exports' are the keys to a rosy future. Perhaps it's not such an imaginative leap to place babies alongside broccoli and pajamas, particularly as babies seem so much more lucrative.[95]

Concerns about the commercialization and commodification of adoption, and consequent involvement of organized crime, also predate the rise in documented adoption rates. After one in a series of failed attempts to centralize the adoption system in the hands of the state in 1991, an official from the Public Ministry told the press that reform was blocked because 'the big fish in child trafficking have intermediaries in congress.'[96] The 'big fish' rumoured in these years include a former Guatemalan ambassador to the United States, the head of the Supreme Court, and wives of a number of high-level military officers.[97] The fattening of babies was more than matched by the fattening of others in the adoption chain. An early claim that birth mothers were paid for their children emerged in a deal that soured in 1992, when, it was reported, a lawyer reneged on his offer to pay a woman for her child and she went to the police.[98] Another birth mother emerged in the press, seemingly on her own volition, to tell her story of selling five of her children to a lawyer for adoption.[99] A number of scenarios of illegality began to emerge through such individual stories. Lawyers, medical personnel, midwives, and birth mothers themselves were variously implicated; nurses, for example, allegedly solicited poor women in maternity wards, while others bought children from women in prisons. 'Substitute mothers,' sometimes called 'kangaroo mothers,' were paid to register the children as their own.[100] Birth certificates and other adoption papers were easily forged, some claimed, increasing the popularity of Guatemala as an easy place for adoption.[101]

'In our country rumours run more rapidly than water in the river and circulate with more efficiency than the national post,' declared a Guatemalan Red Cross official, responding to the organ-theft rumour epidemic of 1994.[102] But popular angst occasionally drew official sanction. In the weeks before the attacks on foreign tourists in the spring of 1994 – the most brutal being the attack on June Weinstock, but there were at least six other incidents – a government child welfare official announced the existence of at least twenty bands of child traffickers in the country that scoured poor neighbourhoods, photographing potential victims.[103] The circulation of the infamous organ price chart, the attacks on foreigners, and the appearance of 'gringo child-stealers' graffiti in Guatemala were all responses to these anxieties. So, too, were increased reports of community panic over the appearance of what Luise White calls, in another context, 'cars out of place.'[104] A black truck with tinted windows set the community of Mazatenango into a panic. When a red truck, without licence plates, roamed around a school in Guatemala City, a crowd of fifty mothers marched to a police station, demanding protection for their children. What they received was not very comforting: an official statement that chided the country for its state of psychosis, and simultaneously warned parents to take precautions to protect their children from strangers bearing cameras.[105]

The attack on June Weinstock was not only a culmination or flashpoint for these anxieties, it was also a turning point. As anthropologist Diane Nelson put it, the attack on Weinstock was 'an action that seems to overflow with significance.'[106] There have been several extremely thoughtful and respectful reflections on this story. Nelson herself has written of how the event shook her own scholarly and political certainties: 'My benevolence (and comfortable position) as an anthropologist in solidarity,' she wrote, 'hits a snag with this violence against another gringa. The highland Maya people usually coded as victims are suddenly perpetrators.'[107] Another anthropologist, Abigail Adams, foregrounded the sexual politics of the story in order to reflect on the peculiar demonization of 'gringas' in the Guatemalan imagination.[108] That George H. Bush was proffered babies to kiss when he visited a poor neighbourhood in Guatemala City several months after the attack on Weinstock is just one of the ways in which power can work in unexpected, and under-theorized, ways. But one didn't have to be an outsider, or a gringa, or even a woman, to feel turned around by this event. A Guatemalan I interviewed, himself an ex-guerilla combatant, told me the same thing. 'I used to think I was fighting for the people,' he said. 'After I watched that attack on television I remember thinking, who *are* the people?' The symbolic possibilities of the story emerged from all parts of the political spectrum, as there was widespread speculation, inside and outside the country, that Weinstock's attackers were incited by members of the Guatemalan military, to sow seeds of doubt about foreign human rights observers during the process of peacemaking.[109]

The widespread media, domestic and international, drawn to the events of March 1994 made less thoughtful judgments. Guatemalan newspapers repeatedly circulated images of Weinstock's broken body, skirt upraised after the attack, then later on a stretcher, almost completely bandaged as she was airlifted out of the country. Images of the shattered courthouse in which she hid were also widely reproduced. Inside Guatemala opinions ranged. Many voiced fury at the official government response, which seemed to privilege the safety of foreign tourists – and the Guatemalan tourist industry – over the security of Guatemalan children. 'Yankee hippies, go home!' read one headline – in English – complaining about the double standard of international travel that prevented Guatemalans from entering the United States but permitted anyone with a 'gringo passport' into Guatemala.[110] An editorial cartoon of this era depicted tourists passing through Guatemalan customs, their knapsacks bulging with babies. 'Anything to declare?' asks the official. 'Not much, just some souvenir handicrafts,' reply the tourists.[111]

For many, transnational adoption provided an instant and easy explanation for the attack. 'It's almost impossible to participate in the adoption process without supporting some sleaziness,' wrote Elizabeth Kadetsky in a *Village Voice* feature on Weinstock. The 'blithe complicity' of adoptive parents in an 'insidious imbalance of power makes the tale of June Weinstock, raped and beaten nearly to death at a pastoral lakeside in the Guatemalan highlands, larger than a lurid bloodletting.'[112] Authorities may have tried to push the child organ-theft rumours off the map of legitimacy, but, as one Guatemalan columnist noted simply, 'someone is making money from the sale of children.'[113]

Thus the kidnap template, which had been building since the 1980s, was entrenched. Kidnap narratives were kept in the public eye by stories of missing children and unregistered foster homes, both staples of Guatemalan journalism, as well as by the arrival of the media-savvy Bruce Harris, an English expatriate, who became the public face of the Guatemalan chapter of Casa Alianza (Covenant House), a Catholic child welfare organization. After the Weinstock story, Casa Alianza broadened its focus from helping street children to publicizing child-snatching. Harris's approach to child advocacy was a peculiar combination of the brave and the bombastic, and always generated attention.

Casa Alianza cooperated with officials in the Solicitor General's Office to investigate a series of trafficking rumours that emanated from the Guatemalan/Mexican border in 1997. This investigation resulted in a barrage of stories of child theft and baby-selling. New scenarios of illegality emerged in these reports: women – sometimes domestic servants, sometimes prostitutes – were held captive and forced to sell their babies. Women were drugged, given caesarean sections, and in this manner had their babies stolen. Harris also gave the anonymous 'big fish' child traffickers names, focusing especially on adoption lawyer Susanna Umaña, wife of the Supreme Court president (who unsuccessfully sued him for libel). A master of the sound bite, Harris was quoted around the world calling Guatemala an 'immense child supermarket' or 'baby factory' for foreigners (a phrase which became popular with Guatemalan government officials) and likening the adoption process to 'ordering a pizza over the telephone.'[114] Tipped off by Harris, in 1996 a British television show, *The Cook Report*, faked a 'rigged' Guatemalan adoption. A couple was planted in the adoption system, and the journalist, Roger Cook, followed them through the process, which included meetings of adoptive parent support groups in England and travel to Guatemala, where they met with their 'stolen' child, secured by, it was alleged, counterfeit documents. While inflammatory stories about baby-selling circulated in the English press, other English reporters claimed that the irregularity in this instance was simply a poorly corrected clerical error in the birth registry.[115]

The difficulty in arbitrating the veracity of individual sensational stories was magnified by the escalating numbers of adoptions, the volume of allegations of impropriety, and the intensification of crime, violence, and impunity after the 1996 peace accords. The post-war culture of impunity made everything believable and possible. *Prensa Libre*, for example, reported that high Guatemalan functionaries were routinely paid off in adoption processes, and that embassies in receiving countries issued entry visas even when the origin of the child was in doubt.[116] In 2000 Guatemalan adoptions received United Nations censure. Ofelia Calcetas-Santos, the UN special rapporteur on the sale of children, child prostitution, and child pornography, spent ten days in Guatemala interviewing government and child welfare officials. Her report was sweeping and damning. 'Legal adoption,' she concluded, 'appears to be the exception rather than the rule.' 'It would seem that, in the majority of cases, international adoption involves a variety of criminal offences, including the buying and selling of children, the falsifying of documents, the kidnapping of children ...'[117] In the intense media commentary which followed this report, UNICEF's representative in Guatemala, Elizabeth Gibbons, poured oil on these fires, telling journalists that 'we don't know which adoptions are legal and which are not.'[118]

The path from this 2000 report to the long sought-after reform legislation, to centralize the process in the state, which finally passed the Guatemalan congress in December 2007, was not exactly inevitable. But a combination of extremely controversial events and circumstances propelled the debate in this direction. The continued lynching of suspected child-snatchers was one. The lynching that greeted me when I came to Guatemala to receive custody of my son in May 2000 occurred around the same time the UN report was released, and had overtones of the Weinstock attack six years earlier. Japanese visitor Saison Tetsuo Yamahiro and Guatemalan bus driver Edgar Castellanos were both killed by a mob in Todos Santos Cuchumatán, victims of a similar tragically mistaken scenario of baby-snatching. That Yamahiro was a foreign tourist guaranteed this story widespread international circulation; that 421 people were lynched in Guatemala between 1996 and 2001 was not so nearly well reported.[119] More visible locally than internationally were those Guatemalans lynched because of their alleged involvement in the baby trade. An unidentified man and woman were burned alive by a crowd in Sumpango, just outside Guatemala City, in April 2006, both suspected child-stealers.[120] Six children had been abducted from the area in the previous six months; in this instance, adoption facilitators told me that the lynching was the result of an adoption negotiation 'gone bad.' Like Weinstock's lynching, this too was widely photographed and filmed, and broadcast repeatedly on Guatemalan television. The burning bodies were of course featured in this iconography, but more prominent was the crowd that circled the bodies; in the front rows were large numbers of children watching the smoldering flames. A few months later, another alleged child trafficker was lynched, while a local midwife narrowly escaped the same fate. A number of women accused of agreeing to sell their children were paraded to the town square, where they were whipped and had their hair shorn.[121]

As the adoption rate climbed – almost doubling between 2002 and 2004, and hitting nearly 5,000 by 2006 – stories of improprieties and enrichment followed suit. The dramatically contested border politics in the United States after 11 September 2001 created new scenarios of illegality. As undocumented immigrant parents working in the United

States found it much more difficult to return to retrieve their children once they established themselves – as had been customary in the past – it was left to professional smugglers – 'coyotes' – to bring children to parents. This may have facilitated familial reunions, but it also facilitated claims that these networks were simply a façade for child-stealers to bring their goods to the United States.[122]

In these years a new figure emerged in the public discussion of adoption networks, the intermediary between birth mothers and the legal system, alternatively called the *buscadora* (looker) or *jaladora* (puller). This figure was always a woman, but these differences in terminology indicated precisely the conflicting understandings of how adoption networks operated. Did adoption go looking for pregnant women, in the form of *jaladoras* who yanked their children away from them? Or, did women go looking for adoption, making contact with local *buscadoras* who linked them with lawyers and the legal and medical apparatus of the adoption system? Certainly the intermediary was on the front lines of the system, incurring the wrath and suspicions of many. 'I call them *jaladoras* because they do a lot more than look,' Casa Alianza's Hector Dionisio told me, citing several scenarios of pressure and manipulation of pregnant women by intermediaries. They function, in Guatemala's kidnap narrative, in much the same way the procuress functioned in Victorian-era white slave narratives: the older woman who presents herself as a trustworthy friend to a poor girl in need, only to abuse this trust in the service of exploitation. 'We have to get them out of the business,' an American orphanage volunteer told me. 'They receive $5,000 a head to stir women up to think about adoption.'

If the money paid intermediaries raised ire, allegations of payments to birth mothers proved even more upsetting. 'In theory the birth mothers don't get money but, for about the past five years, we all know that's not the case,' an American expat who rents rooms to adoptive parents told me. In public discussions, birth mothers are characterized as either baby-sellers or victims of baby-stealers. During the debate on the adoption reform bill in 2007, Norma Cruz's *Sobrevivientes* group organized demonstrations of mothers, who marched outside the National Palace in Guatemala City with empty strollers to dramatize their stories of child theft. 'We aren't against adoption,' Cruz told the BBC. 'We are against the business this has become, where people are getting rich selling kids that have been taken away from their mothers.'[123] Others have claimed that commodification of adoption has created not only theft but also its own market logic, so that women are producing children *for* adoption. A government official instrumental in the adoption reform bill told me casually that he believed fully 80 percent of Guatemalan women want money for their babies. Without a financial incentive, the adoption rate would plummet, he continued, because women can always find an aunt or a mother to look after their children. The same sentiment was voiced by Casa Alianza's Hector Dionisio, who told me Guatemala's adoption rate would be about 80 per cent less than current figures because Guatemalan women 'don't lack affection for [in Spanish *desamor*, literally not-love] their children'; in other words, finances were distorting natural mother-love. Officials from UNICEF's Guatemala office have stated repeatedly that one-third of Guatemalan birth mothers relinquish more than one child for adoption, as though this proves financial motivations for relinquishment.[124] Perhaps the most dismal view of Guatemalan birth mothers – not to mention reproductive complexities in general – came from Hector Julio Perez, vice-president of the Guatemalan Congress: 'If I sell *elotes* [corn on the cob] and they take away my market, what am I going to do? I'm not going to keep producing *elotes*.'[125]

Birth mothers occupy this narrow space between victim and villain, but the space for lawyers is even more confined: they are truly believed to be the scoundrels of the piece. The only person I met in Guatemala who told me adoption reform wasn't necessary was an adoption lawyer. He gave me a tour of his *casa cuna*, located in a gated community in Guatemala City. Behind the high walls was a splendid place filled with toys and Disney-inspired murals; it also housed a well-stocked clinic, not to mention dozens of clean, healthy, adorable babies. It could have been any private First World daycare centre. Paradoxically, this display of abundance, paid for by U.S. parents for their soon-to-be-departing Guatemalan children, shook me as much as the poverty of those remaining, visible everyday on the street. This is what gives the clandestine 'fattening house' trope its power. When children 'go missing' into such luxury, concerns about 'missingness' are not necessarily diminished. The wealthy lawyer stereotype helps also to explain the rumour, which I heard from a number of different people, that some lawyers keep houses of pregnant women, literal baby factories, and that the lawyers themselves act as the studs.

Transnational adoption's negative domestic face has been created not only from these considerable stories of theft and corruption, or even Guatemala's violent history. A central premise of this book is that nations have a powerful stake in their children. Poor nations, like poor people, experience the 'missingness' of children, or their inability to provide hegemonic standards of childhood, in profoundly grievous and symbolic ways. We've seen that Guatemalan officials and tourist industry spokespeople were frantic to restore the country's good name after the lynching of tourists in the spring of 1994, but nationalist responses to adoption don't necessarily have to spring from crude self-interest. 'What's happening to our culture that we don't take care of our children?' asked a Guatemalan government spokesperson to a *New York Times* reporter in 2006. It was a question I heard repeatedly from women's groups and other non-governmental organizations. When a representative from a Guatemalan woman's group invoked the daily departure of Guatemalan children at the airport to explain her concerns about the country's high adoption rate, I don't think she was playing nationalist politics with women's wombs. 'Guatemalans are tired of bad press; during the civil war it was their poor human rights record, and now it is adoption,' reported the BBC. The country has become 'synonymous with stealing and selling children,' read a typical Guatemalan editorial.[126] That the Guatemalan adoption boom was motored exclusively by the United States, after other countries, all Hague Convention signatories, withdrew their programs, helped to merge this discourse of national shame – audible in other sending countries as well – with anti-American and anti-imperial resentments. The Guatemalan press occasionally features big exposés from U.S. adoption agency websites, quoting showroom-like descriptions of available Guatemalan babies. It is instructive to imagine a Guatemalan reading of the vast adoption marketing apparatus some agencies provide. 'Guate-mama' T-shirts and bibs that depict a child holding Guatemalan and U.S. flags together are intended to celebrate roots and multicultural families in the United States, but how can this soften the razor-sharp edges of U.S./Guatemalan history? Almost all of the most critical commentaries about adoption, written by Guatemalans and foreigners alike, take at least one obligatory tour of the 'adoption hotels' that have developed in Guatemala's tourist districts. Perhaps the only figure more popularly symbolic of global inequalities than the American tourist in the Third World is the American adoptive parent in the Third World, and the swimming pools and bars of Guatemala's exclusive hotels provide ample fuel for journalists and others to express antipathy to both.[127] Trying to keep adoption systems open, American adoptive parents organized to send photo albums of their adopted children, enjoying a happy U.S. life, to Wendy Berger, wife of Guatemala's ex-president Oscar Berger and a staunch advocate of adoption reform. The gesture didn't work. 'I don't come to your country and tell you how to do things,' she replied.[128]

Here lies the significance of the symbolic child in the campaign to reform Guatemala's adoption laws. Reform advocates called the day of the congressional vote a 'day of dignity of childhood.' Outside the National Palace, demonstrators dressed in white carried signs which read, 'Vote Guatemala, Vote for Dignity.' While many child welfare advocates told me that adoption reform would never have passed without the threat that the United States would suspend Guatemalan adoptions unless it did, I think the public discussion of the bill provided an important and highly symbolic attempt for Guatemala to re-enter the family of modern nations. Representatives from France, Spain, Britain, and Germany either watched the vote from inside the Congress, or expressed their approval after. Nidia Aguilar del Cid, a long-time Guatemalan child rights advocate declared that the vote 'basically gives our image a whitewash in the eyes of the countries that want to adopt children here.'[129] The words of a prosecutor in a Polish baby-selling scandal in 1993 applied here perfectly: 'This is a civilized country. You can't just walk in here and buy a baby.'[130]

The adoption reform campaign in Guatemala is a perfect example of how children's issues are helping to create new political space, particularly around subjects – children – rarely considered as political actors. Some political scientists, such as Goran Theorborn, have written approvingly of how child politics are making 'important contributions to the constitution of an active civil society.'[131] This may be so, but it also reflects a more complicated development, part of a neo-colonial imposition of a single standard of childhood around the world. When countries commit themselves to dominant notions of childhood in order to affirm their support for democratic renewal or responsible economic policies, what are the implications of this embrace of symbolic children for the lives of actual children? When the fate of the child is taken up as an insult to the nation, as it often is by countries on the 'losing' end of adoption, the issue is infused with great political relevance. However, in practice, the voices of those at the heart of the story are typically marginalized.[132] Birth mothers, for example, were barely heard from in the adoption reform debate in Guatemala, and children not at all.

The Narrow Space for Rescue

And so, what of rescue? In recent years, the case for Guatemalan adoptions as salvation has been made with less volume, but it isn't absent. Inside and outside the country, a few have attempted to stand kidnap on its head, arguing that high international adoption rates are a cause for celebration because it means the country cares for its children. 'The more adoptions there are, the more protection is being achieved,' wrote well-known lawyer Fernando Linares Beltranena in the Guatemalan press, a position echoed in the U.S. press by Elizabeth Bartholet, who recently termed Guatemala a 'model for those who believe in adoption.'[133] Other Guatemalans have, like people the world over, emphasized adoption as literally life-saving. 'We're rescuing these children from death,' declared adoption lawyer Susana Luarca (formerly Urmaña). Other high-profile adoption lawyers argue the practice prevents child prostitution, homelessness, or child labour. 'I feel good when I see these children going off to America,' says adoption lawyer Feliciano Carrillo. 'I think this child has a good future, a secure future, a future that even I wish I would have had.'[134] Such straightforward certainties of rescue occasionally surface in the Guatemalan media. The conservative columnist Karin Escaler, for example, wrote of adoption as a 'gift for generations,' evoking the image of the Guatemalan child in the United States who can 'go to baseball and boy scouts, know family life, go to university, establish a business.'[135]

The kidnap narrative is also challenged by those who are incredulous about its central premises. These direct conflicts between kidnap and rescue reveal the absolute impossibility of choosing a single, linear framework, perhaps especially so in places recovering from the traumas of war. The conditions which create the paradigmatically needy children transnational adoption seeks to rescue also create the conditions which make kidnap plausible and possible – and certainly make empirical certainties impossible. A few examples: The requirement that birth mothers and the child provide DNA samples was instituted first by the Canadian government in the 1990s, amidst rumours of 'kangaroo mothers' hired to pose as birth mothers of stolen children. It was soon taken up by all receiving nations; in the pre-reform controversies of 2007, the U.S. government upped the requirement to two DNA tests. This was meant to provide safeguards and assurances; and, of course, it did. Some point to the DNA requirement as the ultimate answer to kidnap; it's just not possible to imagine how stolen children pass through tightly guarded immigration gates. To others there is no mystery at all; Casa Alianza's Hector Dionisio spent an afternoon with me outlining several scenarios of illegality to trick the DNA requirement. 'It is an open secret,' writes anthropologist Angelina Snodgrass Godoy, 'that many ex-military men are now active in most forms of organized crime,' and have forged strong links to customs, immigration, the judiciary, and the police.[136] Others call it the 'neo-liberalization' of violence, outsourcing what used to be the job of the state.[137]

When the state is widely regarded as second string to the mafia, the scientific assurances of DNA tests inhabit the same realm as the complicated science of organ donation: it doesn't trump the skepticism created by daily life. Similarly, the damning 2000 UNICEF report on adoption was widely criticized, especially by adoptive parents groups, for its obvious lack of empirical rigour. Indeed, the report made sweeping claims about adoption illegalities and irregularities, with no discussion of the evidence gathered to support these conclusions. The author herself agreed with a *Guardian* reporter that it was written in great haste, and that her ten days in Guatemala were hardly sufficient.[138] Yet what has not been widely reported is that a major source of information about illegal adoption for the report was University of San Carlos sociologist Mayra Gutiérrez Hernández, who went missing days after the UNICEF document was publicly announced in Guatemala. Gutiérrez became the subject of an Amnesty International campaign when a cursory police investigation into her disappearance blamed a vengeful ex-boyfriend. 'Yes, I knew Mayra. They usually try a homosexual conspiracy,' said Nidia Aguilar del Cid dryly when I asked her about Gutiérrez's disappearance.[139] 'We all know people are being paid off and babies are stolen. Don't stop adoption, prosecute those who are doing it!' thundered U.S. adoption agency spokesperson Tom DiFilipo, to widespread applause, during an important policy conference on Guatemalan adoption reform in the United States. This level of certainty about the easy separation – not to mention prosecution – of the licit and the illicit in the global circulation of people and goods is simply not universally shared.[140]

This privileged innocence of one party is exactly what makes it possible for lopsided transnational relations to continue. I am reminded of a young American couple I met during my stay at the Hotel Casa Grande, one of Guatemala City's 'baby hotels,' in 2000. During one smiling exchange of compliments about our new children, they blurted out their story. They had been in the adoption system only three months when they received word their documents were ready and their adoption had been approved – an unheard-of interval in a legal process which generally took from six months to a year. Furthermore, they had met their child not, as was customary, when the foster mother brought the baby to the hotel, but rather at the airport when they arrived. As they were waiting for a taxi, a car drove up, a man who identified himself as their lawyer pressed a baby in their arms through the open car window, and drove off. I don't know what they made of this experience. At the time, I remember feeling surprised at the naive way they related the story, seemingly incurious about the various unsavoury possibilities. Some time later, my own imagination expanded.

However, one does not need an unshattered faith in global justice, or even the cultural superiority of the boy scouts and baseball, to believe that adoption provides an important alternative to Guatemalan women. There is a feminist argument for adoption, most evident in the writings of adoptive mothers, but also audible in Guatemala. In *Good-bye Baby: Adoptions from Guatemala,* American filmmaker Patricia Goudvis interviews several women, Americans and Guatemalans alike, who emphasize the sexual irresponsibility and machismo of Guatemalan men to press the case for keeping adoption systems open in the face of mounting commodification. 'If women have a choice of being a paid baby producer or a prostitute, what's the best choice?' asks an American feminist I met in Guatemala; a question for which, of course, there is no right answer. The sexism of Guatemalan men is also used to explain the preponderance of transnational over domestic adoption in Guatemala. Sidestepping the vast history of family-making during the war, as well as the hugely different economies of foreign versus domestic adoption, it is often said simplistically that there is no 'adoption culture' in Guatemala because Guatemalan men refuse to 'raise other men's children.'[141]

Conclusion: Beyond Kidnap and Rescue

What do Guatemalans think about adoption? I've based my story on my reading of the public discussion, inside and outside the country. Rather than evaluate truths or banish lies, I've tried to set this public discussion in the context of Guatemala's own history, as well as a global debate on transnational adoption which privileges narratives of kidnap and rescue, in different places and at different times. I've kept my analysis to the level of the public discussion in order to begin to think about what makes kidnap and rescue narratives believable, but I am more than mindful of just how partial this story is. The Guatemalan-American writer Francisco Goldman says that whispered rumour and gossip are 'probably the most effective form of media in a largely illiterate country.'[142] Studies which foreground the voices – especially the whispers – of Guatemalans are obviously needed. An extremely preliminary survey of Guatemalan perceptions of adoption, by two American psychologists, concluded that the majority of their (small) sample held positive attitudes towards transnational adoption, but a minority expressed concerns about trafficking, child-snatching, and organ theft.[143]

Even more obviously lacking is the perspective of Guatemalan birth mothers, as well as the cultural world they inhabit. In public discussions, birth mothers are caricatured as victims or villains and thus rendered mute, in Guatemala as elsewhere in the world. The social, personal, and psychic consequences of relinquishment have been studied in the First World, where birth mothers have also told their own stories. Understanding the meaning of adoption for birth mothers from other parts of the world is barely beginning.[144] The discourses of kidnap and rescue I have been analysing focus almost solely on Guatemalan children; when the debate expands from babies to mothers, the story gets even more complicated. Does adoption enhance or foreclose on reproductive alternatives for Guatemalan women? As Tobias Hubinette argues for Korea, so too in Guatemala the torrent of harsh criticism for exporting children occurs with little mention of the internal patriarchal structures that are the 'absolute precondition for the practice to exist in the first place.'[145] The full story of transnational adoption is simply unknowable until the conversation includes birth mothers.

In this tremendously complicated and conflict-laden story, the most sophisticated and thoughtful voices I heard were not the public ones. Privately, in the offices of human rights organizations and women's groups, of child welfare advocates and adoption facilitators, I often heard the more nuanced stories, the places kidnap and rescue don't take us. I learned it is possible to lament the hard lives and lack of reproductive choices of women without accepting baby-selling as a reasonable alternative. I learned that the symbolic power of missing babies is not just so much fodder for the election campaigns of nationalist politicians, but also a painful and visible reminder of the ongoing traumas of a war that solved little. While I learned enough to be wary about the zealousness of child savers who reduce pregnant women to vessels for nationalist or anti-imperialist ideologies, I also learned that sometimes the pain of relinquishment is felt even when it's not your own baby.

From Susi Bolaños, a social worker who has facilitated over 250 reunions between birth parents and transnationally adopted children, I learned the absolute futility of imagining adoption as solely kidnap or rescue. Perhaps more than anyone else in Guatemala, Bolaños has seen the best and the worst of the system. She tells extraordinary stories, of a birth mother who found pride and satisfaction in a photo of her daughter growing up outside the country, posed at a piano. She showed the photo to all her neighbours. 'Look,' she'd say, 'this is my daughter playing a piano; no one in her village had even *seen* a piano.' While this vindicated her decision to give her child away, Bolaños is clearly not unmindful of the layers of colonialism embedded in that piano. She also told me the story of a birth mother who balked at being photographed because she feared her daughter – growing up in the splendour of abundance – would find her ugly. Adding yet another level of complication to baby-selling controversies, some birth mothers she has found receive regular remittances from their children's adopted families in the United States. Because of this, she tells me, they have been able to maintain homes for and raise their other children.[146] 'It's much more shameful to give up your child than to be pregnant out of wedlock,' she explains. 'There's a saying here, only animals give up their children.' At the same time, although she's never encountered the mother of a stolen child, she has absolutely no trouble imagining that she could. 'Fear is the ground here,' she says simply. Kidnap and rescue are part of this conversation, but in such overlapping, intersecting, and complicated ways that they cannot be pried apart.

Conclusion: Setting the Agenda for a Happy Childhood

Foreign Children

Little Indian, Sioux, or Crow,
Little frosty Eskimo,
Little Turk or Japanee,
Oh! don't you wish that you were me?

You have seen the scarlet trees
And the lions over seas;
You have eaten ostrich eggs,
And turned the turtle off their legs.

Such a life is very fine,
But it's not so nice as mine:
You must often as you trod,
Have wearied NOT to be abroad.

You have curious things to eat,
I am fed on proper meat;
You must dwell upon the foam,
But I am safe and live at home.
   Little Indian, Sioux or Crow,
   Little frosty Eskimo,
   Little Turk or Japanee,
Oh! don't you wish that you were me?
                – Robert Louis Stevenson, *A Child's Garden of Verses* (1913)

One of the things I did when I returned to Guatemala to research this book was to write the name of the lawyers my Canadian adoption agency used in the front of my notebook. Every time I conducted an interview, opened a report, or read newspaper clippings at the archives, I hoped I wouldn't encounter their names.

I didn't. Nor did I read my agency's name in any of the voluminous reporting of adoption scandals in Guatemala's recent history. My adoption application was processed less than twelve months before the Canadian government cut ties with Guatemala because of its non-ratification of the Hague adoption treaty. I met and received custody of my son two days after a suspected baby-stealer was lynched. A few months before, a respected international agency, UNICEF, condemned transnational adoption almost entirely, and a Guatemalan feminist university professor – the kind of person I'd likely be friends with if I knew her in Canada – went missing, quite possibly for supplying a United Nations inquiry with research about corrupt adoption practices.

I can write this book because I met Hilda, my son's birth mother. We have a photo of her holding him, saying goodbye. Her face is visible in his mouth, his jaw line, and his eyes. Those eyes, in the photo, are sad. The full story of how Jordi Arturo Belyea Dubinsky came to be is not mine to tell. But that I met his mother, and learned her circumstances, makes ours simply another sad adoption story, rather than a 'scandal.' There is a line between these two things, but it's not one that always gives me as much comfort as you might think. I recount my story as a series of fortunate events – for me – based on privilege, luck, timing, and good word-of-mouth about what proved to be an ethical adoption agency. But like many adoptive parents, I had moments of being blinded by 'the force of my own wanting.'[1] What if someone had shoved a baby through a car window into *my* arms?

I wrote this book in order to make sense of the complexities and contradictions of modern adoption and the global politics of childhood. I've dwelt in the murky spaces that the conflicting paradigms of kidnap and rescue don't reach. Kidnap doesn't account for the graciousness of my Spanish teacher, a Mexican immigrant to small-town Ontario, who greeted my son's arrival with a handmade vest, decorated with Canadian flags. Rescue can't explain my son's response when we discussed the teary-eyed photo of his mother's goodbye. 'You'd cry too if you lost me,' he declared, accurately summarizing both the emotions and the politics of adoption.

We need more space in public debate about adoption for these nuances and contradictions. Public discussions of children and borders and adoption in North America, steeped in either feel-good stories of rescue or horrific tales of kidnap, flatten disparate and contradictory stories. During the research for this book, I visited a Latin American adopted children's 'culture camp' with my son, which took place in a Midwestern U.S. city. Latin America as imagined by white people in the suburbs of the United States was not, as it turned out, our cup of tea; we both hated it, albeit for different reasons. And while it is far too easy to heap scorn on well-meaning but superficial moments of multicultural practice like these, the distance between this sanitized, imaginary Guatemala and the real thing was striking. So, too, was the distance between these multicultural families and the immigrant diasporas of their children. The bonds of community – tentative as they may have been – forged a generation ago by white adoptive parents and black community leaders through Montreal's Negro Community have been replaced, today, by the logic of the market. The only Latin American adults I met at Latin American culture camp were the hired help: cooks, dance instructors, and language teachers.[2]

First Nations scholar Patricia Monture, among many others, declares that 'removing children from their homes weakens the entire community.'[3] I think she's right. In this book, we've seen that the circulation or transfer of children between nations or races can be the most powerful weapon, or trophy, imaginable. But like all matters involving the intimate and the imperial, this takes place on so many levels at once. To put it plainly, children, whatever their symbolic status might have been, grow up. Adopted children, and sometimes their families, can create new forms of community, consciousness, and identity. Adult adopted children are leading the way in creating a new way of thinking about adoption, demanding 'justice for an entire community, rather than claiming to save a single child.'[4]

'When we consider transnational adoption,' writes adoptee Molly McCullough, 'we must, inescapably, confront issues that are far more poignant than international politics, far more heart-rending than legal processes; we encounter the profound, emotional, and often overwhelmingly painful conditions that circumscribe the lives of real people.'[5] Adoption, particularly when it's open or visible, simply exposes the painful stories that biological families can more easily keep hidden. It is unsettling to consider the circumstances that produce adoption for many reasons. Among them, we believe we are sparing children brutal details, about their own history or the world in which they live. 'I didn't want to punish him with the truth,' writes Ralph Savarese, explaining his turmoil over recounting his adoptive son's tragic history faithfully.[6] Yet, as we've seen, to collapse a vast world of children into a single, bucolic concept of 'childhood' is more than simply misleading. Robert Louis Stevenson's sorrowful evocation of 'foreign children' a century ago is more than cloying; such sentiments are strategies of control. The myth of the universality of childhood – premised on key concepts such as innocence, dependence, and vulnerability – measures and normalizes the lives of many against the experiences of a tiny few. This keeps development agendas – the ability to set the agenda for 'a happy childhood,' as Jo Boyden calls it – in the hands of the powerful.[7] If we were to invert this pyramid, we might see the vast world of children, living various kinds of 'childhoods,' and be forced to think differently about cherished ideas such as innocence and dependence.

In much of the world, children live, in Carolyn Nordstrom's evocative phrase, on the 'jagged edge of peace.' 'When you walk the streets with homeless children,' Nordstrom observes, 'you see the world from their point of view: it is adults who cause the violence that leaves them homeless. It is children who take them in and help.'[8] In war zones, children organize themselves into self-sufficient communities, attempting to build sane, peaceful alternatives to violent adult worlds they neither create nor control. In post-conflict societies, children put into practice the goals of mediation and reconciliation brokered by adult authorities in far-away jurisdictions. In factories, farms, and streets, child labourers make shrewd calculations that defy their stereotype of mute suffering. Even child sex workers, bearers of perhaps the heaviest symbolic burden of our time, can step off their pedestal and reflect wisely on the political and moral economies which frame their lives.[9] Perhaps it is not so strange to suggest that adopted children are capable of understanding the actual circumstances of their origins, juggling two (or more) families and national identities, and assimilating non-sanitized lessons about poverty, violence, empire, and war. We can't move beyond kidnap and rescue until we also move beyond the adult-created lie of universal, innocent childhood.

I've argued for a clear-eyed assessment of the many ways in which children are inseparably attached to adult political worlds, but the reverse is true as well. Children don't simply absorb or experience adult-initiated political issues. They also sustain them. What Ann Stoler has termed the 'emotional economy' of sexuality, parenting, and domestic arrangements has played a central role in maintaining political authority and economic systems the world over.[10] In this book, I've found, as Stoler has suggested one might, 'unexpected points of congruence and similarities of discourse in seemingly disparate sites.'[11] I've suggested that these convergences tell us something about how adult political conflicts – the Cold War, civil rights and race politics in the 1960s, wars of empire in 1980s Latin America – were fought through and for children. Similarly, when Cynthia Enloe reminds us to pay more attention to what she calls the 'underestimation of power' in relations between and inside nations, she has in mind things like the alleged docility and cheapened labour of young South Korean female factory workers, which has sustained a global empire of tennis shoes.[12] These feminist thinkers are quite right in encouraging us to expand our thinking about governance and global power relations beyond men-in-suits. But, to return to the South Korean example, it's true that we couldn't have the global political economy we have without the labour of female factory workers, which is made cheap by patriarchal ideologies. Yet these ideologies have also produced, as we've seen, the relinquishment of hundreds of thousands of South Korean children born to many of those same Nike-producing factory workers (which is why these children are known in South Korea as IMF orphans). Here power relations have vanished in a double sense, because when children, rather than sneakers, join global circuits of trade and migration, the conditions of exploitation which produced them are instantly erased in favour of sentimental, heroic stories of the rescue of needy children by good-hearted people from the West.

We're blinded by fantasies of rescue because of the symbolic and psychic space children occupy, because we've imagined 'childhood' as a space beyond conflict.[13] But seeking a space beyond conflict is not in itself a bad thing. In pointing to the jumble of contradictions that have accompanied the rise of the global symbolic child, I'm not advocating that we lose the impulses towards care which children evoke, or that we treat children as adults. Perhaps the reverse is true. Maybe we should gather up all the warmth, reverence, and compassion we seem to want to bestow on children – at least for the first few years – and spread this around more evenly towards everyone. One of my favourite theorists of childhood was the late anthropologist Sharon Stephens. She argued that our huge cultural investment in childhood innocence and vulnerability stems from the utopian possibility represented by children, who, we'd like to believe, stand outside of the market and market-driven politics.[14] If 'childhood' is disappearing (though it would be more accurate to say it often never 'appeared') – as children serve in armies and militias, are targeted by death squads and market researchers, create autonomous communities in storm drains and garbage dumps, work in factories, engage in commercialized sex – we seem to lose the ability to discuss the future with anything like hope or optimism. But optimism needs a firmer foundation than the symbolic child provides. An appreciation of the complicated histories of the world's children might help to replace nostalgia with action, in which children and adults together make a better present.

Notes

1. Children and the Stories We Tell about Them

1 Michael O'Brien, 'Of Cats, Historians and Gardeners,' *Journal of American History* 89.1 (2002): 44.

2 Bonnie Smith, *The Gender of History: Men, Women and Historical Practice* (Cambridge: Harvard University Press, 1998); Cecilia Morgan, 'History, Nation, Empire: Gender and the Work of Southern Ontario Historical Societies, 1890 – 1920s,' *Canadian Historical Review* 82.3 (Sept. 2001): 491–528.

3 Elizabeth Larsen, 'Did I Steal My Daughter? The Tribulations of Global Adoption,' *Mother Jones*, Nov./Dec. 2007.

4 As well as a number of individual memoirs, North American birthmothers' stories are well told in Ann Fessler, *The Girls Who Went Away: The Hidden History of Women Who Surrendered Children for Adoption in the Decades before Roe v. Wade* (New York: Penguin, 2006). An important new study of birthmothers in a 'sending' country is Pien Bos, 'Once a Mother: Relinquishment and Adoption from the Perspective of Unmarried Mothers in South India' (Ph.D. diss., Radboud University, 2007). The perspective of adult transnational adoptees can be found in Tobias Hubinette, 'Comforting an Orphaned Nation: Representations of International Adoption and Adopted Koreans in Korean Popular Culture' (Ph.D. diss., Stockholm University, Department of Oriental Languages, 2005); and Jane Jeong Trenka et al., eds, *Outsiders Within: Writing on Transracial Adoption* (Cambridge: South End Press, 2006). See also the recent dissertation by Aboriginal adoptee Raven Sinclair, 'All My Relations – Native Transracial Adoption: A Critical Case Study of Cultural Identity' (Ph.D. diss., University of Calgary, 2007).

5 Leela Ghandi, *Affective Communities: Anticolonial Thought, Fin de Siecle Radi-*

calism, and the Politics of Friendship (Durham, NC: Duke University Press, 2006), p. 2.

6 Barbara Katz Rothman, *Weaving a Family: Untangling Race and Adoption* (Boston: Beacon Press, 2005), p. 9. See also the discussion in Toby Alice Volkman's 'Introduction: New Geographies of Kinship,' in *Cultures of Transnational Adoption*, ed. Toby Alice Volkman, pp. 1–24 (Durham, NC: Duke University Press, 2005).

7 Ruth Behar, *The Vulnerable Observer: Anthropology That Breaks Your Heart* (Boston: Beacon, 1996).

8 Judith Walkowitz, *City of Dreadful Delight* (Chicago: University of Chicago Press, 1993). On the symbolic politics of childhood, see Daniel Cook, ed., *Symbolic Children* (New York: Peter Lang, 2002).

9 Catherine E. McKinley, *The Book of Sarahs* (New York: Counterpoint, 2002), p. 20. McKinley is quoting the writer Anotole Broyard.

10 Maggie Black, *The Children and the Nations: The Story of UNICEF* (Sydney: UNICEF, 1986), p. 415.

11 Roman de la Campa, *Cuba on My Mind: Journeys to a Severed Nation* (London: Verso, 2000), p. 41.

12 See, for example, Arlette Farge and Jacques Revel, *The Vanishing Children of Paris: Rumour and Politics before the French Revolution* (Cambridge: Harvard University Press, 1991); Peter Pierce, *The Country of Lost Children: An Australian Anxiety* (Cambridge: Cambridge University Press, 1999); Sarah Carter, *Capturing Women* (Montreal and Kingston: McGill-Queen's University Press, 1997); and June Namais, *White Captives* (Chapel Hill: University of North Carolina Press, 1993).

13 Marshall Sahlins, *Apologies to Thucydides: Understanding History as Culture and Vice Versa* (Chicago: University of Chicago Press, 2004), p. 169.

14 This chapter of North American adoption history is well told in Veronica Strong-Boag, *Finding Families Finding Ourselves: English Canada Encounters Adoption from the Nineteenth Century to the 1990s* (Toronto: Oxford University Press, 2006); Barbara Melosh, *Strangers and Kin: The American Way of Adoption* (Cambridge: Harvard University Pres, 2002); and Ellen Herman, *Kinship by Design: A History of Adoption in the Modern United States* (Chicago: University of Chicago Press, 2008).

15 'The Scandal of our Orphanages,' *Christian Outlook*, October 1961.

16 'A Canadian Haven for Black U.S. Babies,' *Globe and Mail*, 1 Oct. 2005. See also the response by Karen Balcom and Karen Dubinsky, 'Babies across Borders,' *Globe and Mail*, 13 Oct. 2005.

17 See, for example, Renate Andres, 'The Apprehension of Native Children,' *Ontario Indian* 4.4 (April 1981): 32–46; Brad McKenzie and Pete Hudson,

'Native Children, Child Welfare, and the Colonization of Native People,' in *The Challenge of Child Welfare*, ed. Kenneth L. Levitt and Brian Warf, pp. 125–41 (Vancouver: UBC Press, 1985); and Suzanne Fournier and Ernie Crey, *Stolen from Our Embrace: The Abduction of First Nations Children and the Restoration of Aboriginal Communities* (Vancouver: Douglas and McIntyre, 1997).

18 Strong-Boag, *Finding Families*, p. 52

19 Robert Van Krieken, 'The "Stolen Generations" and Cultural Genocide: The Forced Removal of Australian Indigenous Children from Their Families and Its Implications for the Sociology of Childhood,' *Childhood* 6 (1999): 297–311.

20 Volkman, 'Introduction: New Geographies of Kinship.'

21 E.J. Graff, 'The Lie We Love,' *Foreign Policy*, Nov./Dec. 2008.

22 http://www.amnesty.org/en/library/asset/AMR34/016/2000/en/dom-AMR340162000en.html (accessed 23 July 2008).

23 'Illegal Adoptions,' *Siglo News*, 24 September 1997; Bruce Harris, Letter, International Adoption Forum, Americas.org, November 2000.

24 Nancy Scheper-Hughes, *Death without Weeping: The Violence of Everyday Life in Brazil* (Berkeley: University of California Press, 1992), p. 242.

25 Odd Arne Westad, *The Global Cold War: Third World Interventions and the Making of Our Times* (Cambridge: Cambridge University Press, 2006), p. 9. The classic account of the domestic side of the Cold War is Elaine May, *Homeward Bound: American Families in the Cold War Era* (New York: Basic Books, 1988). See also Sharon Stephens, 'Nationalism, Nuclear Policy and Children in Cold War America,' *Childhood* 4.103 (1997): 103–23; and Elise Chenier, *Strangers in Our Midst: Sexual Deviancy in Postwar Ontario* (Toronto: University of Toronto Press, 2007).

26 Greg Grandin, *The Last Colonial Massacre: Latin America in the Cold War* (Chicago: University of Chicago Press, 2004), p. 4.

27 John McLaren, 'The State, Child Snatching, and the Law: The Seizure and Indoctrination of Sons of Freedom Children in British Columbia, 1950–1960,' in *Regulating Lives: Historical Essays on the State, the Individual and the Law*, ed. John McLaren, Robert Menzies, and Dorothy Chunn, pp. 259–93 (Vancouver: University of British Columbia Press, 2002).

28 Hubinette, 'Comforting an Orphaned Nation,' p. 84

29 *London Times*, 23 September 1957; 'Troops Advance against Children,' *Current Digest of the Soviet Press* 9 (23 Oct. 1957); *Isvestia*, 13 September 1957; all cited in Mary Dudziak, *Cold War Civil Rights: Race and the Image of American Democracy* (Princeton: Princeton University Press, 2000), pp. 120–1.

30 Franca Iacovetta, *Gatekeepers: Reshaping Immigrant Lives in Cold War Canada*

(Toronto: Between the Lines, 2006); Mona Gleason, *Normalizing the Ideal: Psychology, Schooling and the Family in Postwar Canada* (Toronto: University of Toronto Press, 1999).

31 'An Appalling Symbol of Alberta's Injustice,' *Edmonton Journal*, 24 September 1968.

32 C.A. Bayly et al., 'AHR Conversation: On Transnational History,' *American Historical Review* 111.5 (Dec. 2006): 1440–65

33 Elizabeth Chin, 'Children out of Bounds in Globalising Times,' *Postcolonial Studies* 6.3 (2003): 309–25.

34 Helen Brocklehurst, *Who's Afraid of Children? Children, Conflict and International Relations* (Hampshire: Ashgate, 2006), p. 16.

35 Claudia Castañada, *Figurations: Child, Bodies, Worlds* (Durham, NC: Duke University Press, 2002), p. 3.

36 Hugh Cunningham, *The Children of the Poor: Representations of Childhood since the Seventeenth Century* (Oxford: Blackwell, 1991), p. 3. See also Xiaobei Chen, *Tending the Gardens of Citizenship: Child Saving in Toronto, 1880s–1920s* (Toronto: University of Toronto Press, 2005); and Pia Haudrup Christensen, 'Childhood and the Cultural Constitution of Vulnerable Bodies,' in *The Body, Childhood and Society*, ed. Alan Prout, pp. 38–59 (New York: Palgrave Macmillan, 2000).

37 Viviana Zelizer, *Pricing the Priceless Child: The Changing Social Value of Children* (New York: Basic Books, 1985), p. 11.

38 Anne Higonnet, *Pictures of Innocence: The History and Crisis of Ideal Childhood* (London: Thames and Hudson, 1998).

39 Dominique Marshall, 'The Construction of Children as an Object of International Relations: The Declaration of Children's Rights and the Child Welfare Committee of the League of Nations, 1900–1924,' *International Journal of Children's Rights* 7 (1999): 103–47.

40 Rebecca de Schweinitz, 'The "Shame of America": African-American Civil Rights and the Politics of Childhood,' in *The Politics of Childhood: International Perspectives, Contemporary Developments*, ed. Jim Goddard, Sally McNamee, Adrian James, and Allison James, pp. 50–65 (Hampshire: Macmillan, 2005).

41 Afua Twum-Danso, 'A Cultural Bridge, Not an Imposition: Legitimizing Children's Rights in the Eyes of Local Communities,' *Journal of the History of Childhood and Youth* 1.3 (Fall 2008): 391–413.

42 Jo Boyden, 'Childhood and the Policy Makers: A Comparative Perspective on the Globalization of Childhood,' in *Constructing and Reconstructing Childhood: Contemporary Issues in the Sociological Study of Childhood*, ed. Allison James and Alan Prout, pp. 184–215 (New York: Falmer Press, 1990);

Erica Burman, 'Local, Global or Globalized? Child Development and International Child Rights Legislation,' *Childhood* 3.45 (1996): 45–66.

43 Vijay Prashad, *The Darker Nations: A People's History of the Third World* (New York: New Press, 2007), p. 8.

44 Caroline F. Levander, *Cradle of Liberty: Race, the Child and National Belonging from Thomas Jefferson to W.E.B. Du Bois* (Durham, NC: Duke University Press, 2006), p. 6.

45 See, for example, Nira Yuval-Davis, *Gender and Nation* (London: Sage, 1997); and Anne McLintock, *Imperial Leather: Race, Gender and Sexuality in the Colonial Context* (New York: Routledge, 1995).

46 Christina Klein, *Cold War Orientalism: Asia in the Middlebrow Imagination, 1945–61* (Berkeley: University of California Press, 2003).

47 Melani McAlister, *Epic Encounters: Culture, Media and U.S. Interests in the Middle East since 1945* (Berkeley: University of California Press, 2005), p. 209.

48 Emily Noonan, 'Adoption and the Guatemalan Journey to American Parenthood,' *Childhood* 14.3 (2007): 301–19.

49 Moira Maguire, 'Foreign Adoptions and the Evolution of Irish Adoption Policy, 1945–1952,' *Journal of Social History* 36.2 (2002): 5.

50 Karen Balcom, *The Traffic in Babies: Cross Border Adoption, Baby-Selling and Child Welfare in the United States and Canada, 1930–1972* (Toronto: University of Toronto Press, forthcoming).

51 Hubinette, 'Comforting an Orphaned Nation'; Eleana Kim, 'Wedding Citizenship and Culture: Korean Adoptees and the Global Family of Korea,' in Volkman, ed., *Cultures of Transnational Adoption*, pp. 49–81.

52 Sara K. Dorow, *Transnational Adoption: A Cultural Economy of Race, Gender and Kinship* (New York: New York University Press, 2006), p. 79.

53 Rita Arditti, *Searching for Life: The Grandmothers of the Plaza de Mayo and the Disappeared Children of Argentina* (Berkeley: University of California, 1999); Marcelo M. Suarez-Orozco, 'The Treatment of Children in the "Dirty War": Ideology, State Terrorism and the Abuse of Children in Argentina,' in *Child Survival: Anthropological Perspectives on the Treatment and Maltreatment of Children*, ed. Nancy Scheper Hughes, pp. 227–46 (Dordrecht, Holland: D. Reidel, 1987); Tomas Brill Mascarenhas, 'House of Horror,' *New Internationalist*, December 2005, pp. 10–11.

54 Laura Briggs, 'Mother, Child, Race, Nation: The Visual Iconography of Rescue and the Politics of Transnational and Transracial Adoption,' *Gender and History* 15.2 (Aug. 2003): 179–200.

55 Herman, *Kinship by Design*, p. 46.

56 Sherene H. Razack, *Casting Out: The Eviction of Muslims from Western Law and Politics* (Toronto: University of Toronto Press, 2008), p. 149.

57 'Healing Hands,' *People*, 11 December 2001, p. 134
58 Paula Fass, *Children of a New World: Society, Culture and Globalization* (New York: NYU Press, 2007).
59 Linda Gordon, *The Great Arizona Orphan Abduction* (Cambridge: Harvard University Press, 1999).
60 Rickie Solinger, *Beggars and Choosers: How the Politics of Choice Shapes Adoption, Abortion and Welfare in the United States* (New York: Hill and Wang, 2001).
61 Bos, 'Once a Mother.'
62 David Eng, 'Transracial Adoption and Queer Diaspora,' *Social Text* 21.1 (2003): 1–37.
63 Paula Fass, *Children of a New World: Society, Culture and Globalization* (New York: NYU Press, 2007), p. 13.
64 E.J. Graff, 'The Lie We Love,' *Foreign Policy*, November/December 2008.

2. The National Baby: Creating Monumental Children in Cuba, from Operation Peter Pan to EliánGonzález

1 Jon Lee Anderson, 'Castro's Last Battle,' *New Yorker*, 31 July 2006, p. 50.
2 Richard Gott, *Cuba: A New History* (New Haven: Yale University Press, 2004), p. 180.
3 Archives of the State Security Historical Research Centre, Havana, cited in Juan Carlos Rodríguez, *The Bay of Pigs and the CIA* (Melbourne: Ocean Press, 1999), p. 54. Rodriguez includes a sample of other fantastic Radio Swan topics from this era, including news that priests were being arrested for feeding the poor, and that Che Guevera was on his way to Russia, in order to avoid the coming bloodbath in Cuba.
4 David Atlee Phillips, *The Night Watch* (New York: Atheneum, 1977), pp. 13, 45. See also Warren Hinckle and William T. Turner, *Deadly Secrets: The CIA-Mafia War against Castro and the Assassination of J.F.K* (New York: Thunder's Mouth Press, 1981); and Peter Wynden, *Bay of Pigs: The Untold Story* (New York: Simon and Schuster 1979). Of course, U.S. government involvement in orchestrating the coup against Arbenz involved far more than Phillips and his radio station; see Nick Cullather, *Secret History: The CIA's Classified Account of Its Operations in Guatemala 1952–1954* (Stanford: Stanford University Press, 2002); Piero Gleijeses, *Shattered Hope: The Guatemalan Revolution and the United States, 1944–1954* (Princeton: Princeton University Press, 1991); Richard Immerman, *The CIA in Guatemala: The Foreign Policy of Intervention* (Austin: University of Texas Press, 1982).
5 Phillips, *Night Watch*, p. 89.

6 Maria de los Angeles Torres, *The Lost Apple: Operation Pedro Pan, Cuban Children in the U.S. and the Promise of a Better Future* (Boston: Beacon Press, 2003), p. 89. The role of the CIA, and the influence of Operation Peter Pan in the legendary 'scare campaign' against socialist candidate Salvador Allende, is well documented in Margaret Power's *Right-wing Women in Chile: Feminine Power and the Struggle against Allende, 1964–1973* (University Park: Pennsylvania State University Press, 2002), pp. 71–98.

7 'Descubren a Impresores de Copias de una Falsa "Ley,"' *Revolución* 4 (22 Sept. 1961); 'Falacia Infame,' *Bohemia*, 24 September 1961.

8 Lauren Derby, 'Imperial Secrets: Vampires and Nationhood in Puerto Rico,' paper presented at the Berkshire Conference on the History of Women, Claremont, California, July 2005. My thanks to Lauren Derby for sharing this paper with me.

9 Gabriel García Márquez, 'Shipwrecked on Dry Land,' *The Guardian*, 25 March 2000.

10 Interview with Ramón Torreira, 24 January 2004; interview with Marina Ochoa, 15 February 2004.

11 Stephan Palmié, *Wizards and Scientists: Explorations in Afro-Cuban Modernity and Tradition* (Durham, NC: Duke University Press, 2002), pp. 201–59.

12 Derby, 'Imperial Secrets'; Luis White, *Speaking with Vampires: Rumour and History in Colonial Africa* (Berkeley: University of California Press, 2000), p. 44; Lauren Derby, 'Gringo Chickens with Worms: Food and Nationalism in the Dominican Republic,' in *Close Encounters of Empire: Writing the Cultural History of U.S.-Latin American Relations*, ed. Gilbert Joseph, Catherine LeGrand, and Ricardo D. Salvatore, pp. 451–93 (Durham, NC: Duke University Press, 1998).

13 *El Mundo*, 1 December 1960, cited in Torres, *The Lost Apple*, p. 90.

14 'Si de Alguien se ha Ocupado La Revolucion ha sido de Los Niños,' *Bohemia*, 24 September 1961; 'La Patria Potestad,' *Verde Olivo*, October 1961.

15 Fidel Castro, 'Fifith Anniversary of CDR' (Havana, 1965), and 'CDR Main Event' (Havana, 1971), at http://lanic.utexas.edu/la/cb/cuba/castro. See also *Fidel and Religion: Talks with Frei Betto* (Havana: Publications Office of the Council of State, 1987), p. 225.

16 Cuban immigration scholar Antonio Aja Diaz, for example, suggests that in that era, fathers would have, without question, made the decision to send their children, though as most Peter Pan children came from middle-class families, most mothers would have been as antagonistic to the revolution as their husbands (interview with Antonio Aja Diaz, Havana, Cuba, 16 January 2008).

17 Thanks to Cathie Krull, who brought this parallel to my attention. See also
    Marguerite Rose Jiménez, 'The Political Economy of Leisure,' in *Reinvent-
    ing the Revolution: A Contemporary Cuba Reader*, ed. Phillip Brenner et al.,
    pp. 146–55 (Lanham: Rowman and Littlefield, 2008); and Elisa Facio, 'Jine-
    terismo during the Special Period,' in *Cuban Transitions at the Millennium*,
    ed. Eloise Linger and John Cotman, pp. 55–75 (Largo, MD: International
    Development Options, 2000).
18 Ruth Behar, 'Post-Utopia: The Erotics of Power and Cuba's Revolutionary
    Children,' in *Cuba: The Elusive Nation*, ed. Damian J.Vernandez and Made-
    line Camara Betancourt, p. 138 (Gainsville: University Press of Florida,
    2000).
19 Raisa Pagés, 'The Status of Cuban Women,' in Brenner et al., eds, *Reinvent-
    ing the Revolution*, pp. 311–15. On the depiction of González's mother, see,
    for example, Fidel Castro, 'Speech to Children Who Stood on Guard Out-
    side the U.S. Interests Section in Havana,' 23 December 1999, and various
    discussions in Cuban media, assembled in *Batalla por la Liberación de Elián
    González* (Havana: Editora Política, 2000).
20 John Carlos Rowe, *The New American Studies* (Minneapolis: University of
    Minnesota Press, 2004), pp. 195–207.
21 Paul C. Mishler, *Raising Reds: The Young Pioneers, Radical Summer Camps,
    and Communist Political Culture in the United States* (New York: Columbia
    University Press, 1999), p. 16.
22 Dorothy Legarreta, *The Guernica Generation: Basque Refugee Children of
    the Spanish Civil War* (Reno: University of Nevada Press, 1984); Loring
    M. Danforth, '"We Crossed a Lot of Borders": Refugee Children of the
    Greek Civil War,' *Diaspora* 12.2 (2003): 169–209; Lisa Kirschenbaum, *Small
    Comrades: Revolutionizing Childhood in Soviet Russia, 1917–1932* (New York:
    Routledge, 2000).
23 'La Patria Potestad,' *Verde Olivo*, October 1961.
24 Roman de la Campa, *Cuba on My Mind: Journeys to a Severed Nation* (Lon-
    don: Verso, 2000), p. 152.
25 Castro, 'CDR Main Event' (1971).
26 Fidel Castro, 'Women's Rally' (1971), at http://lanic.utexas.edu/la/cb/
    cuba/castro. *Granma* repeated these charges some years later: 'This mon-
    strous and egotistical society converted them into drug addicts, gangsters,
    and the girls into prostitutes' ('Glorificacion de un Crimen,' *Granma*, 19
    September 1986).
27 'Si de Alguien se ha Ocupado La Revolución ha sido de Los Niños,' *Bohe-
    mia*, 24 September 1961.
28 Marvin Leiner, *Children Are the Revolution: Daycare in Cuba* (New York:

Penguin, 1974), p. 131. See also Karen Wald, *Children of Che: Childcare and Education in Cuba* (Palo Alto: Ramparts, 1978).

29 Franca Iacovetta, *Gatekeepers: Reshaping Immigrant Lives in Cold War Canada* (Toronto: Between the Lines, 2006), pp. 21–47.

30 Ron Robin, *The Making of the Cold War Enemy: Culture and Politics in the Military-Intellectual Complex* (Princeton: Princeton University Press, 2001). See also Michael Rogin, *'Ronald Reagan,' the Movie: And Other Episodes in Political Demonology* (Berkeley: University of California Press, 1988).

31 Mary Maxwell, 'The Unaccompanied Cuban Children's Program,' unpublished paper, 29 April 1963, Barry University Archives, Operation Pedro Pan collection.

32 Monsignor Bryan O. Walsh, 'Cuban Refugee Children,' *Journal of Interamerican Studies and World Affairs* 13.3/4 (July–Oct. 1971): 395.

33 Torres, *The Lost Apple*, pp. 74–87.

34 Hugh Thomas, *Cuba; or, The Pursuit of Freedom* (New York: DaCapo Press, 1998), p. 1301. That figure rose to 100,000 by March of 1961. See also Felix Massud-Piloto, *From Welcomed Exiles to Illegal Immigrants: Cuban American Migration to the U.S., 1959–1995* (New York: Rowman and Littlefield, 1995).

35 Torres, *The Lost Apple*, pp. 233–9. Torres also notes that her information request was denied even after the CIA had released thousands of pages of documents about its activities in 1960s Cuba, including material on the Bay of Pigs invasion and the missile crisis. 'Why,' she asks, 'would it be so secretive about the unaccompanied children's program?' (p. 238).

36 Ibid., p. 78

37 See, for example, '8,000 Cuba Children Saved from Castro's Brainwashing,' *Miami Herald*, 8 March 1962.

38 'Hundreds Thank Priest Who Cared,' *Miami Voice*, 3 March 1978.

39 'Cuban Children Meet Snow, Peanut Butter, English Language, and Come through Fine,' *Rockford Observer*, April 1962.

40 Interview with Elly Chovel, 12 January 2005, Miami.

41 Thomas, *Cuba*, p. 1276. 'Cubans,' declared Thomas, 'right and left, were bad at keeping secrets.'

42 Warren Miller, *90 Miles from Home: The Face of Cuba Today* (Boston: Little, Brown, 1961), p. 26.

43 See, for example, 'Operation Pedro Pan: How Thousands of Children Shuffled under Castro's Nose,' *Miami Voice* 3 March 1978. In 1962, Antonio Micocci, a staff member in the Cuban Refugee Program in Washington, wrote to the editor of a Colorado newspaper, calling its recent headline, 'The Story of Cuban Refugees in Colorado May Never Be Told,' 'scary,' and assuring readers that this clandestine understanding of Cuban refugee

children was exaggerated (though he too requested that reporters refrain from printing the names and exact location of unaccompanied children) ('The Story of Cuban Refugees in Colorado May Never Be Told,' *Rocky Mountain News*, 27 February 1962, and 'Letter to the Editor,' ibid., 31 March 1962).

44 In 2001 author Olga Drucker, a Kindertransport veteran, was invited to speak to the OPP group in Miami. In *Operation Pedro Pan: The Untold Exodus of 14,048 Cuban Children* (New York: Routledge, 1999), p. xii, Yvonne Conde cites the Kindertransport as a forerunner. Torres consciously distances herself from this comparison (*The Lost Apple*, p. 248).

45 'They Left Cuban Parents, Came to Miami Alone,' *Miami Daily News*, 18 February 1962.

46 'And Now the Children?' *Time Magazine*, 6 October 1961.

47 '8,000 Cuban Children Find Refuge from Reds,' *Miami Voice*, 9 March 1962; Torres, *The Lost Apple*, p. 59.

48 Gott, *Cuba*, p. 189; Thomas, *Cuba*, p. 1339.

49 de la Campa, *Cuba on My Mind*, p. 59; Ileana Fuentes, 'Portrait of Wendy, at Fifty, with a Bra,' in *Remembering Cuba: Legacy of a Diaspora*, ed. Andrea O'Reilly Herrera, p. 60 (Austin: University of Texas Press, 2002). The biographer of another Peter Pan child, the late artist Ana Mendieta, speculated similarly about the emigration of the upper-class Mendieta daughters: 'Good girls … were still chaperoned when they went to a dance or a movie with a boy and now they would be wrested from the family … to live in promiscuity with other children of unknown provenance, thrown at the mercy of toothless sugar-cane workers' (Robert Katz, *Naked by the Window: The Fatal Marriage of Carle Andre and Ana Mendieta* [New York: Atlantic Monthly, 1990], p. 43). Melina López uses the dispute between a teenage girl and her parents over her desire to join the Literacy Campaign as a dramatic device in her play about Peter Pan, 'Sonia Flew,' performed in Boston's Huntington Theater in 2004 (Flora M. González Mandri, 'Operation Pedro Pan: A Tale of Trauma and Remembrance,' *Latino Studies*, forthcoming). Thanks to Flora González for sharing a prepublication copy of this paper with me.

50 Dana Evan Kaplan, 'Fleeing the Revolution: The Exodus of Cuban Jewry in the Early 1960s,' *Cuban Studies* 36 (2005): 129–54.

51 'Cuban Reds Concentrate on Conquering Children,' *Steubenville Ohio Register*, 22 March 1962; 'Cuban Parents Desperate, We Must Get Our Children Out,' *Miami Herald*, 19 June 1961; Walsh, 'Cuban Refugee Children,' p. 382. The history of relations between the Catholic Church and the revolutionary government is well told in John Kirk, *Between God and the Party: Reli-*

gion and Politics in Revolutionary Cuba (Tampa: University of South Florida Press, 1989).

52 Torres, *The Lost Apple*, p. 111; 'A Return to Cuba, a Search for Himself,' *New York Times*, 21 October 2001.

53 'African Savages Take Over Her School: A Cuban Girl Flees in Terror,' *Miami Herald*, 27 August 1962.

54 Robin, *The Making of the Cold War Enemy*, pp. 167–70. See also Louis Menand, 'Brainwashed,' *New Yorker*, 15 September 2003, pp. 88–91.

55 See, for example, Mary Louise Adams, *The Trouble with Normal: Postwar Youth and the Making of Heterosexuality* (Toronto: University of Toronto Press, 1997); Mark West, *Children, Culture and Controversy* (Hamden: Archon Books, 1988); Mona Gleason, *Normalizing the Ideal: Psychology, Schooling and the Family in Postwar Canada* (Toronto: University of Toronto Press, 1999); Margot Henriksen, *Dr. Strangelove's America: Society and Culture in the Atomic Age* (Berkeley: University of California Press, 1997).

56 I've seen three different versions of this story: 'Displaced Tots Know Horrors of Red Cuba,' *Marathon Keynoter*,1 February 1962; 'Cuban Refugee Children Benefit from Party at Babcock Home,' *Lake Placid Journal*, 13 December 1962; 'Anecdote of the Week,' *Parade Magazine*, 17 February 1963.

57 Carlos Eire, *Waiting for Snow in Havana: Confessions of a Cuban Boy* (New York: Free Press, 2003), p. 87.

58 Louis A. Pérez, Jr, *On Becoming Cuban: Identity, Nationality and Culture* (New York: Harper Collins, 1999), p. 490.

59 Thomas Borstelmann, *The Cold War and the Color Line: American Race Relations in the Global Arena* (Cambridge: Harvard University Press, 2001), pp. 112–13. See also John J. Johnson, *Latin America in Caricature* (Austin: University of Texas Press, 1980).

60 Gott, *Cuba*, p. 175.

61 Elizabeth Sutherland, *The Youngest Revolution: A Personal Report on Cuba* (New York: Dial Press, 1969), p. 95; 'Children's Crusade,' *Newsweek*, 3 April 1961. For exiles' testimony about children in Cuba, see United State Senate, *Cuban Refugee Problem: Hearings before the Judiciary*, 3 and 4 December 1962, p. 383. On the influence of the Cuban Revolution on youth culture in various countries, see, for example, Van Gosse, *Where the Boys Are: Cuba, Cold War America and the Making of a New Left* (London: Verso, 1993); Cynthia Wright, 'Between Nation and Empire: The Making of Canada-Cuba Solidarity,' paper presented at New World Coming: The Sixties and the Shaping of Global Consciousness, Queen's University, June 2007; and Jennifer

Hosek, 'Importing the Revolution One Island at a Time: Rudi Dutschke Reads Che Guevara,' paper presented at New World Coming: The Sixties and the Shaping of Global Consciousness, Queen's University, June 2007. See also Julie Marie Bunk, *Fidel Castro and the Quest for a Revolutionary Culture in Cuba* (University Park: Pennsylvania State University Press, 1994), pp. 21–86.

62 Rafael Hernández, *Looking at Cuba* (Gainsville: University Press of Florida, 2003), p 40.

63 Marina Ochoa, dir., *El Otro Lado de Cristal: Un documental sobre Operación Peter Pan*, ICAIC, Havana, 1994.

64 '8,000 Cuban Children Saved from Castro Brainwashing,' *Miami Herald*, 8 March 1962.

65 'Refugee Cuban Children Need Homes,' *Christian Century*, 4 April 1962.

66 Christina Klein, *Cold War Orientalism: Asia in the Middlebrow Imagination, 1945–61* (Berkeley: University of California Press, 2003).

67 'Many to Offer Homes to Teen-Age Exiles,' *Fort Lauderdale Daily News*, 12 March 1962.

68 'Cuban Reds Concentrate on Conquering Children,' *Steubenville Ohio Register*, 22 March 1962. Twenty-eight Jewish children left Cuba through the Peter Pan program, and Jewish social service agencies helped over one hundred unaccompanied child refugees. Protestant children accounted for 365 of the total. See Torres, *The Lost Apple*, p. 148, on Jewish child refugees; see also Kaplan, 'Fleeing the Revolution,' pp. 142–6.

69 'Catholic Charities Bring Six Cuban Children Here,' *Providence Rhode Island*,13 April 1962.

70 'Cuban Children Meet Snow, Peanut Butter, English Language, and Come Through Fine,' *Rockford Observer*, April 1962; 'New Life for Cuban Boys – for "Gringo" Parents Too,' *Sarasota Herald Tribune*, 16 September 1962.

71 'Cuban Children Meet Snow, Peanut Butter, English Language, and Come Through Fine,' *Rockford Observer*, April 1962.

72 'Armando Codina,' filmed testimonial on the occasion of receiving Florida Entrepreneur Medal, Florida Merchant Builder's Association, 1995.

73 'Eighty Cuban Boys in Miami: A Day in Their New Life,' *Miami Herald*, 8 March 1962.

74 'Young Refugees Here from Cuba,' *Pueblo Star Journal and Sunday Chieftain*, 25 March 1962.

75 'Eight Thousand Unaccompanied Children from Cuba,' *Catholic Virginian*, 16 March 1962.

76 'They Came Alone from Cuba,' *Madison Journal*, 11 February 1963; 'A Place in the Sun for Chico,' *Miami Herald*, 25 June 1963.

77 'Operation Pedro Pan: A New Life for Cuban Children,' *Miami Daily News,* 27 May 1962.

78 Torres, *The Lost Apple,* p. 223.

79 The Operation Pedro Pan Group now has a membership of approximately two thousand.

80 Victor Triay, *Fleeing Castro: Operation Pedro Pan and the Cuban Children's Program* (Miami: University Press of Florida, 1998).

81 Grupo Arieto, *Contra Viento y Marea* (Havana: Casa de las Americas, 1978), pp. 34, 40.

82 Jesús Díaz, dir., *55 Hermanos,* 1978.

83 Ibid. See also Louis Adrian Betancourt, *Por Que Carlos?* (Havana: Editorial Letras Cubanas, 1981).

84 Marta Díaz Fernández, 'Representación de la Emigración en el Cine Cubano Contemporáneo,' paper presented at the Latin American Studies Association Conference, Montreal, 2007. Thanks to Marta Díaz for sharing this paper with me.

85 Teresa de Jesús Fernández, 'From This Side of the Fish Tank,' in *By Heart / De Memoria: Cuban Women's Journeys In and Out of Exile,* ed. Maria de los Angeles Torres, p. 77 (Philadelphia: Temple University Press).

86 Maasud-Piloto, *From Welcomed Exiles to Illegal Immigrants,* p. 77; Torres, *The Lost Apple,* p. 222; Betancourt, *Por Que Carlos?*

87 John G. Hubbell, 'Operation Pedro Pan,' *Readers Digest,* February 1988.

88 'Exile Children Adjust Quickly,' *Miami Herald,* 17 November 1969; 'Bryan Walsh: Clergyman,' *Miami Herald Tropic,* 22 September 1985.

89 See, for example, *Miami Herald* coverage of Martínez's Senate election campaign in 2004, as well as his campaign DVD, 'Mel Martínez for U.S. Senate,' Barry University Archives, Pedro Pan Collection, Individual Files.

90 See, for example, 'Daring Hero Helped 14,000 Children Escape,' *National Enquirer,* n.d. (circa 1986); 'The Daughters of Pedro Pan,' *Miami Herald Tropic,* 18 October 1987; 'Polita Grau Paid with 12 Years of Her Life,' *Miami Weekly Sun,* 20 November 1998. Polita Grau's obituary was published as 'Polita Grau, 85, dies; was First Lady of Cuba,' *Miami Herald,* 23 March 2000. See also Mongo Grau's autobiography, *Cuba desde 1930* (Miami: Dax Books, 1997).

91 'Glorificacion de un Crimen,' *Granma,* 19 September 1986.

92 See interview with Willy Chirino in *The Flight of Peter Pan,* dir. Joe Cardoa and Mario de Varona, PBS, 1999.

93 'Msgr. Walsh Remembered,' *Florida Catholic,* 3 January 2002.

94 'Walsh Respected for More than Pedro Pan,' *Miami Herald,* 25 December

2001; Bryan Walsh, 'Memorial Mass for Archbishop Romero, March 11, 1990,' unpublished paper, Walsh Papers, Barry University Archives.

95 Bryan Walsh, 'The Origins of Operation Pedro Pan,' unpublished paper, presented at Florida International University Pedro Pan Conference, Miami, 20 April 2001.

96 'Cuban Exiles Reunite to Help Dedicate Historic County Park,' *Miami Herald*, 23 November 2004.

97 'The Dark Side of Peter Pan,' *Miami Herald*, 29 November 1990.

98 'Pedro Pan's Heroes,' *Miami Herald*, 3 January 1998.

99 'The Tale of Three Mothers: GOP Reaches Out to Catholic Voters,' *Florida Catholic*, 3 May 2001.

100 Achy Obejas, *Days of Awe* (New York: Ballantine, 2001), p. 237

101 'Nuevas y Escandalosas Revelaciones sobre Acciones Organizadas por el Gobierno de Estados Unidos contra Cuba en los Primeros Años de la Revolución,' *Granma*, 14 January 1998.

102 Ramón Torreira Crespo and Jose Buajasan Marrawi, *Operación Peter Pan: Un Caso de Guerra Psicológica contra Cuba* (Havana: Editora Politica, 2000), p. 125.

103 Interview with Ramón Torreira, 24 January 2004, Havana. Torreira has also made this argument in other publications; see 'First Wave of Cuban Emigrants and the Catholic Church,' *Enfoques*, February 2005, p. 8.

104 'Mel Martinez, Terrorist Candidate for Senate,' *Granma International*, 2 February 2004.

105 'Peter Pan Despojada de la Mascara,' *Juventud rebelde*, 26 March 2000.

106 Torreira and Buajasan, *Operación Peter Pan*, p. 177.

107 'Entre Pillos, Monstruos y Gente sin Alma,' *Granma*, 30 March 2000.

108 'Cuba Intenta Usar la Operación Pedro Pan en el Caso Leían,' *el Nuevo Heráld*, 1 April 2000. On the publicity given to Torreira and Buajasan in Cuba, see, for example, Como Pan Caliente, *Ahora! Órgano Provincial del PCC en Hololguin*, 1 April 2000; *Santa Clara Vanguardia*,15 April 2000; *Cienfuegos Cinco de Septiembre*, 23 June 2000. On publishing in contemporary Cuba, see Maria López Vigil, 'The Cuban Media,' in Brenner et al., eds, *Reinventing the Revolution*, pp. 386–91; and Ezequiel Minaya, 'Authors Who Knew or Know the Limits,' in *Capitalism, God and a Good Cigar: Cuba Enters the Twenty-First Century*, ed. Lydia Chavez, pp. 78–94 (Durham NC: Duke University Press, 2005).

109 Alex Stepick, Guillermo Grenier, Max Castro, and Marvin Dunn, *This Is Our Land: Immigrants and Power in Miami* (Berkeley: University of California Press, 2003), p. 2. Among the volumes of Elián commentary, see

especially Lillian Guerra, 'Elián González and the "Real Cuba" of Miami: Visions of Identity, Exceptionality, and Divinity,' *Cuban Studies* 37 (2007): 1–24; Sarah Banet-Weiser, 'Elián González and "The Purpose of America": Nation, Family and the Child-Citizen,' *American Quarterly* 55.2 (June 2003): 149–77; Ann Louise Bardach, *Cuba Confidential: Love and Vengeance in Miami and Havana* (New York: Vintage, 2003); Miguel A. de la Torre, *La Lucha for Cuba: Religion and Politics on the Streets of Miami* (Berkeley: University of California Press, 2003); Stephen Wilkinson, 'Riding on a Wave of Change: The Elián Crisis and the Prospects for an End to the U.S. Embargo of Cuba,' *Soundings: A Journal of Politics and Culture* 15 (Summer 2000): 27–49; 'Saving Elián,' PBS *Frontline*, 6 February 2001.

110 'I Was an "Elián" of the Early '60s,' *Boston Globe*, 3 February 2000; 'Carta de Una Pedro Pan,' *Nuevo Herald*, 18 April 2000; 'Let Elián Remain Free,' *New York Times*, 12 January 2000.

111 Mari Rodriguez Ichaso, dir., *Made in Cuba: Children of Paradise*, 2001. When I described to a Cuban friend what I'd been learning about life in the transit camps in Miami for the Peter Pan children, he suggested it didn't sound so different from the country boarding schools most of his generation attended in Cuba for high school. Cuban blogger Miriam Celaya makes the same point: 'Surely the CIA could have created an occasional monstrosity called Operation Peter Pan decades ago, but the "educative" work of the Cuban government ... could very well have been plotted by Captain Hook himself' ('Captain Hook,' 28 June 2009, http://desdecuba. com/sin_evasion [accessed 9 Sept. 2009]).

112 'Pedro Pan Exiles Finding Their Past,' *Miami Herald*, 4 December 2000; 'The Passion of Elian,' *Washington Post*, 7 April 2000; 'Meet Miami's Moderates,' *Salon*, 7 April 2000.

113 Flora González Mandri, 'Operation Pedro Pan: A Tale of Trauma and Remembrance,' *Latino Studies* 6.3 (2008): 252–68.

114 See, for example, de la Campa's comments on his exile father and his immigration decisions: 'I slowly came to understand his decision to leave Cuba: how people like him ... got caught in the middle of a nasty Cold War' (de la Campa, *Cuba on My Mind*, p. 120) .

115 Fidel Castro, May Day, Havana, 2000, and 'Speech to Children Who Stood on Guard outside the U.S. Interests Section,' 23 December 1999, at http://lanic.utexas.edu/la/cb/cuba/castro.

116 Maria Christina Garcia, *Havana USA: Cuban Exiles and Cuban-Americans in South Florida 1959–1994* (Berkeley: University of California Press, 1996); Susan Eckstein and Lorena Barbiera, 'Cuban Americans and Their Trans-

national Ties,' and Susan Eckstein, 'Dolllarization and Its Discontents in the Post-Soviet Era,' both in Brenner et al., eds, *Reinventing the Revolution*, pp. 267–74 and pp. 179–92.

117 Diáz, 'Representación ...'

118 'Our Manics in Havana,' *The Guardian*, 2 March 2001.

119 He was interviewed by CBS's *60 Minutes* in 2005 on the occasion of his eleventh birthday ('Elian at 11,' CBSNews.com, 29 September 2005). See also 'Castaway Back in the Spotlight,' *Toronto Star*, 7 October 2005.

120 Robin Blackburn, 'Putting the Hammer Down on Cuba,' *New Left Review* 4 (July/Aug. 2000): 15. On the legacy of González in Cuba, see also Jon Lee Anderson, 'The Old Man and the Boy,' *New Yorker*, 21 February 2000, pp. 224–37; and Bardach, *Cuba Confidential*, pp. 334–59.

121 Denise Blum, 'Cuba: The Post-2001 Notions of Participation, Responsibility and Character Formation,' paper presented at the Latin American Studies Association Conference, Montreal, September 2007. I thank Denise Blum for sharing this paper with me.

122 Torres, *The Lost Apple*, p. 22.

123 Ana Menéndez, *In Cuba I Was a German Shepherd* (New York: Grove Press, 2001), p. 172.

124 Dorothy Legarreta, *The Guernica Generation: Basque Refugee Children of the Spanish Civil War* (Reno: University of Nevada Press, 1984), p. 181.

3. The Hybrid Baby: Domestic Interracial Adoption since the 1950s

1 'SW 55 Conferences,' Child Welfare League of America Archives, Social Welfare History Archives, University of Minnesota.

2 Malcolm X, *Autobiography of Malcolm X*, cited in George Elliott Clarke, *Odysseys Home: Mapping African Canadian Literature* (Toronto: University of Toronto Press, 2002), p. 29.

3 This work is based on a 20 per cent sample of case files from the Montreal Children's Service Centre, between 1956 and 1969, a sample of approximately 800 cases. Of these 800 case files, approximately 100 involved non-white children and/or interracial placements. In Manitoba, I was able to locate the case files of Aboriginal adoptions directly. I read a 13 per cent sample of the extant files of the (former) Manitoba Children's Aid Society, from 1961 to 1980, approximately 200 files.

4 'The Children Nobody Wants,' *Star Weekly*, September 1961.

5 Robert Young, *Colonial Desire: Hybridity in Theory, Culture and Race* (London: Routledge, 1995), p. 10. More likely now to describe cultural, rather than physiological or biologized, moments of cross-racial connection,

recent commentators nevertheless stress the political dimensions of the term. 'Hybridity is constituted and contested through complex hierarchies of power,' write two British postcolonial theorists (Annie E. Coombes and Avtar Brah, 'Introduction: The Conundrum of "Mixing,"' in *Hybridity and Its Discontents: Politics, Science and Culture*, ed. Avtar Brah and Annie E. Coombes, p. 7 [London: Routledge, 2000]).

6 Young, *Colonial Desire*, p. 27.

7 Grace Gallay, 'Community and Family,' paper presented at Mixed Race Adoptions, Open Door Society First International Conference, Montreal, 1969, p. 41. It seems that Montreal was also ahead of the rest of the country in placing black children in white foster homes. As of the late 1950s, the Toronto Children's Aid Society placed children of 'Negroid appearance' in institutions, rather than white foster homes (A. Lenore Schwalbe, 'Negro and Partly-Negro Wards of the Children's Aid Society of Metropolitan Toronto' [MSW thesis, University of Toronto, 1958], p. 24). That Open Door Society parents were the 'first' in North America to adopt transracially comes from Rita J. Simon and Howard Altstein, *Adoption across Borders* (Lanham: Rowman and Littlefield, 2000), p. 1. Sociologist Joyce Ladner found examples of cross-racial placements in two U.S. cities (San Francisco and Minneapolis) at a slightly earlier date, but sees the formation of the ODS in Montreal as an important influence on the 'transracial adoption movement' in the United States (Joyce Ladner, *Mixed Families: Adopting across Racial Boundaries* [Garden City: Anchor Press, 1977], p. 61).

8 Ellen Herman, *Kinship by Design: A History of Adoption in the Modern United States* (Chicago: University of Chicago Press, 2008), p. 122.

9 Rosemary Landsdowne, 'The Concept of Non-Adoptibility' (MSW thesis, University of British Columbia, 1949). See also Herman, *Kinship by Design*.

10 Karen Balcom, *The Traffic in Babies: Cross Border Adoption, Baby-Selling and Child Welfare in the United States and Canada, 1930–1972* (Toronto: University of Toronto Press, forthcoming).

11 Children's Service Centre, *Annual Report*, 1955. These, and all other children's names in this article, are pseudonyms.

12 Some years after the founding of the ODS, an analogous organization, Spadete (Société pour l'adoption d'enfants de toutes ethnies) was founded by a Montreal college teacher – and adoptive parent – explicitly to serve the francophone Catholic population. Spadete worked with the Société d'adoption et de protection de l'enfance in Montreal ('A la société d'adoption Spadete, il n'est jamais question de races,' *Le Petit Journal*, 29 June 1969). On the history of adoption laws in Quebec, see Dominique Goubau and Claire O'Neill, 'L'adoption, l'Eglise et l'Etat: Les origines tumultueuses d'une in-

stitution légale,' in *L'évolution de la protection de l'enfance au Quebec*, ed. Renée Joyal (Sainte-Foy: Presses de l'Université du Quebec, 2000), pp. 97–130; and Ann M. Paquet, 'Study of Current Adoption Law and Practice in the Province of Quebec' (MSW thesis, McGill University, 1959).

13 Charles Saunders, *Share the Care: The Story of the Nova Scotia Home for Coloured Children* (Halifax: Nimbus, 1994), p. 138.

14 Open Door Society, *Mixed Race Adoption: A Community Project*, 1967.

15 Of cross-racially adopting men, 70 per cent had post-secondary education, for example, compared to 48 per cent of same-race adopting men, and 9 per cent of the Canadian labour force (Ethel Roskies, 'An Exploratory Study of the Characteristics of Adoptive Parents of Mixed-Race Children in the Montreal Area' [M.A. thesis, University of Montreal, 1963], p. 40). See also Grace Gallay, 'A Study in the Motivation Expressed by White Couples Who Adopt Non-White Children' (MSW research report, McGill University, May 1963). Sociologist Joyce Ladner found a similar demographic profile among transracially adopting U.S. parents (*Mixed Families*, p. 29).

16 Children's Service Centre case files (hereafter cited as 'CSC case files'). To ensure confidentiality, all identifying information, including file numbers, have been removed from these sources.

17 'We Adopted a Negro,' *Maclean's*, 19 November 1960; 'When Noel Came Home,' *Good Housekeeping*, August 1965; 'Many Interracial Adoptions Are Triggered by Chance,' *Ebony*, August 1961.

18 CSC case file.

19 CSC case file.

20 Interview with Grace Gallay, 27 June 2003, Montreal.

21 CSC case file.

22 *Westmount Examiner*, June 1968.

23 Open Door Society (ODS) correspondence files, October 1961.

24 ODS executive minutes, January 1969, September 1970; ODS correspondence files, September 1970. On advertising children for adoption in Canada, see Veronica Strong-Boag 'Today's Child: Creating the Just Society One Family at a Time in 1960s Canada,' *Canadian Historical Review* 86.4 (Dec. 2005): 673–99.

25 On the racialization of the 'population bomb' in the 1960s, see Laura Briggs, *Reproducing Empire: Race, Sex, Science and U.S. Imperialism in Puerto Rico* (Berkeley: University of California Press, 2002).

26 Clayton Hagen, 'Matching Values,' paper presented at Mixed Race Adoptions, Open Door Society First International Conference, Montreal, 1969, p. 33.

27 'PM Sees Bigotry on the Wane,' *Montreal Star*, 1 February 1966.

28 Barbara Yngvesson, '"Un Nino de Cualquier Color": Race and Nation in Inter-country Adoption,' in *Globalizing Institutions: Case Studies in Regulation and Innovation*, ed. Jane Jenson and Boaventura de Sousa Santos, p. 182 (Aldershot: Ashgate, 2000).

29 Letter to the editor, *Montreal Star*, 7 September 1967; 'Should Whites Adopt Colored Babies,' *Coronet*, December 1964.

30 ODS minutes, 11 June 1965.

31 'New Hope for Canada's Homeless Children,' *Chatelaine*, December 1963; 'Color Keeps Them Apart,' *Toronto Star*, 1 June 1963.

32 CSC case file.

33 Gallay, 'Community and Family,' p. 42; interview with Grace Gallay, 27 June 2003; 'The Scandal of Our Orphanages,' *Christian Outlook*, October 1961.

34 CSC case file.

35 CSC case file.

36 *Montreal Star*, 18 February 1967.

37 Caroline F. Levander, *Cradle of Liberty: Race, the Child and National Belonging from Thomas Jefferson to W.E.B. Du Bois* (Durham, NC: Duke University Press, 2006), p. 6.

38 'Children Have No Prejudice,' *Montreal Monitor*, 18 February 1960. On the raceless baby in advertising, see Patricia Holland, *Picturing Childhood: The Myth of the Child in Popular Imagery* (London: I.B. Tauris, 2004).

39 'A Child Is a Child,' *Toronto Star*, 23 November 1964; 'Interracial Adoptions: How Are They Working?' *Parents Magazine*, February 1971.

40 ODS correspondence, telephone survey, 1971. See also Lawrence Scyner, 'Towards Adolescence and Young Adulthood,' paper presented at the Second International Conference on Transracial Adoption, Boston, November 1970.

41 See, for example, 'Popularity Is Her Only Problem,' *Vancouver Sun*, 10 September 1969; 'Multi-Racial Children – Their Need Is Great!' *North Shore News*, 5 June 1969; Strong-Boag, 'Today's Child'; interview with Irene Henderson, Winnipeg, 23 July 2003.

42 CSC case file.

43 'The Children Nobody Wants,' *Star Weekly*, 23 September 1961.

44 'Adopting Black Babies,' *Newsweek*, 3 November 1969.

45 CSC case file.

46 CSC case file.

47 Rae Tucker Rambally, *Practice Imperfect: Reflections on a Career in Social Work* (Montreal: Shoreline, 2002); interview with Rae Rambally, June 2003.

48 CSC case file.

49 'How We Adopted an Interracial Family,' *Chatelaine*, December 1966; *Montreal Gazette*, 26 October 1965; *Christian Outlook*, October 1961.

50 Ann Stoller, *Carnal Knowledge and Imperial Power: Race and the Intimate in Colonial Rule* (Berkeley: University of California Press, 2002). See also Adele Perry, *On the Edge of Empire: Race, Gender and the Making of British Columbia, 1849–1871* (Toronto: University of Toronto Press, 2001).

51 Renee C. Romano, *Race Mixing: Black-White Marriage in Post War America* (Cambridge: Harvard University Press, 2003), p. 37.

52 *Montreal Gazette*, 28 April 1962.

53 Romano, *Race Mixing*, p. 75.

54 Veronica Strong-Boag, *Finding Families Finding Ourselves: English Canada Encounters Adoption from the Nineteenth Century to the 1990s* (Toronto: Oxford University Press, 2006); Sandra Jarvie, 'Silent, Denigrated and Rendered Invisible: Mothers Who Lost Their Babies to Adoption in the 1960s and 1970s,' in *Home/Bodies: Geographies of Self, Place and Space*, ed. Wendy Schissel, pp. 69–82 (Calgary: University of Calgary Press, 2006); Patti Phillips 'Blood Not Thicker Than Water: Adoption and Nation Building in the Post War Baby Boom' (M.A. thesis, Queen's University, 1995); Barbara Melosh, *Strangers and Kin: The American Way of Adoption* (Cambridge: Harvard University Press, 2002); Julie Berebitsky, *Like Our Very Own: Adoption and the Changing Culture of Motherhood, 1851–1950* (Lawrence: University of Kansas Press, 2000); E. Wayne Carp, *Family Matters: Secrecy and Disclosure in the History of Adoption* (Cambridge: Harvard University Press, 1998); Rickie Solinger, *Wake Up Little Suzy: Single Pregnancy and Race before Roe v. Wade* (New York: Routledge, 1992), and *Beggars and Choosers: How the Politics of Choice Shapes Adoption, Abortion and Welfare in the United States* (New York: Hill and Wang, 2001); Herman *Kinship by Design*.

55 'The West Indians: Our Loneliest Immigrants,' *Maclean's* , 4 November 1961. See also Violet King, 'Calypso in Canada,' *Canadian Welfare* 34 (Nov. 1958); Ian R. Mackenzie, 'Early Movements of Domestics from the Caribbean and Canadian Immigration Policy: A Research Note,' *Alternate Routes* 8 (1988); Dorothy Williams, *The Road to Now: A History of Blacks in Montreal* (Montreal: Vehicule Press, 1997).

56 Children's Service Centre, *Annual Reports*, 1960s.

57 CSC case file.

58 CSC case file.

59 CSC case file.

60 CSC case file.

61 CSC case file.

62 CSC case file.

63 Melosh, *Strangers and Kin*, p. 153.

64 Lost in the volumes of social work literature on black disinterest in the adoption or foster-care system is a U.S. study which revealed that, when class and financial status is taken into account, black families are *more* likely to adopt through the child welfare system than white families. See Elizabeth Herzog and Rose Bernstein, 'Why So Few Negro Adoptions? A Reappraisal of Evidence,' *Children* 12.1 (Jan.-Feb. 1965): 14–18.

65 Since the story of Canada's civil rights movement has yet to be fully told, it is difficult to contextualize groups such as the Open Door Society. Important information about early civil rights campaigns is contained in Constance Backhouse, *Colour-Coded: A Legal History of Racism in Canada, 1900–1950* (Toronto: University of Toronto Press, 1999); Ross Lambertson, *Repression and Resistance: Canadian Human Rights Activists, 1930–1960* (Toronto: University of Toronto Press, 2005); and James St James Walker, *'Race,' Rights and the Law in the Supreme Court of Canada: Historical Case Studies* (Waterloo, ON: Wilfrid Laurier University Press, 1997).

66 Interview with Carole Kristianson, Vancouver, September 2003.

67 'Interracial Adoptions: How Are They Working?' *Parents*, February 1971; Margaret Edgar, 'Black Children – White Family: A Problem of Identity,' unpublished paper, circa 1970; interview with Margaret Edgar, Galiano, September 2003.

68 Herman, *Kinship by Design*, p. 243.

69 Williams, *Road to Now*, pp. 100–74. See also Sean Mills, 'The Empire Within: Montreal, the Sixties, and the Forging of a Radical Imagination' (Ph.D. diss., Queen's University, 2007).

70 Jael Silliman, Marlene Gerber Fried, Loretta Ross, and Elena R. Gutiérrez, *Undivided Rights: Women of Color Organize for Reproductive Justice* (Cambridge: South End Press, 2004), p. 9; Jennifer Nelson, *Women of Color and the Reproductive Rights Movement* (New York: NYU Press, 2003); Kimberly Springer, *Living for the Revolution: Black Feminist Organizations, 1968–1980* (Durham, NC: Duke University Press, 2005).

71 Recent rethinking of the NABSW statement can be found in Laura Briggs, 'Communities Resisting Interracial Adoption: The Indian Child Welfare Act and the NABSW Statement of 1972,' paper presented at the Adoption and Culture Conference, University of Tampa, 2005; and Heather M. Dalmage, 'Interracial Couples, Multiracial People, and the Color Line in Adoption,' in *Adoptive Families in a Diverse Society*, ed. Katrina Wegar, pp. 210–25 (New Brunswick: Rutgers University Press, 2006). There is an extensive literature, mostly in the United States, about this debate. For example, see Amuzie Chimezie, 'Transracial Adoption of Black Children,'

Social Work 20.4 (July 1975): 296–301; Alicia Howard, David D. Royse, and John A. Skerl, 'Transracial Adoption: The Black Community Perspective,' *Social Work* 22.3 (May 1977): 184–9; Bernice Q. Madison and Michael Schapiro, 'Black Adoption – Issues and Policies: Review of the Literature,' *Social Services Review* 47.4 (Dec. 1973): 531–60; Maye H. Grant, 'Perspectives on Adoption: Black into White,' *Black World*, November 1972, pp. 66–75; Ladner, *Mixed Families*; Elizabeth Bartholet, 'Where Do Black Children Belong,' *University of Pennsylvania Law Review* 139.5 (May 1991): 1163–1256, and 'Race Separatism in the Family: More on the Transracial Adoption Debate,' *Duke Journal of Gender, Law and Policy* 2.1 (Spring 1995): 99–105; Peter Hayes, 'The Ideological Attack on Transracial Adoption in the USA and Britain,' *International Journal of Law and the Family* 9.1 (1995): 1–22; Rudolph Alexander, Jr, and Carla M. Curtis, 'A Review of Empirical Research Involving the Transracial Adoption of African American Children,' *Journal of Black Psychology* 22.2 (May 1996): 223–35; Randall Kennedy, *Interracial Intimacies: Sex, Marriage, Identity and Adoption* (New York: Pantheon, 2003); Sandra Patton, *Birth Marks: Transracial Adoption in Contemporary America* (New York: NYU Press), 2000.

72 Howard McCurdy, 'Address,' paper presented at Mixed Race Adoptions, Open Door Society First International Conference, Montreal, 1969, pp. 9–17.

73 Interview with Irene Henderson, Winnipeg, July 2003.

74 Scyner, 'Towards Adolescence and Young Adulthood.'

75 See, for example, Sally Haslinger, 'You Mixed? Racial Identity without Racial Biology,' in *Adoption Matters: Philosophical and Feminist Essays,* ed. Sally Haslinger and Charlotte Witt, pp. 265–91 (Ithaca, NY: Cornell University Press, 2005); Barbara Ballis Lal, 'Learning to Do Ethnic Identity: The Transracial/Transethnic Adoptive Family as Site and Context,' in *Rethinking 'Mixed Race,'* ed. David Parker and Miri Son, pp. 154–72 (London: Pluto Press, 2001); Barbara Katz Rothman, *Weaving a Family: Untangling Race and Adoption* (Boston: Beacon Press, 2005); and Toby Alice Volkman, 'Embodying Chinese Culture: Transnational Adoption in North America,' in *Cultures of Transnational Adoption,* ed. Toby Alice Volkman, pp. 81–116 (Durham, NC: Duke University Press), 2005.

76 Dorothy Roberts, 'Adoption Myths and Racial Realities in the United States,' in *Outsiders Within: Writing on Transracial Adoption,* ed. Jane Jeong Trenka, Julia Chinyete Oparah, and Sun Yung Shin, p. 55 (Cambridge: South End Press, 2006).

77 Jennifer Mills, 'The Congress of Black Women of Canada, 1973–1983,' paper presented at the Legacy of Slavery Conference, Queen's University,

21 November 2007. My thanks to Jennifer Mills for sharing this paper with me. The ODS was invited to the Congress of Black Women founding conference, and this workshop on adoption specifically. Despite receiving assurances from Aileen Williams, the moderator of the conference, that 'this is not a "protest" Congress,' the ODS declined to attend. Their stated reason – financial considerations – seems flimsy given that the conference was held in relatively nearby Toronto.

78 Interview with Jasmine Smith (pseudonym), Kingston, August 2004.

79 Open Door Society correspondence files, Margaret Edgar to Dr David Kirk, 16 February 1972.

80 'Do Black Parents Care?' *UHURU*, 13 July 1970, p. 4. See also 'Black and White Liberals Discuss Black Problems,' *UHURU*, 1 June 1970.

81 Interview with Irene Henderson and Jody Boyer, Kingston, June 2002; interview with Frances Bayne, Montreal. July 2003.

82 Open Door Society correspondence files, 1972.

83 'Article Considered Disservice,' *Contrast*, 2 February 1973.

84 Shandra Spears, 'Strong Spirit, Fractured Identity: An Ojibway Adoptee's Journey to Wholeness,' in *Strong Women Stories*, ed. Kim Anderson and Bonita Lawrence, p. 83 (Toronto: Sumach Press, 2003).

85 Patrick Johnston, in *Native Children and the Child Welfare System* (Toronto: Canadian Council on Social Development, 1983), p. 23, takes the phrase 'the sixties scoop' from a self-reflective British Colombia social worker, herself a participant in the removal of Native children from their communities on what she later termed 'the slightest pretext.' Other important commentaries on the politics of Aboriginal adoption in Canada are Margaret Ward, *The Adoption of Native Canadian Children* (Cobalt: Highway Book Shop, 1984); Brad McKenzie and Pete Hudson, 'Native Children, Child Welfare, and the Colonization of Native People,' in *The Challenge of Child Welfare*, ed. Kenneth L. Levitt and Brian Warf, pp. 125–41 (Vancouver: UBC Press, 1985); Suzanne Fournier and Ernie Crey, *Stolen from Our Embrace: The Abduction of First Nations Children and the Restoration of Aboriginal Communities* (Vancouver: Douglas and McIntyre, 1997); Patricia A. Monture, 'A Vicious Circle: Child Welfare and the First Nations,' *Canadian Journal of Women and the Law* 3.1 (1989): 1–17; Geoffrey York, *The Dispossessed: Life and Death in Native Canada* (Boston: Little Brown, 1990); Christopher Bagley, 'Adoption of Native Children in Canada: A Policy Analysis and a Research Report,' in *Intercountry Adoption: A Multi National Perspective*, ed. Howard Alstein and Rita Simon, pp. 55–79 (New York: Praeger, 1991); Marie Adams, *Our Son a Stranger: Adoption Breakdown and Its Effects on Parents* (Montreal and Kingston: McGill-Queen's University Press, 2002); Wesley

Crichlow, 'Western Colonization as Disease: Native Adoption and Cultural Genocide,' *Critical Social Work* 3.1 (2002): 1–14; Spears, 'Strong Spirit, Fractured Identity.'

86 E.C. Kimelman, *No Quiet Place*, Review Committee on Indian and Métis Adoptions and Placements (Winnipeg: Manitoba Department of Community Services, 1985).

87 Winona LaDuke, 'Foreword,' in *At the Risk of Being Heard: Identity, Indigenous Rights and Postcolonial States*, ed. Bartholomew Dean and Jerome M. Levi, p. 10 (Ann Arbor: University of Michigan Press, 2003).

88 Kenn Richard, 'On the Matter of Cross-Cultural Aboriginal Adoptions,' in *Putting a Human Face on Child Welfare: Voices from the Prairies*, ed. Ivan Brown, Ferzana Chaze, Don Fuchs, Jean Lafrance, Sharon Mckay, and Shelley Thomas-Prokop, p.189 (Regina: Prairie Child Welfare Consortium, 2007).

89 Brad Evenson, 'The Sixties Scoop,' *Calgary Herald*, 19 April 1998.

90 'I deliberately chose to downplay his warning, not because I believed he was necessarily wrong, but because I had faith in the current belief that the environment was more important in the upbringing of all children. His comments still haunt me' (Adams, *Our Son a Stranger*, p. 104).

91 Evenson, 'The Sixties Scoop.'

92 Raven Sinclair, 'All My Relations – Native Transracial Adoption: A Critical Case Study of Cultural Identity' (Ph.D. diss., University of Calgary, 2007), p. 282.

93 Ibid., p. 285.

94 Sara K. Dorow, *Transnational Adoption: A Cultural Economy of Race, Gender and Kinship* (New York: NYU Press, 2006), pp. 55–6.

95 The figures are as follows: total number of children placed outside Manitoba, 4,824; total within Canada, 3,649; total placed in the United States, 1,149; outside North America, 16. Of these placements, 274 were Caucasian, 170 were of unknown racial origin, and the rest were Aboriginal or Métis (Manitoba Department of Family Services, 'Out of Province Adoptions').

96 Suzanne Fournier and Ernie Crey report the following national statistical trend: in 1959, Native children represented 1 per cent of children 'in care'; by 1969 this figure climbed to 30 to 40 per cent (*Stolen from Our Embrace*, p. 83). See also Government of Canada, *Report on the Royal Commission on Aboriginal Peoples, Volume Three: Gathering Strength* (Ottawa: Ministry of Supply and Services, 1996), pp. 24–6; Marlee Kline, 'Child Welfare Law – Best Interests of the Child: Ideology and First Nations,' *Osgood Hall Law Journal* 30 (1992): 375–426.

97 Richard Wagamese, *One Native Life* (Vancouver: Douglas and McIntyre, 2008), p. 227.

98 Another statistical survey of Aboriginal adoption in Manitoba found a higher rate. Using a list from the Department of Indian Affairs in Ottawa, Josette Lukowycz sampled ninety-five adoptions of Aboriginal children between the 1950s and 1984 and found that 80 per cent were non-voluntary relinquishments (Josette Lukowycz, 'An Exploratory Study of the Adoption of Indian Children in Manitoba' [MSW thesis, University of Manitoba, 1985], p. 48).

99 'Calling Forth Our Future: Options for the Exercise of Indigenous Peoples' Authority in Child Welfare,' Union of B.C. Indian Chiefs, 2002, p. 9, http://www.ubcic.bc.ca. See also the various articles in D. Memee Lavell-Harvard and Jeannette Corbiere Lavell, eds, *'Until Our Hearts Are on the Ground': Aboriginal Mothering, Oppression, Resistance and Rebirth* (Toronto: Demeber Press, 2006).

100 All citations from Manitoba Children's Aid Society case files (hereafter cited as 'CAS case files').

101 Claudia Fonseca, 'Patterns of Shared Parenthood among the Brazilian Poor,' in *Cultures of Transnational Adoption,* ed. Toby Alice Volkman, p. 157 (Durham, NC: Duke University Press, 2005). This point has also been made by commentators on Aboriginal adoption; see Pauline Turner Strong, 'To Forget Their Tongue, Their Name, and Their Whole Relation: Captivity, Extra-Tribal Adoption, and the Indian Child Welfare Act,' in *Relative Values: Reconfiguring Kinship Studies,* ed. Sarah Franklin and Susan McKinnon, pp. 468–94 (New York: Oxford University Press, 2001).

102 CAS case file.

103 CAS case file.

104 CAS case file.

105 CAS case file.

106 CAS case file.

107 Drew Hayden Taylor, *Someday* (Saskatoon: Fifth House Press, 1993), p. 14.

108 Andrea Smith, *Conquest: Sexual Violence and American Indian Genocide* (Cambridge: South End Press, 2005).

109 In 1973 the director of the Adoption Resource Exchange of North America (ARENA an extension of the Indian Adoption Project, which promoted cross-border and cross-racial placements) underlined that 'since the Indian people have the same resistance to their children being placed transracially as the blacks, we continue to use the resources of ARENA to make known the need for Indian families' (Balcom, *Traffic in Babies,* p. 451).

110 'Good Intentions Not Enough!' *Akswesasne Notes*, Early Summer, 1974, p. 41. Resolutions calling for Aboriginal control over the child welfare system were passed by the National Association of Native Women and the Indian Homemakers Association of B.C. in 1974. See 'Native Women Exhorted to Become More Active,' *Thunder Bay Chronicle Journal*, 26 August 1974; 'Calling Forth Our Future: Options for the Exercise of Indigenous Peoples' Authority in Child Welfare,' Union of B.C. Indian Chiefs, 2002, p. 15, http://www.ubcic.bc.ca

111 Nancy Janovicek, 'Assisting Our Own: Urban Migration, Self-Governance, and Native Women's Organizing in Thunder Bay, Ontario, 1972–1989,' *American Indian Quarterly* 27.3–4 (Summer/Fall 2003): 548–64.

112 See, for example, the 'Today's Child' column in the *Toronto Native Times*, which ran in the mid-1970s.

113 Scott Rutherford, 'Canada's Other Red Scare: The Anicinabe Park Occupation, Indigenous Radicalism and the Circulation of Global Culture and Politics, 1965–1975' (Ph.D. dissertation in progress, Queen's University).

114 'Another Native People Lose Their Children,' *Akwesasne Notes*, Early Summer, 1975, p. 26.

115 'Department of Social Services Steals Children,' *New Breed*, September 1975.

116 Library and Archives Canada, RG 146, RCMP files, Native People's Friendship Delegation, Vol. 1, p. 14.

117 *New Breed*, November-December 1975.

118 The most complete account of the Indian Child Welfare Act campaign is Steven Unger, 'The Indian Child Welfare Act of 1978: A Case Study' (Ph.D. diss., University of Southern California, 2004). See also Briggs, 'Communities Resisting Interracial Adoption.'

119 Patrick Johnston, *Native Children and the Child Welfare System* (Toronto: Canadian Council on Social Development, 1983), p. 90; Renate Andres, 'The Apprehension of Native Children,' *Ontario Indian* 4.4 (April 1981): 32–46; Hudson and McKenzie, 'Native Children, Child Welfare, and the Colonization of Native People,' p. 137.

120 Strong-Boag, *Finding Families, Finding Ourselves*, p. 169.

121 Review Committee on Indian and Métis Adoptions and Placements, *Transcripts and Briefs* (Winnipeg: Manitoba Community Services, 1985), p. 15.

122 Ibid., p. 464.

123 Fournier and Crey, *Stolen from Our Embrace*, p. 89. The 'foreign car' is shorthand for a globalized fear: see, for example Luis White, 'Cars out of Place: Vampires, Technology and Labor in East and Central Africa,' *Repre-*

sentations 43 (Summer 1993): 27–50; and Abigail Adams, 'Gringas, Ghouls and Guatemala: The 1994 Attacks on North American Women Accused of Body Organ Trafficking,' *Journal of Latin American Anthropology* 4.1 (1999): 112–33.

124 'Child Export for Adoption Riles Natives,' *Winnipeg Free Press*, 4 March 1982; 'Judge to Review Native Adoptions,' *Winnipeg Free Press*, 13 March 1982. One of the dramatically failed Louisiana placements, the story of the Gott children, is explored in Colleen Rajotte's documentary series, 'Confronting the Past.' See www.rajottedocs.com.

125 Sinclair, 'All My Relations,' p. 258.

126 CAS case file.

127 Strong-Boag, *Finding Families*, p. 138.

128 CAS case file.

129 See, for example, Strong-Boag, *Finding Families*; Solinger, *Beggars and Choosers*; Melosh, *Strangers and Kin*; and Berebitsky, *Like Our Very Own*.

130 CAS case file.

131 CAS case file.

132 CAS case files.

133 'Jae Ran Kim, 'Scattered Seeds: The Christian Influence on Korean Adoption,' in Trenka et al., eds, *Outsiders Within*, p. 156.

134 CAS case file.

135 Review Committee, *Transcripts and Briefs*, p. 12.

136 CAS case file.

137 CAS case file.

138 CAS case file. This corresponds with the situation in the United States, where adoptive parents made their decisions to choose Aboriginal children largely at the encouragement of their adoption agency (Heidi Kiiwetinepinesiik Stark and Keke Jason Todd Stark, 'Flying the Coop: ICWA and the Welfare of Indian Children,' in Trenka et al., eds, *Outsiders Within*,p. 129).

139 CAS case file.

140 'Plan Seeks Metis, Indian Adoptions,' *Calgary Herald*, 8 May 1968; 'Pilot Project Seeks Homes for Indian Children,' *Kingston Whig Standard*, 8 May 1968.

141 CAS case file.

142 CAS case file.

143 Kenneth Plett, 'Transracial Adoption: A Study of the Placement of Native Indian Children with Caucasian Couples' (MSW thesis, University of Manitoba, 1979), p. 45. The survey was based on seventy-five respondents.

144 Raven Sinclair, 'Identity Lost and Found: Lessons from the Sixties Scoop,'
     First Peoples Child and Family Review 3.1 (2007): 73.
145 Unger, 'The Indian Child Welfare Act of 1978,' p. 347.
146 Cindy Blackstock, Nico Trocmé, and Marlyn Bennett, 'Child Maltreat-
     ment Investigations among Aboriginal and Non-Aboriginal Families in
     Canada,' *Violence against Women* 10 (2004): 901–16.
147 Sinclair, 'All My Relations,' p. 24.
148 Nicholas Sammond, *Babes in Tomorrowland: Walt Disney and the Making
     of the American Child, 1930–1960* (Durham, NC: Duke University Press,
     2009), p. 3.

**4. The Missing Baby: Transnational Adoption and the Vanishing Children
of Guatemala**

 1 Ellen Herman, *Kinship by Design: A History of Adoption in the Modern United
    States* (Chicago: University of Chicago Press, 2008), p. 228.
 2 Howard Alstein and Rita J. Simon, *Intercountry Adoption: A Multinational
    Perspective* (New York: Praeger, 1991), p. 1. See also Everett M. Ressler, Neil
    Boothby, and Daniel J Steinbock, *Unaccompanied Children: Care and Protec-
    tion in Wars, Natural Disasters, and Refugee Movements* (New York: Oxford
    University Press, 1988). While popular, this origin story ignores earlier
    child migration schemes – such as the poor white children who moved
    from Britain throughout the Empire in the nineteenth and twentieth
    centuries. See, for example Veronica Strong-Boag, *Finding Families Finding
    Ourselves: English Canada Encounters Adoption from the Nineteenth Century
    to the 1990s* (Toronto: Oxford University Press, 2006); Jon Lawrence and
    Pat Starkey, *Child Welfare and Social Action in the Nineteenth and Twentieth
    Centuries: International Perspectives* (Liverpool: Liverpool University Press,
    2001); Joy Parr, *Labouring Children: British Immigrant Apprentices to Canada,
    1869–1924* (Montreal: McGill-Queen's University Press, 1980).
 3 Karen Balcom *The Traffic in Babies: Cross Border Adoption, Baby-Selling and
    Child Welfare in the United States and Canada, 1930–1972* (Toronto: Univer-
    sity of Toronto Press, forthcoming).
 4 Alstein and Simon, *Intercountry Adoption*, p. 2.
 5 Sara K. Dorow, *Transnational Adoption: A Cultural Economy of Race, Gender
    and Kinship* (New York: New York University Press, 2006), pp 35–64; Elaine
    May, *Barren in the Promised Land: Childless Americans and the Pursuit of
    Happiness* (Cambridge: Harvard University Press, 1995); Veronica Strong-
    Boag, 'Home Dreams: Women and the Suburban Experiment in Canada,
    1945–60,' *Canadian Historical Review* 72.4 (Dec. 1991): 471–504.

6 Tobias Hubinette, 'Comforting an Orphaned Nation: Representations of International Adoption and Adopted Koreans in Korean Popular Culture' (Ph.D. diss., Stockholm University, Department of Oriental Languages, 2005), pp. 28–9.

7 Ibid., pp. 61–2. See also Jae Ran Kim, 'Scattered Seeds: The Christian Influence on Korean Adoption,' in *Outsiders Within: Writing on Transracial Adoption*, ed. Jane Jeong Trenka, pp. 151–62 (Cambridge: South End Press, 2006).

8 Strong-Boag, *Finding Families*, p. 195. Families for Children was started by Naomi Bronstein (12 children, of which 7 were adopted), Bonnie Cappuccinno (19 adopted children), and Sandra Simpson (32 children, including 28 adopted). See 'The Little Family That Grew and Grew,' *Chatelaine*, December 1990; 'Searching Far and Wide for a Child,' *Toronto Star*, 24 October 1988; and 'Mother Lode,' *Montreal Gazette*, 3 October 1999. The origins of transnational adoption in Canada are explored in Tarah Brookfield, '"Our Deepest Concern Is for the Safety of Our Children and Their Children": Canadian Women Respond to Cold War Fears at Home and Abroad, 1950–1980' (Ph.D. diss., York University, 2008). My thanks to Tarah Brookfield for sharing her research with me.

9 Adam Pertman, *Adoption Nation* (Boston: Basic, 2000), p. 76; Barbara Melosh, *Strangers and Kin: The American Way of Adoption* (Cambridge: Harvard University Press, 2002) p. 160.

10 Signe Howell, *The Kinning of Foreigners: Transnational Adoption in a Global Perspective* (New York: Berghahn Books, 2006), p. 19.

11 On Spain, see Howell, *Kinning of Foreigners*, p. 21. The complicated history of the two-way traffic of adoption across the Canada/U.S. border is explored in Balcom, *The Traffic in Babies*. On the United States as a 'sending' nation, see 'A Canadian Haven for Black U.S. Babies,' *Globe and Mail*, 1 October 2005.

12 Laura Briggs 'Mother, Child, Race, Nation: The Visual Iconography of Rescue and the Politics of Transnational and Transracial Adoption,' *Gender and History* 15.2 (Aug. 2000): 180.

13 Kirsten Lovelock, 'Intercountry Adoption as a Migratory Practice: A Comparative Analysis of Intercountry Adoption and Immigration Policy and Practice in the United States, Canada and New Zealand in the Post W.W. II Period,' *International Migration Review* 34.3 (Autumn 2000): 910. See also Richard Weil, 'International Adoptions: The Quiet Migration,' *International Migration Review* 18.2 (Summer 1984): 276–93.

14 Dorow, *Transnational Adoption*, p. 54.

15 Kim, 'Scattered Seeds,' pp. 152–61; Ellen Herman, 'Bertha and Harry Holt,' Adoption History Project, http://www.uoregon.edu/~adoption/

16 Strong-Boag, *Finding Families*. pp. 203–7.
17 Sheila Gormely, 'Canada Brings In 100 Babies from War-Torn Asian Lands', *Toronto Star*, 3 February 1973, cited in Brookfield, p. 56.
18 Lisa Cartwright, 'Images of "Waiting Children," Spectatorship and Pity in the Representation of the Global Social Orphan in the 1990s,' in *Cultures of Transnational Adoption*, ed. Toby Volkman, pp. 185–212 (Durham, NC: Duke University Press, 2005); Strong-Boag, *Finding Families*, p. 205; Geraldine Sherman, 'From Russia (or China or Peru or Bucharest) with Love,' *Toronto Life*, November 1995, pp. 1–9.
19 Dorow, *Transnational Adoption*, pp. 37, 62.
20 Erica Burman, 'Innocents Abroad: Western Fantasies of Childhood and the Iconography of Emergencies,' *Disasters* 18.3 (2007): 241.
21 'Families Give Globalization Added Meaning,' *Globe and Mail*, 5 December 2002.
22 Dorow, *Transnational Adoption*, p. 10.
23 Laura Briggs, 'Making "American" Families: Transnational Adoption and U.S. Latin American Policy,' in *Haunted by Empire: Geographies of Intimacy in North American History*, ed. Ann Laura Stoler, p. 346 (Durham, NC: Duke University Press, 2006). An insightful analysis of adoptive parents narratives is Emily Noonan, 'Adoption and the Guatemalan Journey to American Parenthood,' *Childhood* 14.3 (2007): 301–19.
24 Emily Prager, *Wuhu Diari: On Taking My Adopted Daughter Back to Her Hometown in China* (New York: Random House, 2001); Karen Evans, *The Lost Daughters of China: Abandoned Girls, Their Journey to America and the Search for a Missing Past* (New York: Putnam, 2000); Martin Goldfarb, 'We Fell in Love with Her,' *Globe and Mail*, 27 October 2001.
25 John Towriss, 'A Personal Adoption Story,' CNN.com., May 2001.
26 Lea Marenn, *Salvador's Children: A Song for Survival* (Columbus: Ohio State University Press, 1993). Another self-reflective adoptive parent memoir is Chris Winston, *A Euro-American on a Korean Tour at a Thai Restaurant in China* (El Dorado: KAAN, 2006).
27 Bruce Porter, 'I Met My Daughter at the Wuhan Foundling Hospital,' *New York Times Magazine*, 11 April 1993, p. 46.
28 Elizabeth Bartholet, *Family Bonds: Adoption, Infertility and the New World of Child Production* (Boston: Beacon Press, 1993), p. 36.
29 This point is well made by Briggs, 'Making "American' Families,'" pp. 346–7
30 Claudia Casteñeda, *Figurations: Child, Bodies, Worlds* (Durham, NC: Duke University Press, 2002), p. 94.

31 Pertman, *Adoption Nation*, pp. 265–78; 'Families Give Globalization Added Meaning,' *Globe and Mail*, 5 December 2002.

32 The creation of adoptive family communities and networks is a phenomenon just beginning to be explored by researchers. For example, see Ann Anagnost, 'Maternal Labor in a Transnational Circuit,' in *Consuming Motherhood*, ed. Janelle S. Taylor, Linda Layne, and Danielle F. Wozniak, pp. 139–67 (New Brunswick: Rutgers University Press, 2004); Barbara Yngvesson, 'Going "Home": Adoption, Loss of Bearings and the Mythology of Roots,' Eleana Kim, 'Wedding Citizenship and Culture: Korean Adoptees and the Global Family of Korea,' and Toby Volkman, 'Embodying Chinese Culture: Transnational Adoption in North America,' all in Volkman, ed., *Cultures of Transnational Adoption*, pp. 25–48, 49–80, and 81–116; and Dorow, *Transnational Adoption*, pp. 205, 262. See also 'Culture Club,' *Globe and Mail*, 2 September 2006; 'Weekend at Culture Camp,' *Mother Jones*, 24 October 2007; and 'Summers at Camp Ethnicity,' *Salon.com*, 12 August 2002.

33 *Oprah Winfrey Show*, air date, 25 October 2006. Of the volumes of commentary on this incident, see especially Adam Elkus, 'Celebrity Colonialism in Africa,' *ZNET*, 4 November 2006. That Madonna's second attempt to adopt from Malawi was more complicated also suggests that a simple-minded embrace of the rescue paradigm is declining ('Madonna Denied Adoption in Africa,' *Globe and Mail*, 4 April 2009).

34 'I Wanted to Save an Orphan from War and Hunger,' *Guardian*, 1 November 2007; 'Chad Parents Await Child Row Outcome,' BBC News, 1 November 2007; 'Chad Orphan Scandal a "Kafkaesque" Nightmare,' National Public Radio, 5 November 2007; 'The Orphans Who Didn't Need Saving,' *New York Times*, 4 November 2007.

35 'In Another Era, Orphan Airlift Would Have Been Lauded,' *Toronto Star*, 3 November 2007.

36 Personal communication, 4 November 2007.

37 Hubinette, ' Comforting an Orphaned Nation,' p. 70; Damien Ngabonziza, 'Inter-country Adoption: In Whose Best Interests?' *Adoption and Fostering* 12.1 (1988): 35–40.

38 'The Great Sale of Children Takes Place in Tijuana,' *Excelsior*, 13 January 1987, cited in 'Protecting Children's Rights in International Adoption,' *Defence for Children International*, Geneva, 1989, p. 11; 'Mexican Mother Sued Adoption Agency Allegedly Involved in Baby Smuggling,' 18 September 2002, Knight Ridder / Tribune News Service.

39 'Brazilian Babies Sold and Killed in Europe for Transplant Organs,' *Guardian*, 24 September 1990.

40 James Fahz, *Adopting from Latin America* (Springfield: Charles C. Thomas, 1988), p. 25.

41 M.E. Fieweger, 'Stolen Children and International Adoptions,' *Child Welfare* 70.2 (March/April 1991): 285–91.

42 'Stealing Children,' *New Internationalist*, no. 245 (July 1993); 'Child-Snatchers Send In the Clowns,' *Independent*, 5 November 1995.

43 'Adoptions in Paraguay: Mothers Cry Theft,' *New York Times*, 19 March 1996.

44 'Where Are My Babies?' *Toronto Star*, 19 November 2000.

45 'Secretive Network: Salvadoran "Baby Scam" Flourishing,' *Los Angeles Times*, 5 December 1986; 'What Did You Do in the War, Mama?' *New York Times Magazine*, 7 February 1999; 'Hunt for Stolen War Children,' *Guardian*, 19 June 2000; 'Separated by War, Reunited through DNA,' *New York Times*, 22 December 2006.

46 'France Moves against Vietnam's Baby Trade,' *Guardian*, 4 May 1999; 'Vietnamese Women Jailed over Baby Sales,' Radio Australia News, 26 May 2001; 'Adoption Agency Acts on Baby-Buying Claims,' *Toronto Star*, 26 August 2001; 'Vietnam Tightens Adoption Controls,' *Guardian*, 22 July 2002; 'Cambodian Parents Forced to Sell Babies,' *www.canoe.com*, 3 February 2001 (retrieved 6 September 2002); 'Empty Cribs,' *Philadelphia Inquirer*, 2 April 2002; 'Where Do Babies Come From?' *New York Times Magazine*, 16 June 2002; 'Chinese Stonewall on Baby Smuggling,' *Globe and Mail*, 15 December 2005; 'Chinese Officials Sentenced for Selling Stolen Babies,' CBC News, 25 February 2006.

47 'Psst! Babies for Sale,' *Time*, 21 October 1991; 'Police Target Malaysia Baby Snatchers,' BBC News, 22 July 2002.

48 'Stop Baby Trade from Romania,' *Toronto Star*, 8 April 1991; 'Foreigners "Purchasing" Romanian Babies, U.N. Told,' *Toronto Star*, 1 August 1991; 'Adoption Racket Role Denied,' *Vancouver Sun*, 15 July 1994; 'Pair Accused of Smuggling Baby Go Home,' *Montreal Gazette*, 30 November 1994.

49 'Russians Torn over Adoption of Orphans,' *Toronto Star*, 22 November 1992; 'Police Raids Uncover "Orphans for Sale" Racket,' *Guardian*, 24 February 2001.

50 'Ex-lawyer Who Deals in Babies,' *Toronto Star*, 3 July 1993; 'Ontario Ex-lawyer Charged in Polish Baby Ring,' *Toronto Star*, 9 December 1993; 'A World of Hope; the Search for Babies to Adopt Has Become a Global Quest,' *Los Angeles Times*, 18 June 1996; 'Canadian Held in Jail in Baby-Smuggling Case,' *Globe and Mail*, 20 November 2000.

51 'Adoption Doctor Found Guilty,' *Budapest Sun*, 1 August 2002.

52 'Pakistan Gang Buys, Sells Children,' *Seattle Times*, 17 March 2002.

53 David Smolin,'The Two Faces of Intercountry Adoption: The Significance of the Indian Adoption Scandals,' *Seton Hall Law Review* 35 (2004–5): 403–93.

54 Ibid., p. 403.

55 See, for example, Karen Balcom, '"Phoney Mothers" and Border-Crossing Adoptions: The Montreal–to–New York Black Market in Babies in the 1950s,' *Journal of Women's History* 19.1 (Spring 2007): 107–17; Patricia T. Rook and R. Schnell, 'Charlotte Whitton and the "Babies for Export" Controversy,' *Alberta History* 30.1 (1982): 11–16; Linda Tollet Austin, *Babies for Sale: The Tennessee Children's Home Adoption Scandal* (Westport: Praeger, 1993); Herman, *Kinship by Design,* pp. 31–9.

56 'Where Do Babies Come From?' *New York Times Magazine,* 16 June 2002.

57 Steven Maynard, 'Through a Hole in the Lavatory Wall: Homosexual Subcultures, Police Surveillance and the Dialectics of Discovery: Toronto, 1890–1930,' *Journal of the History of Sexuality* 5.3 (1994): 207–42; Matt Houlbrook, *Queer London* (Chicago: University of Chicago Press, 2005).

58 For an analysis of adoption stories in contemporary media, see Adam Pertman, 'Adoption in the Media: In Need of Editing,' and Christine Ward Gailey, 'Urchins, Orphans, Monsters, and Victims: Images of Adoptive Families in U.S. Commercial Films, 1950–2000,' both in *Adoptive Families in a Diverse Society,* ed. Katarina Wegar, pp. 60–70 and pp. 71–91 (New Brunswick: Rutgers University Press, 2006).

59 Tobias Hecht, 'Children and Contemporary Latin America,' in *Minor Omissions: Children in Latin American History and Society,* ed. Tobias Hecht, p. 242 (Madison: University of Wisconsin Press, 2002).

60 Rosa Perla Resnick, 'Latin American Children in Intercountry Adoption,' in *Adoption : Essays in Social Policy, Law and Society,* ed. Philip Bean, p. 275 (London: Tavistock, 1984).

61 Greg Grandin, *Empire's Workshop* (New York: Metropolitan Books, 2006), p. 4.

62 Greg Grandin, *The Last Colonial Massacre* (Chicago: University of Chicago Press, 2004), pp. 44, 59.

63 Aryeh Neier, 'Foreword,' in Beatriz Manz, *Paradise in Ashes: A Guatemalan Journey of Courage, Terror and Hope* (Berkeley: University of California Press, 2004), p. xiii.

64 George Lovell, *A Beauty That Hurts: Life and Death in Guatemala* (Toronto: Between the Lines, 1995), p. 162. The most commonly cited sources for the statistics of the civil war are two post-war reports: Commission for Historical Clarification (CEH), *Guatemala: Memory of Silence* (Guatemala

City: CEH, 1999); and Recovery of Historical Memory Project (REMHI), *Guatemala Never Again!* (Guatemala City: ODHAG, 1999).

65 Grandin, *The Last Colonial Massacre*, p. 3. See also Susanne Jonas, *The Battle for Guatemala* (Boulder: Westview Press, 1991); and Robert M. Carmack, ed., *Harvest of Violence: The Maya Indians and the Guatemalan Crisis* (Norman: University of Oklahoma Press, 1988).

66 Victoria Sanford, *Buried Secrets: Truth and Human Rights in Guatemala* (New York: Palgrave, 2003), p. 14.

67 Victor Perera, *Unfinished Conquest: The Guatemalan Tragedy* (Berkeley: University of California Press, 1993). See also Nancy Leigh Tierney, *Robbed of Humanity: Lives of Guatemalan Street Children* (Saint Paul: Pangaea, 1997).

68 REMHI, *Guatemala Never Again!* pp. 29–39

69 *Hasta Encontrarte* 3rd edn (Guatemala City: ODHAG, 2005), pp. 30–4, 43. See also Manz, *Paradise in Ashes*; and Ricardo Falla, *Massacres in the Jungle* (Boulder: Westview Press, 1994).

70 'New Hope for Missing Kids,' *San Francisco Gate,* 7 September 2000; interview with Nidia Aguilar del Cid, Procuraduría de los Derechos Humanos, Defensor de la niñez, Guatemala City, May 2006. The figure 438 represents the number of adoptions documented by the U.S. State Department between 1979 and 1983.

71 'Hunt for Stolen War Children,' *Guardian,* 19 June 2000.

72 *Demos a la niñez un futuro de paz* (Guatemala City: ODHAG, 2006). ODHAG is the Oficina de Derechos Humanos del Arzobispado de Guatemala (Human Rights Office of the Archbishopric of Guatemala).

73 *Discovering Dominga,* directed by Patricia Flynn, Public Broadcasting System, POV, 2003. On the Rio Negro massacres, see Jesús Tecú Osorio, *The Rio Negro Massacres* (Washington, DC: Rights Action, 2003).

74 Interview with Norma Cruz, 2 May 2006. Cruz is featured in the NFB film *Killer's Paradise* (2006), directed by Giselle Portenier, which documents the femicide rate.

75 Of the many accounts of the legacy of Guatemala's civil war, I'm especially influenced by Francisco Goldman, *The Art of Political Murder: Who Killed the Bishop* (New York: Grove, 2007); Angelina Snodgrass Godoy, *Popular Injustice: Violence, Community and Law in Latin America* (Stanford: Stanford University Press, 2006); Linda Green, *Fear as a Way of Life: Mayan Widows in Rural Guatemala* (New York: Columbia University Press, 1999); Susan C. Peacock and Adriana Beltrán, *Hidden Powers in Post-Conflict Guatemala* (Washington, DC: Washington Office on Latin America, 2003); Sanford, *Buried Secrets;* and Daniel Wilkinson, *Silence on the Mountain: Stories of Terror, Betrayal and Forgetting in Guatemala* (Boston: Houghton Mifflin, 2002).

76 ILPEC (Latin American Institute for Education and Communications), 'Adoption and the Rights of the Child in Guatemala,' unpublished report for UNICEF, Guatemala, 2000; 'Exportación de Niños,' *Siglo XXI*, 11 July 2005; 'Exportador de bebes,' *Prensa Libre*, 9 June 2006.

77 'Se violan dereches del niños,' *Prensa Libre*, 21 November 2007. The Guatemalan adoption system is explained (and contested) in ILPEC, 'Adoption and the Rights of the Child in Guatemala'; and 'UNICEF, Guatemalan Adoption, and the Best Interests of the Child: An Informative Study,' *Families without Borders*, November 2003.

78 Cynthia Enloe, *The Curious Feminist: Searching for Women in a New Age of Empire* (Berkeley: University of California Press, 2004), p. 193.

79 Jose De la Cruz, Letter to the editor, *El Periodico*, 12 December 2007.

80 Izvestia ,25 July 1985, cited in Veronique Campion-Vincent, *Organ Theft Legends* (Jackson: University of Mississippi Press, 2005), p. 9

81 Todd Levanthal, 'The "Baby Parts" Myth: The Anatomy of a Rumor,' unpublished report, United States Information Agency, 20 May 1994; 'Too Good to Be True,' *Newsweek*, International Edition, 26 June 1995.

82 'Stroock: No hay trafico de ninos,' *El Grafico*, 15 October 1992. See also *Prensa Libre*, 16 October 1992.

83 Sanford, *Buried Secrets*, pp. 58–9; Sister Dianna Ortiz, *The Blindfold's Eye* (Maryknoll: Orbis, 2002). Of course, this is just one of countless such examples of U.S. government denial in these years. For others, see, for example, Jean Marie Simon, *Guatemala: Eternal Spring, Eternal Tyranny* (New York: Norton, 1987).

84 Castañeda, *Figurations*, p. 130.

85 '94 Beating Victim Still in Nursing Home,' *Fairbanks Daily News-Miner*, 13 June 2004.

86 'Se ha hecho frecuente la compra de niños para mutilarlos' *Prensa Libre*, 13 March 1994; 'Witch Hunt,' *Washington Post*, 22 May 1994.

87 'Trasplante de órganos es un proceso muy complejo,' *Prensa Libre*, 8 April 1994.

88 *Diario Centro America*, 14 April 1994; 'Niños y Seguridad,' *La Hora*, 14 April 1994.

89 Peter Burger, 'Organ Snatcher Myth,' alt.folklore.urban, 13 January 1998.

90 Nancy Scheper-Hughes, 'Theft of Life,' *Anthropology Today* 12.3 (June 1996): 5. See also 'The New Cannibalism,' *New Internationalist*, April 1998, pp. 14–17; and 'The Global Traffic in Human Organs,' *Current Anthropology* 41.2 (April 2000): 191–224.

91 Stephen Fraser, 'Myth, Fact and Confusion in the Disappearances of Children in Guatemala,' *Lulu Press*, 24 May 1994, p. 9.

92 'Crece robo de recién nacidos,' *El Grafico*, 13 October 1993.

93 See, for example, *El Grafico*, 21 April 1992.

94 'Se venden niños, bonitos y baratos,' *Prensa Libre*, 25 October 1992.

95 Duncan Green, *Silent Revolution: The Rise and Crisis of Market Economics in Latin America* (New York: Monthly Review Press, 2003); Edward F. Fischer and Peter Benson, *Broccoli and Desire: Global Connections and Maya Struggles in Postwar Guatemala* (Stanford: Stanford University Press, 2006).

96 *La Hora*, 27 December 1991.

97 'Guatemala: Political Violence Finds a New Cover,' *Los Angeles Times*, 17 December 1995.

98 'Policía descubrió un nuevo caso de tráfico de niños,' *Prensa Libre*, 25 August 1992.

99 'La venta de niños, un negocio de adultos,' *Siglo XXI*, 20 September 1993.

100 'Robo de niños se ha vuelto gran negocio,' *La República*, 16 August 1993.

101 'Se venden niños, bonitos y baratos,' *Prensa Libre*, 25 October 1992.

102 'Rumores de robo de órgano,' *Diario de Centro America*, 14 April 1994.

103 'Carranza: Los traficantes de niños fotografían potenciales víctimas,' *Siglo XXI*, 15 January 1994.

104 Luise White, 'Cars out of Place: Vampires, Technology and Labor in East and Central Africa,' *Representations*, no. 43 (Summer 1993): 27–50.

105 'Crece preocupación por robo de niños,' *La Republica*, 18 March 1994. See also 'Title Missing,' *La Hora*, 18 March 1994; 'Title Missing,' *Siglo XXI*, 24 March 1994.

106 Diane M. Nelson, *A Finger in the Wound: Body Politics in Quincentennial Guatemala* (Berkeley: University of California Press, 1999), p. 68.

107 Ibid., p. 47

108 Abigail Adams, 'Gringas, Ghouls and Guatemala: The 1994 Attacks on North American Women Accused of Body Organ Trafficking,' *Journal of Latin American Anthropology* 4.1 (1999): 112–33. Weinstock's story has also been explored in Anne Collinson, 'The Littlest Immigrants: Cross-Border Adoption in the Americas,' *Journal of Women's History* 19.1 (2007): 132–41.

109 'GAM: Linchamiento de extranjeros puede bloquear la verificación,' *Siglo Vienteuno*, 31 March 1994; 'Child Kidnapping Rumors Fuel Attacks on Americans,' *Los Angeles Times*, 2 April 1994; 'The Baby-Snatching Hysteria,' *Miami Herald*, 4 April 1994; 'Behind the Kidnapping of Children for Their Organs,' *Los Angeles Times*, 1 May 1994.

110 'Yankee hippies, go home!' *La Republica*, 12 April 1994; 'Turismo o Respeta Para la Vida,' *Prensa Libre*, 9 April 1994.

111 *Le Republica*, 4 August 1994.

112 'Guatemala Inflamed,' *Village Voice*, 31 May 1994.

113 'Niños y Seguridad,' *La Hora*, 14 April 1994. See also 'Los rumores, y la adopción illegal,' *Siglo Vienteuno*, 14 April 1994.

114 See, for example, Harris's interview in the wildly alarmist NFB film *The Baby Business* (1975); 'Expose on Child Trafficking Hits Press,' *Siglo News*, 24 September 1997; 'With Babies in Demand, Kidnappers Are on the Prowl,' *Houston Chronicle*, 1 November 1997; 'Selling Babies, an Interview with Bruce Harris,' *Cerigua Weekly Briefs*, no. 39 (9 Oct.1997); 'Buy Baby Buy,' *Guardian*, 27 August 1999; 'Baby Snatchers Who Thrive on Poverty,' *National Post*, 29 July 1999; Bruce Harris, Letter, International Adoption Forum, *Americas.org*, November 2000; 'Robbing the Cradle: Adoptions under Fire in Guatemala,' *Newday.com*, 2 November 2003.

115 'Cooks Baby Trade Expose a Scoop Too Far,' *Observer*, 28 July 1996. See also reports in the *Evening Standard*, 14 May 1996, and the *Daily Mirror*, 13 May 1996.

116 'Millones en adopciones,' *Prensa Libre*, 29 June 1998, cited in Derek Honeyman, 'Lynch Mobs and Child Theft Rumours in the Guatemala Highlands' (M.A. thesis, University of Alberta, 1999).

117 United Nations Commission on Human Rights, 'Report of the Special Rapporteur on the Sale of Children, Child Prostitution and Child Pornography,' 27 January 2000.

118 'Adoption vs. trafficking in Guatemala,' *Christian Science Monitor*, 17 October 2000.

119 As well as the barrage of press coverage, a thoughtful analysis of the Todos Santos lynching was written by Robert Sittler in 'Understanding Death in a Mayan Market,' *Community College Humanities Review* 22.1 (Fall 2001): 88–98. The lynching figures are from the United Nations Commission for Guatemala, cited in Jim Handy, 'Chicken Thieves, Witches, and Judges: Vigilante Justice and Customary Law in Guatemala,' *Journal of Latin American Studies* 36 (2004): 535.

120 There had been fifty-seven lynchings in the previous year and a half, by no means all of them related to child-stealing ('Casos más recientes,' *Prensa Libre*, 5 May 2006).

121 'Disburbios: Un muerto y 28 casas quemadas,' *Prensa Libre*, 2 October 2006.

122 'Child-Smuggling Ring Broken Up by the U.S. Immigration Agency,' *New York Times*, 13 August 2002; 'El problema es tener que basarnos en leyes caducas y obsoletas,' *Prensa Libre*, 1 July 2007.

123 'Madres exigen acabar con el robo de niños,' *Prensa Libre* 19 November 2007; 'Guatemala Adoptions: A Baby Trade?' BBC News, 17 December 2007.

124 Latin American Institute for Education and Communications for UNICEF, 'Adoption and the Rights of the Child in Guatemala,' 2000; Dr Manuel Manrique, 'Future of Guatemalan Adoptions,' panel, Adoption, Ethics and Accountability Conference, Arlington, Virginia, October 2007.

125 'Guatemala Adoptions: A Baby Trade?' BBC News, 17 December 2007; 'Inside Guatemala's Adoption Pipeline,' *Chicago Tribune*, 11 November 2007.

126 'Guatemala System Is Scrutinized as Americans Rush In to Adopt,' *New York Times*, 5 November 2006; 'Guatemala's Baby Business,' BBC News, 1 September 2000; 'La adopción fue desnaturalizada,' *el Periodico*, 12 December 2007.

127 See, for example, Jacob Wheeler, 'Baby Hotel: The Gateway to Guatemalan Adoption' *Worldpress.org*, 9 October 2006; Maeve Garigan, 'Guatemala's Adoption Industry,' *SAIS Review* 27.2 (Summer/Fall 2007): 179–81.

128 Jacob Wheeler, 'Banana Republic to Baby Republic,' *In These Times*, 5 November 2007.

129 'Guatemala: Whitewash for "Adoption Paradise,"' *Inter Press Service*, 17 December 2007; 'Congreso aprueba la ley de adopciones,' *Prensa Libre*, 11 December 2007; 'New Guatemala Adoption Law Approved,' *Associated Press*, 11 December 2007.

130 'Ex-lawyer Who Deals in Babies,' *Toronto Star*, 3 July 1993.

131 Goran Theorborn, 'Child Politics: Dimensions and Perspectives,' *Childhood* 3 (1996): 29–44.

132 I am inspired here by the arguments Cynthia Enloe has made about how crimes against women are taken up in nationalist conflicts (Enloe, *The Curious Feminist*, pp. 69–82).

133 'Guatemala Protects Children in Adoption More than Nicaragua,' *el Periodico*, 22 October 2004; 'Slamming the Door on Adoption,' *Washington Post.com*, 4 November 2007.

134 'Inside Guatemala's Adoption Pipeline,' *Chicago Tribune*, 11 November 2007.

135 'Guatemala System Is Scrutinized as Americans Rush In to Adopt,' *New York Times*, 5 November 2006; 'Opinión,' *Siglo XXI*, 31 January 2005.

136 Angelina Snodgrass Godoy, *Popular Injustice: Violence, Community and Law in Latin America* (Stanford: Stanford University Press, 2006.), p. 50.

137 Fischer and Benson, *Broccoli and Desire*, p. 96.

138 'Guatemala Babies 'Sold to Highest Bidders,' *Guardian*, 13 June 2000.

139 On Gutiérrez, see http://www.amnesty.org/en/library/info/AMR34/016/2000. Aguilar is referring to the most prominent homosexual conspiracy designed to cover official involvement in political assassination in Guatemala, the death of Archbishop Juan Gerardi.

140 Tom DiFilipo, 'Future of Guatemalan Adoptions,' panel, Adoption, Ethics and Accountability Conference, Arlington, Virginia, October 2007. See Carolyn Nordstrom's important *Global Outlaws: Crime, Money and Power in the Contemporary World* (Berkeley: University of California Press, 2007).

141 'Adoption vs. trafficking in Guatemala,' *Christian Science Monitor*, 17 October 2000. On informal adoption and family-making during the war, see Falla, *Massacres in the Jungle*.

142 Goldman, *Art of Political Murder*, p. 91.

143 Samantha L. Wilson and Judith L. Gibbons, 'Guatemalan Perceptions of Adoption,' *International Social Work* 48.6 (2005): 742–52.

144 Important sources on birth mothers' perspectives from developing countries are Pien Bos 'Once a Mother: Relinquishment and Adoption from the Perspective of Unmarried Mothers from South India' (Ph.D. diss., Radboud University, Nijmegan, 2007); and Claudia Fonseca, 'Patterns of Shared Parenthood among the Brazilian Poor,' in Volkman, ed., *Cultures of Transnational Adoption*, pp. 142–61. On First World stories, see Ann Fessler's sensitive collection of interviews with birth mothers, *The Girls Who Went Away: The Hidden History of Women Who Surrendered Children for Adoption in the Decades before Roe v. Wade* (New York: Penguin, 2006).

145 Hubinette, 'Comforting an Orphaned Nation,' p. 87.

146 The complications of remittances between adoptive and birth families is also discussed in 'Looking for Their Children's Birth Mothers,' *New York Times*, 28 October 2007.

Conclusion: Setting the Agenda for a Happy Childhood

1 Elizabeth Larsen, 'Did I Steal My Daughter? The Tribulations of Global Adoption,' *Mother Jones*, November/December 2007.

2 There are of course exceptions to my observation about the disconnectedness between adoptive families and immigrant communities. For an important account of efforts to connect adoptive families with immigrant groups, see Chris Winston, *A Euro-American on a Korean Tour at a Thai Restaurant in China: Perspective of an Adoptive Parent of Korean Kids* (El Dorado Hills: KAAN, 2006).

3 Patricia Monture, 'A Vicious Circle: Child Welfare and the First Nations,' *Canadian Journal of Women and the Law* 3.1 (1989): 3.

4 Jane Jeong Trenka, Julia Chinyere Oparah, and Sun Yung Shin, eds, *Outsiders Within: Writing on Transracial Adoption* (Cambridge: South End Press, 2006), p. 7.

5 Molly McCullough, 'A Long Way from Home: A Glimpse at Transnational Adoption,' Women's Studies 323 essay, University of Victoria, April 2008.

This essay won the Canadian Women's Studies Association Undergraduate Essay Prize, 2008.

6 Ralph Savarese, *Reasonable People: A Memoir of Autism and Adoption* (New York: Other Press, 2007), p. 158.

7 Jo Boyden, 'Childhood and the Policy Makers: A Comparative Perspective on the Globalization of Childhood,' in *Constructing and Reconstructing Childhood: Contemporary Issues in the Sociological Study of Childhood*, ed. Allison James and Alan Prout, pp. 184–215 (New York: Falmer Press, 1990).

8 Carolyn Nordstrom, 'The Jagged Edge of Peace: The Creation of Culture and War Orphans of Angola,' in *Troublemakers or Peacemakers? Youth and Post-Accord Peace Building*, ed. Siobhan McEvoy-Levy, pp. 99–116 (Notre Dame: University of Notre Dame Press, 2006).

9 These are huge topics. A partial list of sources includes Jo Boyden and Joanna de Berry, eds, *Children and Youth on the Front Line: Ethnography, Armed Conflict and Displacement* (Oxford: Berghahn Books, 2004); Julia O'Connel Davidson, *Children in the Global Sex Trade* (Cambridge: Polity Press, 2005); Duncan Green, *Hidden Lives; Voices of Children in Latin America and the Caribbean* (Toronto: Between the Lines, 1988); McEvoy-Levy, ed., *Troublemakers or Peacemakers? Youth and Post-Accord Peace Building;* Heather Montgomery, *Modern Babylon? Prostituting Children in Thailand* (Oxford: Berghahn Books, 2001); Jeremy Seabrook, *Children of Other Worlds: Exploitation in the Global Market* (London: Pluto Press, 2001); Nancy Scheper-Hughes and Carolyn Sargent, eds, *Small Wars: The Cultural Politics of Childhood* (Berkeley: University of California Press, 1999).

10 Ann Stoler, 'Intimidations of Empire: Predicaments of the Tactile and Unseen,' in *Haunted by Empire: Geographies of Intimacy in North American History*, ed. Ann Stoler, p. 14 (Durham, NC: Duke University Press, 2006).

11 Ann Stoler, 'Tense and Tender Ties: The Politics of Comparison in North American History and (Post) Colonial Studies,' in Stoler, ed., *Haunted by Empire*, p. 40.

12 Cynthia Enloe, *The Curious Feminist: Searching for Women in a New Age of Empire* (Berkeley: University of California Press, 2004), pp. 19–57.

13 Patricia Holland, *Picturing Childhood: The Myth of the Child in Popular Imagery* (London: I.B. Tauris, 2004), p. 111.

14 Sharon Stephens, 'Children and the Politics of Culture in "Late Capitalism,"' in *Children and the Politics of Culture*, ed. Sharon Stephens, pp. 3–47 (Princeton: Princeton University Press, 1995).

Selected Bibliography

Adams, Abigail. 'Gringas, Ghouls and Guatemala: The 1994 Attacks on North American Women Accused of Body Organ Trafficking.' *Journal of Latin American Anthropology* 4.1 (1999): 112–33.

Adams, Marie. *Our Son a Stranger: Adoption Breakdown and Its Effects on Parents.* Montreal and Kingston: McGill-Queen's Press, 2002.

Adams, Mary Louise. *The Trouble with Normal: Postwar Youth and the Making of Heterosexuality.* Toronto: University of Toronto Press, 1997.

Alstein, Howard, and Rita J. Simon. *Intercountry Adoption: A Multinational Perspective.* New York: Praeger, 1991.

Anagnost, Ann. 'Maternal Labor in a Transnational Circuit.' In *Consuming Motherhood,* ed. Janelle S. Taylor, Linda Layne, and Danielle F. Wozniak, pp. 139–67. New Brunswick, NJ: Rutgers University Press, 2004.

Arditti, Rita. *Searching for Life: The Grandmothers of the Plaza de Mayo and the Disappeared Children of Argentina.* Berkeley: University of California Press, 1999.

Atlee Phillips, David. *The Night Watch.* New York: Atheneum, 1977.

Austin, Linda Tollet. *Babies for Sale: The Tennessee Children's Home Adoption Scandal.* Westport: Praeger, 1993.

Bagley, Christopher. 'Adoption of Native Children in Canada: A Policy Analysis and a Research Report.' In *Intercountry Adoption: A Multinational Perspective,* ed. Howard Alstein and Rita Simon, pp. 55–79. New York: Praeger, 1991.

Balcom, Karen. *The Traffic in Babies: Cross Border Adoption, Baby-Selling, and Child Welfare in the United States and Canada, 1930–1972.* Toronto: University of Toronto Press, forthcoming.

Banet-Weiser, Sarah. 'Elián González and "The Purpose of America": Nation, Family and the Child-Citizen.' *American Quarterly* 55.2 (June 2003): 149–77.

Bardach, Ann Louise. *Cuba Confidential: Love and Vengeance in Miami and Havana*. New York: Vintage, 2003.

Bartholet, Elizabeth. 'Where Do Black Children Belong?' *University of Pennsylvania Law Review* 139.5 (May 1991): 1163–1256.

– *Family Bonds: Adoption, Infertility and the New World of Child Production*. Boston: Beacon Press, 1993.

Batalla por la Liberación de Elián González. Havana: Editora Política, 2000.

Bayly, C.A., et al. 'AHR Conversation: On Transnational History.' *American Historical Review* 111.5 (Dec. 2006): 1440–65.

Behar, Ruth. *The Vulnerable Observer: Anthropology That Breaks Your Heart*. Boston: Beacon, 1996.

– 'Post-Utopia: The Erotics of Power and Cuba's Revolutionary Children.' In *Cuba: The Elusive Nation*, ed. Damian J.Vernandez and Madeline Camara Betancourt, pp. 134–54. Gainsville: University Press of Florida, 2000.

Berebitsky, Julie. *Like Our Very Own: Adoption and the Changing Culture of Motherhood, 1851–1950*. Lawrence: University Press of Kansas, 2000.

Betancourt, Louis Adrian. *Por Que Carlos?* Havana: Editorial Letras Cubanas, 1981.

Black, Maggie. *The Children and the Nations: The Story of UNICEF*. Sydney: UNICEF, 1986.

Blackburn, Robin. 'Putting the Hammer Down on Cuba.' *New Left Review* 4 (July/August 2000): 5–36.

Blackstock, Cindy, Nico Trocmé, and Marlyn Bennett. 'Child Maltreatment Investigations among Aboriginal and Non-Aboriginal Families in Canada.' *Violence against Women* 10 (2004): 901–16.

Blum, Denise. 'Cuba: The Post-2001 Notions of Participation, Responsibility and Character Formation.' Paper presented at the Latin American Studies Association Conference, Montreal, September 2007.

Borstelmann, Thomas. *The Cold War and the Color Line: American Race Relations in the Global Arena*. Cambridge: Harvard University Press, 2001.

Bos, Pien. 'Once a Mother: Relinquishment and Adoption from the Perspective of Unmarried Mothers in South India.' Ph.D. diss., Radboud University, 2007.

Boyden, Jo. 'Childhood and the Policy Makers: A Comparative Perspective on the Globalization of Childhood.' In *Constructing and Reconstructing Childhood: Contemporary Issues in the Sociological Study of Childhood*, ed. Allison James and Alan Prout, pp. 184–215. New York: Falmer Press, 1990.

Boyden, Jo, and Joanna de Berry, eds. *Children and Youth on the Front Line: Ethnography, Armed Conflict and Displacement*. Oxford: Berghahn Books, 2004.

Briggs, Laura. *Reproducing Empire: Race, Sex Science and U.S. Imperialism in Puerto Rico*. Berkeley: University of California Press, 2002.

– 'Mother, Child, Race, Nation: The Visual Iconography of Rescue and the Politics of Transnational and Transracial Adoption.' *Gender and History* 15.2 (Aug. 2003): 179–200.

– 'Communities Resisting Interracial Adoption: The Indian Child Welfare Act and the NABSW Statement of 1972.' Paper presented at the Adoption and Culture Conference, University of Tampa, October 2005.

– 'Making "American" Families: Transnational Adoption and U.S. Latin American Policy.' In *Haunted by Empire: Geographies of Intimacy in North American History*, ed. Ann Laura Stoler, pp. 344–65. Durham, NC: Duke University Press, 2006.

Brocklehurst, Helen. *Who's Afraid of Children? Children, Conflict and International Relations*. Hampshire: Ashgate, 2006.

Brookfield, Tarah. '"Our Deepest Concern Is for the Safety of Our Children and Their Children": Canadian Women Respond to Cold War Fears at Home and Abroad, 1950–1980.' Ph.D. diss., York University, 2008.

Bunk, Julie Marie. *Fidel Castro and the Quest for a Revolutionary Culture in Cuba*. University Park: Pennsylvania State University Press, 1994.

Burman, Erica. 'Local, Global or Globalized? Child Development and International Child Rights Legislation.' *Childhood* 3.45 (1996): 45–66.

– 'Innocents Abroad: Western Fantasies of Childhood and the Iconography of Emergencies.' *Disasters* 18.3 (2007): 241–59.

Campion-Vincent, Veronique. *Organ Theft Legends*. Jackson: University of Mississippi Press, 2005. French edition, Société d'Edition Les Belles Lettres, 1997.

Carmack, Robert M., ed. *Harvest of Violence: The Maya Indians and the Guatemalan Crisis*. Norman: University of Oklahoma Press, 1988.

Carp Wayne. *Family Matters: Secrecy and Disclosure in the History of Adoption*. Cambridge: Harvard University Press, 1998.

Cartwright, Lisa. 'Images of "Waiting Children": Spectatorship and Pity in the Representation of the Global Social Orphan in the 1990s.' In *Cultures of Transnational Adoption*, ed. Toby Volkman, pp. 185–212. Durham, NC: Duke University Press, 2005.

Castañada, Claudia. *Figurations: Child, Bodies, Worlds*. Durham, NC: Duke University Press, 2002.

Chen, Xiaobei. *Tending the Gardens of Citizenship: Child Saving in Toronto, 1880s–1920s*. Toronto: University of Toronto Press, 2005.

Chimezie, Amuzie. 'Transracial Adoption of Black Children.' *Social Work* 20.4 (July 1975): 296–301.

Chin, Elizabeth. 'Children out of Bounds in Globalising Times.' *Postcolonial Studies* 6.3 (2003): 309–25.

Christensen, Pia Haudrup. 'Childhood and the Cultural Constitution of Vulnerable Bodies.' In *The Body, Childhood and Society*, ed. Alan Prout, pp. 38–59. New York: Palgrave Macmillan, 2000.

Collinson, Anne. 'The Littlest Immigrants: Cross-Border Adoption in the Americas.' *Journal of Women's History* 19.1 (2007): 132–41.

Commission for Historical Clarification (CEH). *Guatemala: Memory of Silence*. Guatemala: CEH, 1999.

Coombes, Annie E., and Avtar Brah. 'Introduction: The Conundrum of "Mixing."' In *Hybridity and Its Discontents: Politics, Science and Culture*, ed. Avtar Brah and Annie E. Coombes, pp. 1–16. London: Routledge, 2000.

Crichlow, Wesley. 'Western Colonization as Disease: Native Adoption and Cultural Genocide.' *Critical Social Work* 3.1 (2002): 1–14.

Cullather, Nick. *Secret History: The CIA's Classified Account of Its Operations in Guatemala 1952–1954*. Stanford: Stanford University Press, 2002.

Cunningham, Hugh. *The Children of the Poor: Representations of Childhood since the Seventeenth Century*. Oxford: Blackwell, 1991.

Dalmage, Heather M. 'Interracial Couples, Multiracial People, and the Color Line in Adoption.' In *Adoptive Families in a Diverse Society*, ed. Katrina Wegar, pp. 210–25. New Brunswick: Rutgers University Press, 2006.

Danforth, Loring M. '"We Crossed a Lot of Borders": Refugee Children of the Greek Civil War.' *Diaspora* 12.2 (2003): 169–209.

de la Campa, Roman. *Cuba on My Mind: Journeys to a Severed Nation*. London: Verso, 2000.

de la Torre, Miguel A. *La Lucha for Cuba: Religion and Politics on the Streets of Miami*. Berkeley: University of California Press, 2003.

de Schweinitz, Rebecca. 'The "Shame of America": African-American Civil Rights and the Politics of Childhood.' In *The Politics of Childhood: International Perspectives, Contemporary Developments*, ed. Jim Goddard, Sally McNamee, Adrian James, and Allison James, pp. 50–65. Hampshire: Macmillan, 2005.

Demos a la niñez un futuro de paz. Guatemala: ODHAG, 2006.

Derby, Lauren. 'Gringo Chickens with Worms: Food and Nationalism in the Dominican Republic.' In *Close Encounters of Empire: Writing the Cultural History of U.S.- Latin American Relations*, ed. Gilbert Joseph, Catherine LeGrand, and Ricardo D. Salvatore, pp. 451–93. Durham, NC: Duke University Press, 1998.

– 'Imperial Secrets: Vampires and Nationhood in Puerto Rico.' Paper presented at the Berkshire Conference on the History of Women, Claremont, California, July 2005.

Diáz, Marta. 'Representación de la emigración en el cine Cubano Contemporáneo.' Paper presented at the Latin American Studies Association conference, Montreal, September 2007.

Discovering Dominga. Directed by Patricia Flynn. Public Broadcasting System, POV, 2003.

Dorow, Sara K. *Transnational Adoption: A Cultural Economy of Race, and Kinship Gender.* New York: New York University Press, 2006.

Dudziak, Mary. *Cold War Civil Rights: Race and the Image of American Democracy.* Princeton: Princeton University Press, 2000.

Eckstein, Susan. 'Dollarization and Its Discontents in the Post-Soviet Era.' In *Reinventing the Revolution: A Contemporary Cuba Reader,* ed. Phillip Brenner, Marguerite Rose Jiménez, John Kirk, and William LeoGrande, pp. 179–92. Latham: Roman and Littlefield, 2007.

Eckstein, Susan, and Lorena Barbiera. 'Cuban Americans and Their Transnational Ties.' In *Reinventing the Revolution: A Contemporary Cuba Reader,* ed. Phillip Brenner, Marguerite Rose Jiménez, John Kirk, and William LeoGrande, pp. 267–74, 179–92. Latham: Roman and Littlefield, 2007.

Eire, Carlos. *Waiting for Snow in Havana: Confessions of a Cuban Boy.* New York: Free Press, 2003.

El Otro Lado de Cristal: Un Documental sobre Operación Peter Pan. Directed by Marina Ochoa. ICAIC, Havana, 1994.

Elkus, Adam. 'Celebrity Colonialism in Africa,' *ZNET,* 4 November 2006.

Eng, David. 'Transracial Adoption and Queer Diaspora.' *Social Text* 21.1 (2003): 1–37.

Enloe, Cynthia. *The Curious Feminist: Searching for Women in a New Age of Empire.* Berkeley: University of California Press, 2004.

Evans, Karen. *The Lost Daughters of China: Abandoned Girls, Their Journey to America and the Search for a Missing Past.* New York: Putnam, 2000.

Facio, Elisa. 'Jineterismo during the Special Period.' In *Cuban Transitions at the Millennium,* ed. Eloise Linger and John Cotman, pp. 55–75. Largo, MD: International Development Options, 2000.

Falla, Ricardo. *Massacres in the Jungle.* Boulder: Westview Press, 1994.

Fass, Paula. *Children of a New World: Society, Culture and Globalization.* New York: NYU Press, 2007.

Fernández, Teresa de Jesús. 'From This Side of the Fish Tank.' In *By Heart / De Memoria: Cuban Women's Journeys in and out of Exile,* ed. Maria de los Angeles Torres, pp. 75–84. Philadelphia: Temple University Press, 2003.

Fessler, Ann. *The Girls Who Went Away: The Hidden History of Women Who Surrendered Children for Adoption in the Decades Before Roe v. Wade*. New York: Penguin, 2006.

Fidel and Religion: Talks with Frei Betto. Havana, Publications Office of the Council of State, 1987.

Fieweger, M.E. 'Stolen Children and International Adoptions.' *Child Welfare* 70.2 (March/April 1991): 285–91.

Fischer, Edward F., and Peter Benson. *Broccoli and Desire: Global Connections and Maya Struggles in Postwar Guatemala*. Stanford: Stanford University Press, 2006.

Fonseca, Claudia. 'Patterns of Shared Parenthood among the Brazilian Poor.' In *Cultures of Transnational Adoption*, ed. Toby Alice Volkman, pp. 142–61. Durham, NC: Duke University Press, 2005.

Fournier Suzanne, and Ernie Crey. *Stolen from Our Embrace: The Abduction of First Nations Children and the Restoration of Aboriginal Communities*. Vancouver: Douglas and McIntyre, 1997.

Fraser, Stephen. 'Myth, Fact and Confusion in the Disappearances of Children in Guatemala.' *Lulu Press*, 24 May 1994.

Gallay, Grace. 'A Study in the Motivation Expressed by White Couples Who Adopt Non-White Children.' MSW research report, McGill University, May 1963.

Garcia, Maria Christina. *Havana USA: Cuban Exiles and Cuban-Americans in South Florida 1959–1994*. Berkeley: University of California Press, 1996.

Garigan, Maeve. 'Guatemala's Adoption Industry.' *SAIS Review* 27.2 (Summer/Fall 2007): 179–81.

Gleason, Mona. *Normalizing the Ideal: Psychology, Schooling and the Family in Postwar Canada*. Toronto: University of Toronto Press, 1999.

Gleijeses, Piero. *Shattered Hope: The Guatemalan Revolution and the United States, 1944–1954*. Princeton: Princeton University Press, 1991.

Godoy, Angelina Snodgrass. *Popular Injustice: Violence, Community and Law in Latin America*. Stanford: Stanford University Press, 2006.

Goldman, Francisco. *The Art of Political Murder: Who Killed the Bishop*. New York: Grove, 2007.

González Mandri, Flora M. 'Operation Pedro Pan: A Tale of Trauma and Remembrance.' *Latino Studies* 6.3 (2008): 252–68.

Gordon, Linda. *The Great Arizona Orphan Abduction*. Cambridge: Harvard University Press, 1999.

Gott, Richard. *Cuba: A New History*. New Haven: Yale University Press, 2004.

Goubau, Dominique, and Claire O'Neill. 'L'adoption, l'Eglise et l'Etat: Les origines tumultueuses d'une institution légale.' In *L'évolution de la protection de l'enfance au Quebec*, ed. Renée Joyal, pp. 97–130. Sainte-Foy: Presses de l'Université du Québec, 2000.

Government of Canada. *Report on the Royal Commission on Aboriginal Peoples, Volume Three: Gathering Strength*. Ottawa: Ministry of Supply and Services, 1996.

Graff, E.J. 'The Lie We Love.' *Foreign Policy*, November/December 2008.

Grandin, Greg. *The Last Colonial Massacre: Latin America in the Cold War*. Chicago: University of Chicago Press, 2004.

– *Empire's Workshop*. New York: Metropolitan Books, 2006.

Grant, Maye H. 'Perspectives on Adoption: Black into White.' *Black World*, November 1972, pp. 66–75.

Green, Duncan. *Hidden Lives: Voices of Children in Latin America and the Caribbean*. Toronto: Between the Lines, 1988.

– *Silent Revolution: The Rise and Crisis of Market Economics in Latin America*. New York: Monthly Review Press, 2003.

Green, Linda. *Fear as a Way of Life: Mayan Widows in Rural Guatemala*. New York: Columbia University Press, 1999.

Grupo Arieto. *Contra Viento y Marea*. Havana: Casa de las Americas, 1978.

Guerra, Lillian. 'Elián González and the "Real Cuba" of Miami: Visions of Identity, Exceptionality, and Divinity.' *Cuban Studies* 37 (2007): 1–24.

Handy, Jim. 'Chicken Thieves, Witches, and Judges: Vigilante Justice and Customary Law in Guatemala.' *Journal of Latin American Studies* 36 (2004): 535–79.

Hasta Encontrarte. 3rd edn. Guatemala City: ODHAG, 2005.

Hecht, Tobias. 'Children and Contemporary Latin America.' In *Minor Omissions: Children in Latin American History and Society*, ed. Tobias Hecht, pp. 242–51. Madison: University of Wisconsin Press, 2002.

Herman, Ellen. 'Bertha and Harry Holt.' Adoption History Project. http://www.uoregon.edu/~adoption/

– *Kinship by Design: A History of Adoption in the Modern United States*. Chicago: University of Chicago Press, 2008.

Hernández, Rafael. *Looking at Cuba*. Gainsville: University Press of Florida, 2003.

Herrera, Andrea O'Reilly, ed. *Remembering Cuba: Legacy of a Diaspora*. Austin: University of Texas Press, 2002.

Herzog, Elizabeth, and Rose Bernstein. 'Why So Few Negro Adoptions? A Reappraisal of Evidence.' *Children* 12.1 (Jan.-Feb. 1965): 14–18.

Higonnet, Anne. *Pictures of Innocence: The History and Crisis of Ideal Childhood*. London: Thames and Hudson, 1998.

Hinckle, Warren, and William T. Turner. *Deadly Secrets: The CIA-Mafia War against Castro and the Assassination of J.F.K.* New York: Thunder's Mouth Press, 1981.

Holland, Patricia. *Picturing Childhood: The Myth of the Child in Popular Imagery.* London: I.B. Tauris, 2004.

Honeyman, Derek. 'Lynch Mobs and Child Theft Rumours in the Guatemala Highlands.' M.A. thesis, University of Alberta, 1999.

Hosek, Jennifer. 'Importing the Revolution One Island at a Time: Rudi Dutschke Reads Che Guevara.' Paper presented at New World Coming: The Sixties and the Shaping of Global Consciousness, Queen's University, June 2007.

Howard, Alicia, David D. Royse, and John A. Skerl. 'Transracial Adoption: The Black Community Perspective.' *Social Work* 22.3 (May 1977): 184–9.

Howell, Signe. *The Kinning of Foreigners: Transnational Adoption in a Global Perspective.* New York: Berghahn Books, 2006.

Hubinette, Tobias. 'Comforting an Orphaned Nation: Representations of International Adoption and Adopted Koreans in Korean Popular Culture.' Ph.D., diss., Stockholm University, Department of Oriental Languages, 2005.

Iacovetta, Franca. *Gatekeepers: Reshaping Immigrant Lives in Cold War Canada.* Toronto: Between the Lines, 2006.

ILPEC (Latin American Institute for Education and Communications). 'Adoption and the Rights of the Child in Guatemala.' Unpublished report for UNICEF, Guatemala, 2000.

Immerman, Richard. *The CIA in Guatemala: The Foreign Policy of Intervention.* Austin: University of Texas Press, 1982.

Janovicek, Nancy. 'Assisting Our Own: Urban Migration, Self-Governance, and Native Women's Organizing in Thunder Bay, Ontario, 1972–1989.' *American Indian Quarterly* 27.3–4 (Summer/Fall 2003): 548–64.

Jarvie, Sandra. 'Silent, Denigrated and Rendered Invisible: Mothers Who Lost Their Babies to Adoption in the 1960s and 1970s.' In *Home/Bodies: Geographies of Self, Place and Space*, ed. Wendy Schissel, pp. 69–82. Calgary: University of Calgary Press, 2006.

Jiménez, Marguerite Rose 'The Political Economy of Leisure.' In *Reinventing the Revolution: A Contemporary Cuba Reader*, ed. Phillip Brenner, Marguerite Rose Jiménez, John Kirk, and William LeoGrande, pp. 146–55. Latham: Roman and Littlefield, 2007.

Johnson, John J. *Latin America in Caricature.* Austin: University of Texas Press, 1980.

Johnston Patrick. *Native Children and the Child Welfare System.* Toronto: Canadian Council on Social Development, 1983.

Jonas, Susanne. *The Battle for Guatemala.* Boulder: Westview Press, 1991.

Kaplan, Dana Evan. 'Fleeing the Revolution: The Exodus of Cuban Jewry in the Early 1960s.' *Cuban Studies* 36 (2005): 129–54.

Katz, Robert. *Naked by the Window: The Fatal Marriage of Carle Andre and Ana Mendieta*. New York: Atlantic Monthly, 1990.

Killer's Paradise. Directed by Giselle Portenier. National Film Board of Canada, 2006.

Kim, Eleana. 'Wedding Citizenship and Culture: Korean Adoptees and the Global Family of Korea.' In *Cultures of Transnational Adoption*, ed. Toby Volkman, pp. 49–81. Durham, NC: Duke University Press, 2005.

Kimelman, E.C. *No Quiet Place*. Review Committee on Indian and Métis Adoptions and Placements. Winnipeg: Manitoba Department of Community Services, 1985.

Kirk, John. *Between God and the Party: Religion and Politics in Revolutionary Cuba*. Tampa: University of South Florida Press, 1989.

Kirschenbaum, Lisa. *Small Comrades: Revolutionizing Childhood in Soviet Russia, 1917–1932*. New York: Routledge, 2000.

Klein, Christina. *Cold War Orientalism: Asia in the Middlebrow Imagination, 1945–61*. Berkeley: University of California Press, 2003.

Kline, Marlee. 'Child Welfare Law – Best Interests of the Child: Ideology and First Nations.' *Osgood Hall Law Journal* 30 (1992): 375–426.

Ladner, Joyce. *Mixed Families: Adopting across Racial Boundaries*. Garden City, NJ: Anchor, 1977.

LaDuke, Winona. 'Foreword.' In *At the Risk of Being Heard: Identity, Indigenous Rights and Postcolonial States*, ed. Bartholomew Dean and Jerome M. Levi. Ann Arbor: University of Michigan Press, 2003.

Landsdowne, Rosemary. 'The Concept of Non-Adoptibility.' MSW thesis, University of British Columbia, 1949.

Larsen, Elizabeth. 'Did I Steal My Daughter? The Tribulations of Global Adoption.' *Mother Jones*, November/December, 2007.

Lavell-Harvard, D. Memee, and Jeannette Corbiere Lavell, eds. *'Until Our Hearts Are on the Ground': Aboriginal Mothering, Oppression, Resistance and Rebirth*. Toronto: Demeter Press, 2006.

Lawrence, Jon, and Pat Starkey. *Child Welfare and Social Action in the Nineteenth and Twentieth Centuries: International Perspectives*. Liverpool: Liverpool University Press, 2001.

Legarreta, Dorothy. *The Guernica Generation: Basque Refugee Children of the Spanish Civil War*. Reno: University of Nevada Press, 1984.

Leiner, Marvin. *Children Are the Revolution: Daycare in Cuba*. New York: Penguin, 1974.

Levander Caroline F. *Cradle of Liberty: Race, the Child and National Belonging from Thomas Jefferson to W.E. B Du Bois*. Durham, NC: Duke University Press, 2006.

Levanthal, Todd. 'The "Baby Parts" Myth: The Anatomy of a Rumor.' Unpublished report, United States Information Agency, 20 May 1994.

Lovell, George. *A Beauty That Hurts: Life and Death in Guatemala*. Toronto: Between the Lines, 1995.

Lovelock, Kirsten. 'Intercountry Adoption as a Migratory Practice: A Comparative Analysis of Intercountry Adoption and Immigration Policy and Practice in the United States, Canada and New Zealand in the Post W.W. II Period.' *International Migration Review* 34.3 (Autumn 2000): 910–34.

Lukowycz, Josette. 'An Exploratory Study of the Adoption of Indian Children in Manitoba.' MSW thesis, University of Manitoba, 1985.

Madison, Bernice Q., and Michael Schapiro. 'Black Adoption – Issues and Policies: Review of the Literature.' *Social Services Review* 47.4 (Dec. 1973): 531–60.

Maguire, Moira. 'Foreign Adoptions and the Evolution of Irish Adoption Policy, 1945–1952.' *Journal of Social History* 36.2 (2002): 5–30.

Manz, Beatriz. *Paradise in Ashes: A Guatemalan Journey of Courage, Terror and Hope*. Berkeley: University of California Press, 2004.

Marenn, Lea. *Salvador's Children: A Song for Survival*. Columbus: Ohio State University Press, 1993.

Marshall, Domenique. 'The Construction of Children as an Object of International Relations: The Declaration of Children's Rights and the Child Welfare Committee of the League of Nations, 1900–1924.' *International Journal of Children's Rights* 7 (1999): 103–47.

Mascarenhas, Tomas Brill. 'House of Horror.' *New Internationalist*, December 2005, pp. 10–11.

Massud-Piloto, Felix. *From Welcomed Exiles to Illegal Immigrants: Cuban American Migration to the U.S.,1959–1995*. New York: Rowman and Littlefield, 1995.

May, Elaine. *Barren in the Promised Land: Childless Americans and the Pursuit of Happiness*. Cambridge: Harvard University Press, 1995.

McAlister, Melani. *Epic Encounters: Culture, Media and U.S. Interests in the Middle East since 1945*. Berkeley: University of California Press, 2005.

McCullough, Molly. 'A Long Way from Home: A Glimpse at Transnational Adoption.' Unpublished Women's Studies 323 essay, University of Victoria, April 2008.

McEvoy-Levy, Siobhan, ed. *Troublemakers or Peacemakers? Youth and Post-Accord Peace Building*. Notre Dame: University of Notre Dame Press, 2006.

McKenzie, Brad, and Pete Hudson. 'Native Children, Child Welfare, and the

Colonization of Native People.' In *The Challenge of Child Welfare*, ed. Kenneth L. Levitt and Brian Warf, pp. 125–41.Vancouver: UBC Press, 1985.

McLaren, John. 'The State, Child Snatching, and the Law: The Seizure and Indocrination of Sons of Freedom Children in British Columbia, 1950–1960.' In *Regulating Lives: Historical Essays on the State, the Individual and the Law*, ed. John McLaren, Robert Menzies ,and Dorothy Chunn, pp. 259–93. Vancouver: University of British Columbia Press, 2002.

Melosh, Barbara. *Strangers and Kin: The American Way of Adoption*. Cambridge: Harvard University Press, 2002.

Menéndez, Ana. *In Cuba I Was a German Shepherd*. New York: Grove Press, 2001.

Miller, Warren. *90 Miles from Home: The Face of Cuba Today*. Boston: Little, Brown, 1961.

Mills, Sean. 'The Empire Within: Montreal, the Sixties, and the Forging of a Radical Imagination.' Ph.D. diss., Queen's University, 2007.

Minaya, Ezequiel. 'Authors Who Knew or Know the Limits.' In *Capitalism. God and a Good Cigar: Cuba Enters the Twenty-First Century*, ed. Lydia Chavez, pp. 78–94. Durham NC: Duke University Press, 2005.

Mishler, Paul C. *Raising Reds: The Young Pioneers, Radical Summer Camps, and Communist Political Culture in the United States*. New York: Columbia University Press, 1999.

Monture, Patricia A. 'A Vicious Circle: Child Welfare and the First Nations.' *Canadian Journal of Women and the Law* 3.1 (1989): 1–17.

Nelson, Diane M. *A Finger in the Wound: Body Politics in Quincentennial Guatemala*. Berkley: University of California Press, 1999.

Nelson, Jennifer. *Women of Color and the Reproductive Rights Movement*. New York: NYU Press, 2003.

Ngabonziza, Damien. 'Inter-country Adoption: In Whose Best Interests?' *Adoption and Fostering* 12.1 (1988): 35–40.

Nordstrom, Carolyn. *Global Outlaws: Crime, Money and Power in the Contemporary World*. Berkeley: University of California Press, 2007.

Obejas, Achy. *Days of Awe*. New York: Ballantine, 2001.

O'Brien, Michael. 'Of Cats, Historians and Gardeners.' *Journal of American History* 89.1 (2002): 44–59.

Ortiz, Dianna. *The Blindfold's Eye*. Maryknoll: Orbis, 2002.

Palmié, Stephan. *Wizards and Scientists: Explorations in Afro-Cuban Modernity and Tradition*. Durham, NC: Duke University Press, 2002.

Paquet, Ann M. 'Study of Current Adoption Law and Practice in the Province of Quebec.' MSW thesis, McGill University, 1959.

Peacock, Susan C., and Adriana Beltrán. *Hidden Powers in Post-Conflict Guatemala*. Washington: Washington Office on Latin America, 2003.

Perera, Victor. *Unfinished Conquest: The Guatemalan Tragedy*. Berkeley: University of California Press, 1993.

Perez, Louis A. *On Becoming Cuban: Identity, Nationality and Culture*. New York: Harper Collins, 1999.

Perry, Adele. *On the Edge of Empire: Race, Gender and the Making of British Columbia, 1849–1871*. Toronto: University of Toronto Press, 2001.

Pertman, Adam. *Adoption Nation*. Boston: Basic, 2000.

Phillips, Patti. 'Blood Not Thicker Than Water: Adoption and Nation Building in the Post War Baby Boom.' M.A. thesis, Queen's University, 1995.

Plett, Kenneth. 'Transracial Adoption: A Study of the Placement of Native Indian Children with Caucasian Couples.' MSW thesis, University of Manitoba, 1979.

Prashad, Vijay. *The Darker Nations: A People's History of the Third World*. New York: New Press, 2007.

Pien, Bos. 'Once a Mother: Relinquishment and Adoption from the Perspective of Unmarried Mothers from South India.' Ph.D. diss., Radboud University, Nijmegan, 2007.

Power, Margaret. *Right-wing Women in Chile: Feminine Power and the Struggle against Allende, 1964–1973*. University Park: Pennsylvania State University Press, 2002.

Prager, Emily. *Wuhu Diari: On Taking My Adopted Daughter Back to Her Hometown in China*. New York: Random House, 2001.

Razack, Sherene. *Casting Out: The Eviction of Muslims from Western Law and Politics*. Toronto: University of Toronto Press, 2008.

'Report of the Special Rapporteur on the Sale of Children, Child Prostitution and Child Pornography in Guatemala.' United Nations Commission on Human Rights, 27 January 2000.

Resnick, Rosa Perla. 'Latin American Children in Intercountry Adoption.' In *Adoption: Essays in Social Policy, Law and Society*, ed. Philip Bean, pp. 275–89. London: Tavistock, 1984.

Ressler, Everett M., Neil Boothby, and Daniel J. Steinbock. *Unaccompanied Children: Care and Protection in Wars, Natural Disasters, and Refugee Movements*. New York: Oxford University Press, 1988.

Richard, Kenn. 'On the Matter of Cross-Cultural Aboriginal Adoptions.' In *Putting a Human Face on Child Welfare: Voices from the Prairies*, ed. Ivan Brown, Ferzana Chaze, Don Fuchs, Jean Lafrance, Sharon Mckay, and Shelley Thomas-Prokop, pp. 189–202. Regina: Prairie Child Welfare Consortium, 2007.

Robin, Ron. *The Making of the Cold War Enemy: Culture and Politics in the Military-Intellectual Complex.* Princeton: Princeton University Press, 2001.

Rodriguez, Juan Carlos. *The Bay of Pigs and the CIA.* Melbourne: Ocean Press, 1999.

Romano, Renee C. *Race Mixing: Black-White Marriage in Post War America.* Cambridge: Harvard University Press, 2003.

Rook, Patricia T., and R. Schnell. 'Charlotte Whitton and the "Babies for Export" Controversy.' *Alberta History* 30.1 (1982): 11–16.

Roskies, Ethel. 'An Exploratory Study of the Characteristics of Adoptive Parents of Mixed-Race Children in the Montreal Area.' M.A. thesis, University of Montreal, 1963.

Rothman, Barbara Katz. *Weaving a Family: Untangling Race and Adoption.* Boston: Beacon Press, 2005.

Rowe, John Carlos. *The New American Studies.* Minneapolis: University of Minnesota Press, 2004.

Rutherford, Scott. 'Canada's Other Red Scare: The Anicinabe Park Occupation, Indigenous Radicalism and the Circulation of Global Culture and Politics, 1965–1975.' Ph.D. dissertation in progress, Queen's University.

Sahlins, Marshall. *Apologies to Thucydides: Understanding History as Culture and Vice Versa.* Chicago: University of Chicago Press, 2004.

Sanford, Victoria. *Buried Secrets: Truth and Human Rights in Guatemala.* New York: Palgrave, 2003.

Saunders, Charles. *Share the Care: The Story of the Nova Scotia Home for Coloured Children.* Halifax: Nimbus, 1994.

Savarese, Ralph. *Reasonable People: A Memoir of Autism and Adoption.* New York: Other Press, 2007.

'Saving Elián.' PBS *Frontline*, 6 February 2001.

Scheper-Hughes, Nancy. *Death without Weeping: The Violence of Everyday Life in Brazil.* Berkeley: University of California Press, 1992.

– 'Theft of Life.' *Anthropology Today* 12.3 (June 1996): 3–11.

– 'The Global Traffic in Human Organs.' *Current Anthropology* 41.2 (April 2000): 191–224.

Scheper Hughes, Nancy, and Carolyn Sargent, eds. *Small Wars: The Cultural Politics of Childhood.* Berkeley: University of California Press, 1999.

Schwalbe A. Lenore. 'Negro and Partly-Negro Wards of the Children's Aid Society of Metropolitan Toronto.' MSW thesis, University of Toronto, December, 1958.

Scyner, Lawrence. 'Towards Adolescence and Young Adulthood.' Paper presented at the Second International Conference on Trans Racial Adoption, Boston, November, 1970.

Seabrook, Jeremy. *Children of Other Worlds: Exploitation in the Global Market.* London: Pluto Press, 2001.

Silliman, Jael, Marlene Gerber Fried, Loretta Ross, and Elena R. Gutiérrez. *Undivided Rights: Women of Color Organize for Reproductive Justice.* Cambridge: South End Press, 2004.

Simon, Jean Marie. *Guatemala: Eternal Spring, Eternal Tyranny.* New York: Norton, 1987.

Simon, Rita J., and Howard Altstein. *Adoption across Borders.* Lanham: Rowman and Littlefield, 2000.

Sinclair, Raven. 'All My Relations -- Native Transracial Adoption: A Critical Case Study of Cultural Identity.' Ph.D. diss., University of Calgary, 2007.

– 'Identity Lost and Found: Lessons from the Sixties Scoop.' *First Peoples Child and Family Review* 3.1 (2007): 72–8.

Sittler, Robert. 'Understanding Death in a Mayan Market.' *Community College Humanities Review* 22.1 (Fall 2001): 88–98.

Smith, Andrea. *Conquest: Sexual Violence and American Indian Genocide.* Cambridge: South End Press, 2005.

Smith, Bonnie. *The Gender of History: Men, Women and Historical Practice.* Cambridge: Harvard University Press, 1998.

Smolin, David. 'The Two Faces of Intercountry Adoption: The Significance of the Indian Adoption Scandals.' *Seton Hall Law Review* 35 (2004–5): 403–93.

Solinger, Rickie. *Wake Up Little Suzy: Single Pregnancy and Race before Roe v. Wade.* New York: Routledge, 1992.

– *Beggars and Choosers: How the Politics of Choice Shapes Adoption, Abortion and Welfare in the United States.* New York: Hill and Wang, 2001.

Spears, Shandra. 'Strong Spirit, Fractured Identity: An Ojibway Adoptee's Journey to Wholeness.' In *Strong Women Stories*, ed. Bonita Lawrence and Kim Anderson, pp. 81–94. Toronto: Sumach Press, 2003.

Springer, Kimberly. *Living for the Revolution: Black Feminist Organizations, 1968–1980.* Durham, NC: Duke University Press, 2005.

Stephens, Sharon. 'Children and the Politics of Culture in "Late Capitalism."' In *Children and the Politics of Culture*, ed. Sharon Stephens, pp. 3–47. Princeton: Princeton University Press, 1995.

Stepick, Alex, Guillermo Grenier, Max Castro, and Marvin Dunn. *This Is Our Land: Immigrants and Power in Miami.* Berkeley: University of California Press, 2003.

Stoller, Ann. *Carnal Knowledge and Imperial Power: Race and the Intimate in Colonial Rule.* Berkeley: University of California Press, 2002.

Strong-Boag, Veronica. 'Home Dreams: Women and the Suburban Experiment in Canada, 1945–60.' *Canadian Historical Review* 72.4 (Dec. 1991): 471–504.

– 'Today's Child: Creating the Just Society One Family at a Time in 1960s Canada.' *Canadian Historical Review* 86.4 (Dec. 2005): 673–99.

– *Finding Families Finding Ourselves: English Canada Encounters Adoption from the Nineteenth Century to the 1990s.* Toronto: Oxford University Press, 2006.

Suarez-Orozco, Marcelo M. 'The Treatment of Children in the "Dirty War": Ideology, State Terrorism and the Abuse of Children in Argentina.' In *Child Survival: Anthropological Perspectives on the Treatment and Maltreatment of Children*, ed. Nancy Scheper Hughes, pp. 227–46. Dordrecht, Holland: D. Reidel, 1987.

Sutherland, Elizabeth. *The Youngest Revolution: A Personal Report on Cuba.* New York: Dial Press, 1969.

Taylor, Drew Hayden. *Someday.* Saskatoon: Fifth House Press, 1993.

Theorborn, Goran. 'Child Politics: Dimensions and Perspectives.' *Childhood* 3 (1996): 29–44.

Thomas, Hugh. *Cuba; or, The Pursuit of Freedom.* New York: DaCapo Press, 1998.

Tierney, Nancy Leigh. *Robbed of Humanity: Lives of Guatemalan Street Children.* Saint Paul: Pangaea, 1997.

Torreira Crespo, Ramón. 'First Wave of Cuban Emigrants and the Catholic Church.' *Enfoques*, February 2005, pp. 8–14.

Torreira Crespo, Ramón, and Jose Buajasan Marrawi. *Operación Peter Pan: Un Caso de Guerra Psicológica contra Cuba.* Havana: Editora Politica, 2000.

Torres, Maria de los Angeles. *The Lost Apple: Operation Pedro Pan, Cuban Children in the U.S. and the Promise of a Better Future.* Boston: Beacon Press, 2003.

Trenka, Jane Jeong, Julia Chinyere Oparah, and Sun Yung Shin, eds. *Outsiders Within: Writing on Transracial Adoption.* Cambridge: South End Press, 2006.

Triay, Victor. *Fleeing Castro: Operation Pedro Pan and the Cuban Children's Program.* Miami: University Press of Florida, 1998.

Tucker Rambally, Rae. *Practice Imperfect: Reflections on a Career in Social Work.* Montreal: Shoreline, 2002.

Turner Strong, Pauline. 'To Forget Their Tongue, Their Name, and Their Whole Relation: Captivity, Extra-Tribal Adoption, and the Indian Child Welfare Act.' In *Relative Values: Reconfiguring Kinship Studies*, ed. Sarah Franklin and Susan McKinnon, pp. 468–94. New York: Oxford University Press, 2001.

Twum-Danso, Afua. 'A Cultural Bridge, Not an Imposition: Legitimizing Children's Rights in the Eyes of Local Communities.' *Journal of the History of Childhood and Youth* 1.3 (Fall 2008): 391–413.

Unger, Steven. 'The Indian Child Welfare Act of 1978: A Case Study.' Ph.D. diss., University of Southern California, 2004.

Van Krieken, Robert. 'The "Stolen Generations" and Cultural Genocide: The Forced Removal of Australian Indigenous Children from their Families and Its Implications for the Sociology of Childhood.' *Childhood* 6 (1999): 297–311.

Volkman Toby, ed. *Cultures of Transnational Adoption.* Durham, NC: Duke University Press, 2005.

Wagamese, Richard. *One Native Life.* Vancouver: Douglas and McIntyre, 2008.

Wald, Karen. *Children of Che: Childcare and Education in Cuba.* Palo Alto: Ramparts, 1978.

Walkowitz, Judith. *City of Dreadful Delight.* Chicago: University of Chicago Press, 1993.

Walsh, Monsignor Bryan O. 'Cuban Refugee Children.' *Journal of Interamerican Studies and World Affairs* 13.3–4 (July-Oct. 1971): 382–95.

Ward, Margaret. *The Adoption of Native Canadian Children.* Cobalt: Highway Book Shop, 1984.

Weil, Richard. 'International Adoptions: The Quiet Migration.' *International Migration Review* 18.2 (Summer 1984): 276–93.

Westad, Odd Arne. *The Global Cold War: Third World Interventions and the Making of Our Times.* Cambridge: Cambridge University Press, 2006.

Wheeler, Jacob. 'Baby Hotel: The Gateway to Guatemalan Adoption.' Worldpress.org, 9 October 2006.

– 'Banana Republic to Baby Republic.' *In These Times,* 5 November 2007.

White, Luise. 'Cars Out of Place: Vampires, Technology and Labor in East and Central Africa.' *Representations,* no. 43 (Summer 1993): 27–50.

– *Speaking with Vampires: Rumour and History in Colonial Africa.* Berkeley: University of California Press, 2000.

Wilkinson, Daniel. *Silence on the Mountain: Stories of Terror, Betrayal and Forgetting in Guatemala.* Boston: Houghton Mifflin, 2002.

Wilkinson, Stephen. 'Riding on a Wave of Change: The Elián Crisis and the Prospects for an End to the U.S. Embargo of Cuba.' *Soundings: A Journal of Politics and Culture* 15 (Summer 2000): 27–49.

Williams, Dorothy. *The Road to Now: A History of Blacks in Montreal.* Montreal: Vehicule Press, 1997.

Wilson, Samantha L., and Judith L. Gibbons. 'Guatemalan Perceptions of Adoption.' *International Social Work* 48.6 (2005): 742–52.

Winston, Chris. *A Euro-American on a Korean Tour at a Thai Restaurant in China: Perspective of an Adoptive Parent of Korean Kids.* El Dorado Hills: KAAAFN, 2006.

Wright, Cynthia. 'Between Nation and Empire: The Making of Canada-Cuba Solidarity.' Paper presented at New World Coming: The Sixties and the Shaping of Global Consciousness, Queen's University, June 2007.

Yngvesson, Barbara. '"Un Nino de Cualquier Color": Race and Nation in Inter-country Adoption.' In *Globalizing Institutions: Case Studies in Regulation and Innovation,* ed. Jane Jenson and Boaventura de Sousa Santos, pp. 179–204. Aldershot: Ashgate, 2000.

– 'Going "Home": Adoption, Loss of Bearings and the Mythology of Roots.' In *Cultures of Transnational Adoption,* ed. Toby Volkman, pp. 25–48. Durham, NC: Duke University Press, 2005.

Young, Robert. *Colonial Desire: Hybridity in Theory, Culture and Race.* London: Routledge, 1995.

Yuval-Davis, Nira. *Gender and Nation.* London: Sage, 1997.

Zelizer, Viviana. *Pricing the Priceless Child: The Changing Social Value of Children.* New York: Basic Books, 1985.

Index